NATURE IN PROCESS

NATURE IN PROCESS

Organic Proposals in Philosophy, Society, and Religion

Andrew M. Davis
Maria-Teresa Teixeira
Wm. Andrew Schwartz
Editors

ANOKA, MINNESOTA 2022

Nature in Process: Organic Proposals in Philosophy, Society, and Religion

© 2022 Process Century Press

All rights reserved. Except for brief quotations in critical publications and reviews, no part of this book may be reproduced in any manner without prior permission from the publisher.

Process Century Press
RiverHouse LLC
802 River Lane
Anoka, MN 55303

Process Century Press books are published in association with the International Process Network.

Cover: Susanna Mennicke

VOLUME XXII:
TOWARD ECOLOGICAL CIVILIZATION SERIES
JEANYNE B. SLETTOM, GENERAL EDITOR

ISBN 978-1-940447-53-7
Printed in the United States of America

SERIES PREFACE: TOWARD ECOLOGICAL CIVILIZATION

We live in the ending of an age. But the ending of the modern period differs from the ending of previous periods, such as the classical or the medieval. The amazing achievements of modernity make it possible, even likely, that its end will also be the end of civilization, of many species, or even of the human species. At the same time, we are living in an age of new beginnings that give promise of an ecological civilization. Its emergence is marked by a growing sense of urgency and deepening awareness that the changes must go to the roots of what has led to the current threat of catastrophe.

In June 2015, the 10th Whitehead International Conference was held in Claremont, CA. Called "Seizing an Alternative: Toward an Ecological Civilization," it claimed an organic, relational, integrated, nondual, and processive conceptuality is needed, and that Alfred North Whitehead provides this in a remarkably comprehensive and rigorous way. We proposed that he could be "the philosopher of ecological civilization." With the help of those who have come to an ecological vision in other ways, the conference explored this Whiteheadian alternative, showing how it can provide the shared vision so urgently needed.

The judgment underlying this effort is that contemporary research and scholarship is still enthralled by the seventeenth-century view of nature articulated by Descartes and reinforced by Kant. Without freeing our minds of this objectifying and reductive understanding of the world, we are not likely to direct our actions wisely in response to the crisis to which this tradition has led us. Given the ambitious goal of replacing now dominant patterns of thought with one that would redirect us toward ecological civilization, clearly more is needed than a single conference. Fortunately, a larger platform is developing that includes the conference and looks beyond it. It is named Pando Populus (pandopopulous.com) in honor of the world's largest and oldest organism, an aspen grove.

As a continuation of the conference, and in support of the larger initiative of Pando Populus, we are publishing this series, appropriately named "Toward Ecological Civilization."

~John B. Cobb, Jr.

OTHER BOOKS IN THIS SERIES
An Axiological Process Ethics, Rem B. Edwards
Panentheism and Scientific Naturalism, David Ray Griffin
Organic Marxism, Philip Clayton & Justin Heinzekehr
Theological Reminiscences, John B. Cobb, Jr.
Integrative Process, Margaret Stout & Jeannine M. Love
Replanting Ourselves in Beauty, Jay McDaniel & Patricia Adams Farmer, eds.
For Our Common Home, John B. Cobb, Jr., & Ignacio Castuera, eds.
Whitehead Word Book, John B. Cobb, Jr.
The Vindication of Radical Empiricism, Michel Weber
Intuition in Mathematics and Physics, Ronny Desmet, ed.
Reforming Higher Education in an Era of Ecological Crisis and Growing Digital Insecurity, Chet Bowers
Protecting Our Common, Sacred Home, David Ray Griffin
Educating for an Ecological Civilization, Marcus Ford & Stephen Rowe, eds.
Socialism in Process, Justin Heinzekehr & Philip Clayton, eds.
Two Americas, Stephen C. Rowe
Rebuilding after Collapse, John Culp, ed.
Putting Philosophy to Work, John B. Cobb Jr. & Wm. Andrew Schwartz, eds.
What Is Ecological Civilization, Philip Clayton & Wm. Andrew Schwartz
Conceiving an Alternative, Demian Wheeler & David Conner, eds.
Rethinking Consciousness, John H. Buchanan & Christopher Aanstoos, eds.
Unprecedented Evolution, Spyridon Koutroufinis & René Pikarski, eds.

Contents

Acknowledgements
Introduction: From Mechanism to Organism 1

Part One: Organic Philosophy

1. Whitehead, Biosemiotics and Value 13
   John Pickering

2. Nature and Experience: Between Process Philosophy and Phenomenology 35
   Luca Vanzago

3. Memory and Thought 53
   Jason Brown

4. The Anthropocene, Ecozoic Era, and Organic Philosophy: A Provocative Trio in Hamilton, Berry, and Whitehead 71
   Herman F. Greene

5. Cause and Influence in Whitehead 95
   John B. Cobb, Jr.

Part Two: Organic Society

6. Growth, Commodification, and Property Rights 107
   Maria-Teresa Teixeira

7. Nature-based Solutions and the Complex Relation Between Society and Nature 119
   Moirika Reker

8. The Good and Prudent Handling of Things:
   The Need for an Ecological Management   131
   Mark Dibben

9. Re-Embedding the Market: Institutionalizing Effective
   Environmentalism   145
   Arran Gare

10. A Jurisprudence for Human Homeostasis with Nature   171
    Charles Walter

Part III: Organic Religion

11. Divine Wilder/ness: Nature, Panentheism, and
    Eco-Theological Ethics   199
    Andrew M. Davis

12. Images of Lions: Psalm 104 as a Metaphor for a
    Processual View of Creation   225
    Robert Gnuse

13. Toward an Ecologically Awakened Islamic Humanism   233
    Farhan A. Shah

14. A Shortcut on the Jain Path of Liberation:
    Aparigraha **as** Ahimsā in Process Philosophy   243
    Wm. Andrew Schwartz

15. A Process-Akashic Religious Naturalism   259
    Leslie A. Muray

Contributors   271

Acknowledgements

The contributions comprising this volume originated at the 2017 International Whitehead Conference. The editors acknowledge in gratitude the University of Azores for hosting the conference; the International Process Network and the conference organizers and section chairs for their leadership; and Dr. John Becker for his early editorial work on some of the chapters of this book. We acknowledge in fond memory the life of Leslie A. Muray (1948–2019) whose own chapter culminates the volume. His vision of a "caring universe" remains a reflection of the kindness and care he showed others through the years.

INTRODUCTION

From Mechanism to Organism

MECHANISTIC VIEWS OF NATURE have long been discredited, yet they still linger in our ways of thinking, in popular science as well as in formal educational curricula. Descartes's mechanistic doctrine described nature in purely deterministic, physical terms, and it is directly related to the forms of dualism and substantialism that have prevailed in our culture to this day. Newton's physics, despite its success, ultimately led to a meaningless and valueless concept of nature. The prevalent idea of science as a manifold of barren, disconnected, valueless abstractions jeopardizes its role as the foundational knowledge for technical, social, ethical, and ecological issues.

The new physics, however, beginning in the early twentieth century, caused a rupture in the longstanding mechanistic paradigm, opening up novel paths of unprecedented discovery and new possibilities for deeper, organic ways of understanding. The emergence of Alfred North Whitehead's "philosophy of organism" was contemporary to the new physics and inaugurated a novel vision of nature through scientific, social, and metaphysical theories. Whitehead effectively saw that addressing the mechanistic rupture required an innovative, organic departure. His critique of abstractions, his refusal to bifurcate nature, and his famous formulation of the fallacy of misplaced concreteness (among others) unveiled the inadequacies of mechanistic thought, the value of an organic paradigm, and a profoundly ecological vision of science, philosophy, and civilization.

The shift to organic modes of thought undergirding Whitehead's philosophy continues to blossom with fresh possibilities for rethinking the world of nature, the place of human beings, and our current ecological precarity. This shift is being felt across disciplines, from philosophy to economics, society, and religion, as scholars are making new connections, challenging older contentions, and working together to realize an ecological civilization. Addressing the ecological crisis is not the domain of a single discipline, but rather requires creative interdisciplinary collaboration, such that metaphysical commitments, calculated scientific judgments, personal and corporate responsibility and, of course, hope—come together to build a peaceful, sustainable, and equitable future.

The contributions to this volume exemplify the interdisciplinary nature of this quest. Written by authors from around the world, and having first emerged at the 2017 International Whitehead Conference at the University of the Azores, Portugal, these organic proposals now appear in this book and are flexibly positioned across three broad themes: Organic Philosophy, Organic Society, and Organic Religion.

Part I: Organic Philosophy

What are the fundamental commitments, priorities, and implications of the development of an *organic philosophy*? Part I offers five chapters, each drawing out key insights that together begin to form a set of answers to this question. Engaging the pervasiveness of process, creativity, interrelation, experience, memory, value, and sympathetic causality in nature, these chapters are rooted in Whiteheadian insights, but not confined to them.

In chapter one, "Whitehead, Biosemiotics, and Value," John Pickering argues for an integrated ecology that allows for the reintegration of rational scientific facts and normative human values such that Hume's famed guillotine between "is" and "ought" is evaded. Pickering brings together key insights from A. N. Whitehead, C. S. Peirce, and biosemiotics to offer a practical vision that could have real geopolitical effects in our time. This vision looks to the ubiquity of subjectivity in nature and thus also the ubiquity of value and purposive causality. As such, it renders coherent the normative world of human values, which must otherwise appear to be an alien feature in a mechanical cosmos devoid of value. In reconnecting what Hume disconnected, Pickering draws on a variety of voices and calls for a metaphysics that transcends conventional boundaries between the mental and the physical and the factual and the normative. He envisions the human self as a semiotic process emerging from the biosemiotic and axiological nature of a truly organic cosmos.

In chapter two, "Nature and Experience: Between Process Philosophy and Phenomenology," Luca Vanzago draws together vital phenomenological and process insights into an engaging discussion as to the ontological status of nature and the place of phenomenal experience. Built on Husserl and influenced by Whitehead, Merleau-Ponty's phenomenology of embodied subjectivity paves the way for a deeper inquiry into a processual conception of nature as a means of renovating phenomenological ontology. In Whitehead, Merleau-Ponty saw nature as that which communicates with itself and, thus, is neither pure object nor pure subject. Approached through a phenomenological perspective, the meaning of nature is always to be conceived in terms of concrescent experience. Vanzago's chapter is an informative look at the influence of Whitehead on Merleau-Ponty and the possibilities of process phenomenology emerging between them.

In chapter three, "Thought and Memory," Jason Brown engages key notions of pastness and presentness, receptiveness and agency, as they relate to memory, thought, and experience in a processual world. For Brown, the complexities of memory have largely been glossed over in cognitive theory, particularly the continuity of thought and perception. He argues that the "endogenous substrate of perception" is in fact memorial, such that conscious thought occurs as an "enhancement at pre-terminal phases in revival." In light of this, he shows that these memorial traces cannot refer to some localized storehouse, but, in fact, repeat the trajectory of the process of actualization in the original experience of perception. Conceived as such, Brown argues that the notion of forgetting is to be conceived not as decay, but as incomplete revival. Distinctions of thought and memory thus depend not only on novelty and a departure from reproduction, but also on the "feeling of presentness" for thought, and a feeling of "pastness for memory." For Brown, a thought image felt in the present has some feeling of agency, which occurs primarily with a lack of resolution or a direction to the future, while the pastness of memory deprives images of volition, even though a sense of effort can still accompany attempts to resurrect past experiences. Brown concludes by applying these insights to the analysis of *déjà vu* in human experience.

In chapter four, "The Anthropocene, Ecozoic Era, and Organic Philosophy: A Provocative Trio in Hamilton, Berry, and Whitehead," Herman F. Greene triangulates Clive Hamilton, Thomas Berry, and A. N. Whitehead in order to reenvision the future. Particularly, when seen together, the respective insights belonging to notions of the Anthropocene, the Ecozoic era, and organic philosophy harbor relevant insights and possibilities for mutual depth. Greene hails Hamilton the *explainer,* because of his vivid explanations of the scientific understanding of the Anthropocene and the ruptures of the Earth system. He calls Berry the *describer* and the *ecological poet,* because of his mythic vision of a transmutation from a terminal Cenozoic era to a newly emerging Ecozoic era. Incorporating both, Greene calls Whitehead the *grand philosopher,* both explainer and describer (and poet), who, contrary to critiques of dryness and impenetrability, actually transforms a world of moving dead objects into a world of processual emotion, intensity, purpose, and value. For Greene, Whitehead's organic vision provides the needed philosophy for the Anthropocene.

In chapter five, "Cause and Influence in Whitehead," John B. Cobb Jr. looks to new social, economic, and political trajectories tied to Whitehead's understanding of cause and influence in his philosophy of organism. For Cobb, many Whiteheadians working in social and political theory have held back from recognizing the actual effects of the characteristics of societies on their members. Cobb links this to a deeper problem regarding what Whitehead says about causality, leading to a distortion that has undermined the use of Whitehead's philosophy in social thought. In recounting how these problems emerge, Cobb points the way forward through a deeper analysis of causality and influence in Whitehead and the resulting economic and political implications for society.

Part II: Organic Society

What changes to communal, cultural, economic, political, and legal life support a turn to an *organic society*? Part II offers five chapters that consider requisite adjustments to how we approach key societal concerns. These include growth and property rights, the relation between society and nature, the need for robust ecological management, the re-embedding of market environmentalism, and the development of an integral jurisprudence of human homeostasis with nature.

In chapter six, "Growth, Commodification and Property Rights," Maria-Teresa Teixeira argues against the delusion of an endless economic growth that is grounded in the notion of production as an endless process and nature as an unlimited resource. Related to the mythology of limitless growth is the endless profit trade of commodification, which produces fragmented and value-deficient societies, particularly with respect to land and property rights. Using essential Whiteheadian insights, Teixeira articulates how we might overcome both growth economies and commodification and develop new holistic models for property rights.

In chapter seven, "Nature-based Solutions and the Complex Relation Between Society and Nature," Moirika Reker scrutinizes the notion of "Nature-based solutions" (NBS) as put forth by the International Union of Nature Conservation, and its wide usage in literature and in reframing environmental policy. What is meant by "nature" in these "solutions," however? Reker follows this question into the various ways in which the concept of nature has been conceived and related to society at large. She concedes the good intentions of NBS but holds that it suffers from anthropocentricism in focusing upon how human beings can benefit from nature. It remains unclear for Reker whether NBS are really a help or hindrance in our complex relation to the natural world.

In chapter eight, "The Good and Prudent Handling of Things: The Need for an Ecological Management," Mark Dibben takes as his starting point the Western infatuation for economic models that equate "growth" and "success," such that management is the architect of "success." Coupled together, these models have played a huge role in the emergence of the Anthropocene, in which human beings retain the power to rapidly alter the biosphere in ways hitherto inconceivable. Human "management" needs transformation. Dibben thus looks to the inherent role of management in nature and animal species; the role of scientism and human management in the modern age; the causes and effects of neo-naturalism; and the failures of human management. In considering proper requisites for an ecological management, Dibben argues that anthropocentrism needs to be supplanted by *biocentrism*, which embeds humans in nature and better supports its transgenerational wellbeing. What is needed is management for *Earthism*, not economism. While this may be radical, it seems for Dibben the only route to human survival.

In chapter nine, "Re-Embedding the Market: Institutionalizing Effective Environmentalism," Arran Gare traces the difficult history which led to the disembedding of the market from communities and the radical economic fluctuations, severe depressions, and social dislocations that resulted. For Gare, this exemplifies Whitehead's fallacy of misplaced concreteness. In disembedding the market from communities, communities where then subjected to a supposedly autonomous market. Gare looks to insights of Karl Polanyi, Arild Vatn, Whitehead, and others in considering what is required to re-embed the market in communities and institute a more effective environmentalism. For Gare, the power of transnational corporations and financial institutions needs to be undermined so that power is returned to the population and a new future forged.

In chapter ten, "A Jurisprudence for Human Homeostasis with Nature," Charles Walters navigates a host of scientific, philosophical, historical, statistical, and legal resources, including the importance and translatability of process philosophy and sociobiology, in order to propose a global jurisprudence of ecological revival and human survival. Walters argues that a necessary condition for sustainability of the Earth's resources is homeostasis between nature and human beings. In order to avoid death and human extinction, he is adamant that we require a "synergistic disystem," where nature is in control and humans are as slaves. In developing his vision of a worldwide ecocentric jurisdiction, he looks to the constitutional principles enacted in both Ecuador and Bolivia. Building on these, Walters sets forth ten additional "Earth Constitution" provisions and statutes to achieve homeostasis. After a year of some two million COVID-19 deaths, nature has yet again reminded human beings who is in control. Indeed, for Walters, the COVID-19 pandemic should compel the world's population to establish an integral ecological jurisprudence before it is too late.

Part III: Organic Religion

What kind of religious and theological resources are needed to support the development of *organic religion*? Part III offers five chapters which draw out relevant ecological possibilities from religious and theological traditions. These include considerations of an ecological God, attention to biblical metaphors of processual creation, the possibilities of an Islamic eco-humanism, a modified process Jainism, and the development of an integrative religious naturalism.

In chapter eleven, "Divine Wilder/ness: Nature, Panentheism, and Eco-Theological Ethics," Andrew M. Davis examines the ecological insights of key philosophers and theologians to articulate the value of "panentheism" as an eco-theological vision harboring great ethical relevance. Davis looks to what he calls "the theological pillars of ecological passivity" as they are exemplified in much popular cultural theology. He focuses principally upon the negative ecological consequences of monarchial omnipotence and divine externality. He then explores the positive ecological value intrinsic to panentheism's vision of divine proximity as inclusion, immanence, and evolution. From these convictions, Davis develops an eco-theological vison of divine attributes and activity, and the human ethical imperative. These include eco-sacramental suffering; divine persuasion and the omnipotentiality of love; divine call and creaturely response; and the divine-human collaborative ethic that Davis calls "ethical theosis."

In chapter twelve, "Images of Lions: Psalm 104 as a Metaphor for a Processual View of Creation," Robert Gnuse recounts his own involvement in the creation-evolution controversy and responds to the claim that evolution replaces God with a process of violent competitive survival. Gnuse looks to biblical passages, particularly Psalm 104, that accept and even embrace the natural violence inherent among the predator-prey relations of a healthy ecological order. For Gnuse, there are biblical passages that express this reality in a laudatory fashion as part of the presence and activity of God in creation. Gnuse holds that this is consistent with a processual view of creation. While Psalm 104 is largely dedicated to the theological praise of God's created order, the psalmist also affirms the messier aspects of creation: the story of predatorial killing and eating. Nevertheless, Gnuse stresses that God is present in the cycle of life and death that is the process of creation.

In chapter thirteen, "Toward an Ecologically Awakened Islamic Humanism," Farhan A. Shah develops the outlines of an Islamic eco-humanism based upon the process philosophy of Muhammad Iqbal. He insists that the Qur'an itself imagines the whole of creation on the analogy of a tree of life, or a single organism, emerging from and returning to its divine source. For Shah, an Islamic humanism affirms the value of human life and human rights as situated *within*, rather than apart from, the larger becoming whole of reality. As such, Shah claims that anthropocentric renderings of humanism are foreign to Islam. In joining qur'anic insights with Iqbal's temporal process philosophy, he seeks a constructive postmodernism that encourages the development of ecological worldviews stressing interrelationality and just and sustainable communities across the world. For Shah, Islam, as interpreted by Iqbal, can offer a powerful contribution to an ecologically awaked humanism.

In chapter fourteen, "A Shortcut on the Jain Path of Liberation: Aparigraha **as** Ahimsā in Process Philosophy," Wm. Andrew Schwartz argues for the relevance of process metaphysics for reimagining and accelerating the Jain path of liberation. Schwartz claims that a substance-based metaphysic—so predominant in the West—introduces unnecessary stumbling blocks on the Jain path. By contrast, a process metaphysics of panexperientialism makes it easier to practice two of the most important vows of Jainism: *aprarigraha* (nonpossession) and *ahimsā* (nonviolence). When one recognizes that the world is not a "collection of objects to own, but a community of subjects to be known," Schwartz holds that the compassion and sympathetic feeling at the heart of both process philosophy and the Jain vows of nonpossession and nonviolence are elevated to new significance. For Schwartz, practicing *aparigraha* as *ahimsā*, grounded in a process view of nature, theoretically multiplies karmic shedding and thus offers a more expedient and efficient path toward liberation.

In chapter fifteen, "A Process-Akashic Religious Naturalism," Leslie A. Muray looks to central insights of Frederick Ferré, Alfred North Whitehead, Erving László, Shubert Ogden, and others to aid the development of a process-akashic vision of religious naturalism. This vision holds to a personalist and organicist understanding of human and nonhuman beings and understands "God" as the creativity of the cosmos, as well as the "Akashic Field" in which the universe preserves and remembers all experiences. For Muray, this vision of a creative, sensitive, and responsive universe that cares for all inhabitants through both influence and reception is similar to Whitehead's understanding of the primordial and consequent natures of God. Yet, Muray follows Ferré, Donald Crosby, and Jerome Stone in identifying "God" with the *drive* toward novelty, beauty, and complexity in the natural order. Still, he insists that there is a caring in the nature of things, a creativity, sensitivity, and responsiveness that calls forth and lures the development of human and nonhuman persons.

The proposals that comprise this volume are not neutral. They recognize the uniqueness of this historical moment and together call for an organic reconception of our philosophical, societal, and religious framing. Far from ousting creativity, experience, mind, feeling, and value, the organic shift represented in these chapters reintegrates what was lost in the mechanistic paradigm. But, in these precarious ecological times, we should remember that a change in the dominant modes of thought, if not accompanied by action, is vacuous—a mere theoretical exercise without practical implementation. We require collective action and individual responsibility stimulated by an overriding sense of worth in achieving an ecological civilization.

Andrew M. Davis
Maria-Teresa Teixeira
Wm. Andrew Schwartz

PART ONE
Organic Philosophy

ONE

Whitehead, Biosemiotics, and Value

John Pickering

'Tis all in pieces, all coherence gone,
All just supply, and all relation . . .
-John Donne, *An Anatomy of the World* (1611)

DONNE WAS RESPONDING to something he saw at the core of the new philosophy of nature that was gaining ground in his time. He intuitively grasped that what was taking shape would utterly change the way people experienced their place in the cosmos. The Earth and the souls on it would no longer be at the center of a universe where everything that existed and all that happened fitted into a wider web of meaning. The new worldview lacked any value-giving framework and would leave the universe devoid of purpose. Without a sense of what was "just supply," the cosmos would be open to plunder. His theological and visceral instincts rebelled.

What Donne feared has duly arrived. We can recognize it in something said by an indigenous inhabitant of the South American rainforest, *apropos* the men whose machines were destroying the life of his region. The remark, perhaps made as much in perplexity as in anger, was "Why don't they *know* what they're doing is wrong?" Here "wrong" doesn't mean "They shouldn't be wrecking our land." but rather "How is it that these men no longer know the difference between wrong and right?"

This loss of the moral intelligence that makes people feel that destroying the natural world is wrong is one reason that human activity is doing so much damage to the world's living systems. It reflects an alienation from nature that is increasing as more and more people live urbanized, technologized lives. The emotional appeal of TV programs celebrating the natural world is a poignant signal that the sensibilities of natural habitation have not been entirely extinguished, even among the urbanized moderns. What Donne saw was that the loss of these sensibilities, the framework of unifying meaning, would lead to people ill-treating the world, as it were. Heidegger pointed to something very like this in his questioning of technology and what it does to human consciousness.[1]

Once the web of the world is cut into manipulable pieces, it reveals itself differently to human consciousness. When nature is no longer valued for its interconnected wholeness, then it no longer has an intrinsic right to proper treatment. Instead, nature is approached as a standing resource, the value of which is its utility for human purposes. The result is that, for well over a century, human beings in technologized societies have been taking more than the world can afford to offer.

The impact of human action on the living world shows all too clearly how destructive this change in consciousness is. Taking more from the living systems of the world, more than the natural rate of re-growth can replace, is eating into our natural capital and profoundly damaging the biosphere. Moreover, the effects of that damage are borne disproportionately by those who have not caused it. Technological advances made by the more developed nations have made possible lifestyles not available to less-developed nations. These latter bear the worst of the damage and get few to none of the benefits. The situation is not only an environmental tragedy but is also unjust.

Destructive over-consumption is a collective mental illness. A remedy is sorely needed that will help to find more sustainable ways for all people to live on the planet. Integral ecology is, or should be, a part of such a remedy, since it appears to offer the unified worldview that Donne feared to lose. As the introduction to this section puts it, integral ecology is based on the view that "everything in nature is constitutively interrelated and requires a systemic, holistic, and dynamic approach—a process-relational ontology—to be properly understood." These are brave words, but ones that might also be adopted by contemporary physical scientists since they, too, seek to create just such a worldview. However, the trouble with their efforts is that questions of value fall by the wayside. The work of physical scientists is done in the long shadow of David Hume's remark on the necessary separation of rational scientific facts and normative human values, often compressed into the slogan "You can't get from is to ought."

What is needed is to ignore Hume's objection and to make from integral ecology a rational worldview that is not only compatible with scientific findings but also with normative human values. A suggestion as to how to do this will be sketched in what follows, using ideas from A. N. Whitehead, C. S. Peirce, and biosemiotics. It is not offered simply as an academic exercise, but as something that might have some purchase for the geopolitical realities of our time.

To begin, the next section attempts to extract some ideas from Whitehead's somewhat challenging conceptual vocabulary.

What Whitehead Does Not Offer to Integral Ecology

Whitehead claims "Nobody can be a good reasoner unless by constant practice he has realized the importance of getting hold of the big ideas and of hanging on to them like grim death."[2] His work shows that he tried to follow his own advice, but while that may have made for consistency, it did not help with accessibility. Whitehead's influence, though enduring and perhaps resurgent, is minor. This is in part because much of his writing, *Process and Reality* being the obvious example, can be notoriously obscure.[3] If integral ecology is to help remedy the geopolitical problems of our time, there is little in Whitehead's more advanced conceptual writings that is of much direct use.

Even so, it is worth hanging on to Whitehead's "big ideas." Perhaps one of his biggest, and one that is particularly relevant here, is that the ultimate constituents of nature are not objects but subjects. The essential property of subjects is the capacity for intentionality, that is, a qualitative link to what surrounds them that guides action, much as Merleau-Ponty proposed.[4] This subjective intentionality is what renders the cosmos open and intrinsically creative, as Merleau-Ponty recognized in his later work, on which Whitehead had a clear influence.[5] While to claim that the ultimate constituents of nature are intentional subjects somewhat oversimplifies the vast sweep of Whitehead's work, it is accurate enough and points to a vital issue. That is, Whitehead gives to subjectivity the same ontological status given to the purely material particles, field, forces and the like that are dealt with by natural science. In passing, it is worth noting that panpsychism is regaining ground in contemporary philosophy.[6]

Accepting this ontological status means to accept that intentionality is *ubiquitous* in nature. Whitehead goes further, proposing that the simple intentionality of nature's ultimate constituents can coalesce into the more complex intentionality of what he calls societies, collectives with an enduring self-identity and a shared project, which would more generally be called organisms. This led Whitehead to the view that "Biology is the study of the larger organisms; whereas physics is the study of the smaller organisms."[7] This claim must have seemed strange in 1926, but at the present time it is perhaps less so, particularly in the light of some recent discussions of panpsychism[8] and of panprotopsychism, which is "roughly, the view that fundamental entities are proto-conscious, that is, that they have certain special properties that are precursors to consciousness and that can collectively constitute consciousness in larger systems."[9]

Here are big ideas that seem worth clinging to, especially as they complement another enduring feature of Whitehead's philosophy; namely, that it is a mistake to consider any aspect of reality apart from the whole of it. Thus: "The misconception which has haunted philosophic literature throughout centuries is the notion of independent existence. There is no such mode of existence. Every entity is only to be understood in terms of the way in which it is interwoven with the rest of the universe."[10] Here, there is a clear echo of a principal feature of Integral Ecology noted above, namely, that "everything in nature is constitutively interrelated."

These two ideas, the *ubiquity of subjectivity* and the *interrrelated continuity* of the natural order, taken together, hint at how the findings of science might be more fully integrated with questions of value, and hence with human norms. If subjectivity, which is intrinsically value-laden, is ubiquitous, and if everything that exists is in some way linked, then values are as ubiquitous as subjectivity. More will be said on this later, but presently, the task is to see past Whitehead's often challenging terminology to the bigger ideas, and to see how they might help to find more sustainable ways for human beings to live.

Examples of his more specific terminology might be, among many others, "aim," "prehension," "causal efficacy," or "actual entity." Searching through his writings, one discovers few illustrative examples that would allow these ideas to be applied more easily. Furthermore, this terminology is often somewhat circular. For example, "aim" is defined as an aspect of "prehension," while "prehension" is something akin to an action with a purpose directed "at that complex of feelings which is the enjoyment of those data in that way."[11] Thus defined, both "aim" and "prehension" seem to require each other to be understood, with "aim" being more of a mental event and "prehension" referring to both mental and physical levels. Rarely are these terms made any more explicit with examples. Both "aim" and "prehension" seem to be critically related to "intentionality," as used by Husserl and Merleau-Ponty. But in Whitehead their definition is multilayered and, in many places, becomes bound up with other equally crucial terms such as "actual entity." But, once again, trying to clarify what those terms mean leads in turn into ever-denser terminology, as here: "Thus an actual entity has a three-fold character: (1) it has the character 'given' for it by the past; (2) it has the subjective character aimed at it in its process of concrescence; (3) it has the superjective character, which is the pragmatic value of its specific satisfaction qualifying the transcendent creativity."[12]

But what do "concrescence" and "superjective character" mean? With steady application and scholarly resources, these terms do in fact come together to provide the organic process worldview for which Whitehead is justly celebrated. But for the more immediate business of finding some remedy for our present geopolitical problems, the exercise is of little help. What might help would be to combine Whitehead's big ideas with other ideas that would make them more applicable, which is what the next section tries to do, using the conceptual resources of biosemiotics.

How to Make Whitehead's Ideas More Applicable

Whitehead's somewhat complex terminology is about three very fundamental questions which, once properly understood, are quite simple ones: (1) what is the world made of? (2) how do things happen? and (3) why? Whitehead's answer to the first has already been sketched above, in caricature as it were. It is the claim that the ultimate constituents of nature are not objects, that is, substances, but rather *events*. Moreover, these are said to have a subjective, purposive aspect. Here "purposive" has to be treated with caution to avoid a homunculus like regress. Whitehead does not propose that the ultimate constituents of the universe have humanlike abilities to, for example, plan actions and make choices. The idea is that all events, even at the smallest dimensions, retain some vestigial aspects of intentionality, and hence, of purpose.

The second question goes to the heart of what is meant by "organic." It is ironic that the oxymoron "organic mechanism" is occasionally used to describe Whitehead's system. Mechanistic is exactly what it is not. Interpreted mechanistically, things happen as they must, just as classical physics describes the movements of planets or of billiard balls on the table. But billiard balls go where they are driven by the actions of the players and, apart from a diminishing number of diehard mechanists, few believe those actions are determined in the same way as the movements of the planets in their orbits. Newtonian mechanics may determine the movements in the solar system, but on the billiard table, things happen as the players intend, as they exercise their skills with foresight and pleasure.

The actions of billiard players, people in general, nonhuman animals, and even plants when seen in the right time frame, are patently *intentional*, both in the more precise sense used by philosophers in the line of Husserl and Merleau-Ponty, and in the more everyday sense referring to an act carried out for some purpose, something the actor *means to do*. Here "means" is of more than usual significance. Used in human terms, the word is Janus-like; it faces both towards and away from the human subject. It stands for the interpretation given to the sensory impressions received from the world around us, such as the words we hear, what we read, and the signs we see around us. Of all these things it can be asked: "What do they mean?" It also stands for *purposiveness*. When we act with an aim in mind, we say of that action that it is something we "mean" to do. In *meaning* an action we own it, which is something that even quite young children know. A child who realizes that something they've done has got them in to trouble will probably try to disown the act by saying "I didn't *mean* it."

Thus, "meaning" brackets subjectivity, since it is used to stand for what the world does to the subject and what the subject does to the world. Meaning, in these senses, is bound up with signs. What a sign "means" is what it *stands for*. As C. S. Peirce put it, with uncharacteristic simplicity, a sign is "something that stands for something, to someone in some capacity."[13] This triadic definition is a productive advance on Saussure's distinction between a sign and what is signified. Although Saussure helped to lay the foundations of modern semiotics, the application of his system is limited by its being dyadic and, consequently, synchronic. That is, it offers a rich vocabulary with which to capture the structure of the sign world at a given moment, especially that part which involves language. But unless extended by the resources of transformational grammars, for example, it fails to capture the way signs function in systems that change over time, or to extend the use of semiotic ideas to embrace all of nature.

Remarkably, a treatment of semiosis that does just that had been put forward by a contemporary of Donne's, the Portuguese scholar John Poinsot, a Dominican Thomist. Poinsot's semiotics was, in fact, an ontological system, and signs were not merely human conventions but were fundamental to the dynamics and the coherence of his worldview. It was just this worldview that Donne feared to lose. As John Deely puts it in his magisterial survey of Western philosophy, Poinsot showed that "the story even of the sign begins with the discovery of nature as a reality prior to and in various ways escaping human purposes."[14] This is very like what is being put forward here, with the help of Peirce's triadic semiotic system.

Peirce, working independently of Saussure and in the tradition of American Pragmatism, developed a semiotic system that, like Poinsot's, was intended to be a complete ontology. For that to be possible, he recognized that as well as distinguishing signs from what they signify, his system also had to include the actual act of interpreting the sign, as below:

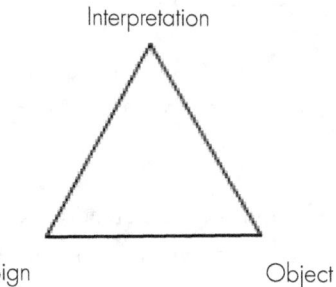

Diagram 1. Legend: Peirce's triadic model of signification.

Moreover, and crucially, the act of interpretation may in turn become a sign for further interpretation, as below:

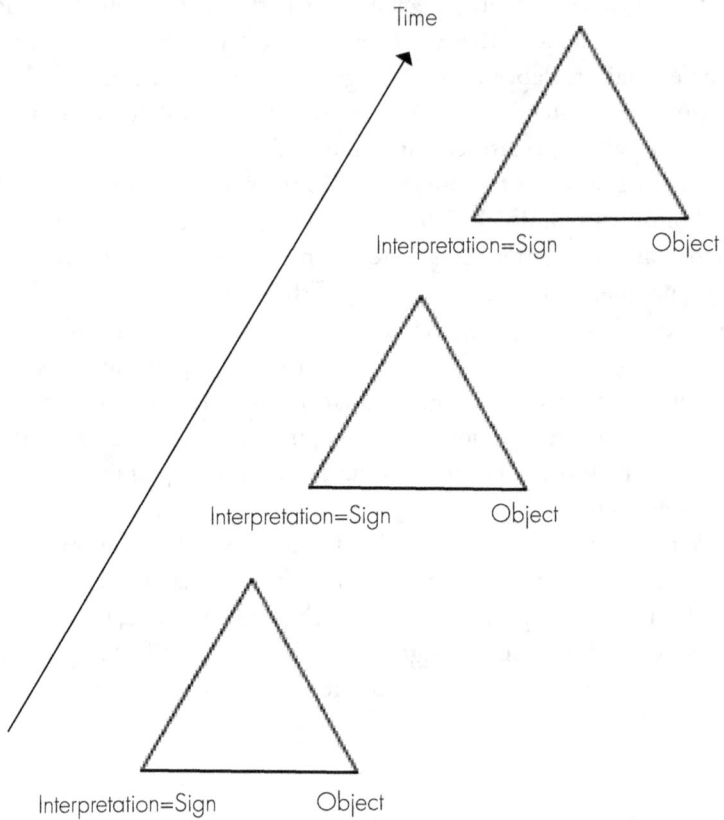

Diagram 2. Legend: Peirce's diachronic model of signification

It is this chaining of signification that renders Peirce's system diachronic, in critical contrast to the essential synchronicity of Saussure's. The contrast is crucial for what is being proposed here. It takes semiotic understanding beyond Saussure's relatively static description of language to deal with the dynamics of change in any system, whether natural or human made. Diachronicity captures the essence of organic action, which is intentional, progressive change.

This is the essence, too, of the flow of human reflexive consciousness. As an illustration of what is meant here, imagine a reader deeply engaged in her book. As her eyes flick over the pages, the words are read without much conscious effort. In skilled readers, this interpretation of signs with conventional meanings is automatic, at least in its initial stages. It is also likely to be much the same for all readers in a particular linguistic community. But it will prompt a flow of thoughts and images which will be unique to the individual reader. These in turn will be further interpreted in light of her feelings about what she's reading and the associations she makes with other things she's read, and with what she knows and feels more generally. All this will shape her interpretation of words and phrases subsequently encountered, much as Peirce conceived chained signification to work.

Let us now imagine that a faint but persistent sound appears in the background. If the reader is deeply engaged with the book, she may preconsciously reject it; that is, in some sense, choose not to hear the sound, or dimly to hear, but ignore it. If it persists, she may gradually allow it, or it may force its way into consciousness. At this point, once it makes it over some threshold of significance, she recognizes that it is her cell phone that she's left in another room; a sudden reorientation of consciousness occurs, and she jumps up to get it. The sound is a sign whose initial interpretation may simply have been as just another background noise of no particular significance. But as it persisted and commanded more and more interpretive attention, it gained meaning and prompted action.

The flow of events here is bound up in many layers of conventional signs that perfuse the human world. But it is reasonable to suppose that similar sequences of perception and action occur in the nonhuman world. Grazing animals, for example, are probably aware of various sounds and sights around them, but although they monitor them at a low level of attention, they remain unconcerned until something makes it over a threshold of significance and prompts action of some sort.

In the middle of the twentieth century, heroic attempts were made by behaviorists to reduce the actions of animals to mere chains of stimuli and responses. A recognition of the many limitations of such an approach was surprisingly long in coming, considering that far richer and realistic ones had been available well before the behaviorist era. For example, naturalists and ethologists, especially those who, like Konrad Lorenz, were influenced by the seminal work of Jacob von Uxeküll, approached animals, plants, and all levels of the living world as active organic beings whose relationship to the world around them was based on action and meaning, not mere stimulation and response. For them, animals and plants were essentially interrelated, that is, coevolved, and, for von Uxeküll, the basis of the interrelation was essentially semiotic.[15]

Biosemiotics, originating in the middle part of the twentieth century, takes von Uxeküll's project on.[16] In doing so, it broadens the treatment of meaning to cover a spectrum of phenomena ranging from the dynamics of human personalities at the most culturally bound end[17] to cellular process at the purely biological end.[18]

Contemporary biosemiotics has developed this project substantially and now combines elements from Peirce and von Uxeküll with cultural studies and systems thinking more generally. It offers a unified view of the interrelatedness of the natural world. Once interrelatedness is understood in semiotic terms, it opens the way to a deeper understanding of the origins of the cultural world, which is the domain of meanings created by human beings and, at a simpler level, by some social animals.

It is in this cultural world that the above example of interrupted reading is set. While it is intended to illustrate the richness of Peirce's treatment of unfolding signification, it also raises a critical question. Is Peirce's chain-like picture of semiosis rich enough? Chained events are necessarily sequential. But semiosis, both in nature and in the human sphere, is more often net-like; that is, it is necessarily parallel. William James recognized this when dealing with consciousness and selective attention, proposing that "the mind is at every stage a theatre of simultaneous possibilities."[19]

Within the sphere of human psychology, there is substantial evidence to back this up. Subliminal presentation of a word with multiple meanings appears to activate all its meanings. Freudian slips show that, in addition to what someone consciously intends to say, there may be other streams of thought that are denied entry to consciousness. The unique talent of the mathematician Ramanujan seemed to involve a parallel search through a space of possibilities that was driven by aesthetics as much as by logic. These and many more examples suggest that, in the human case, the flow of mental experience is parallel rather than sequential. In which case, the semiotic chains suggested by Peirce are better seen as a linear slice through a vast parallel network. In it, patterns of activity form and reform. In keeping with Peirce's pragmatism, it may be taken that patterns compatible with the patterns around them persist, and patterns that are not compatible, fade.

David Bohm's hypothesis of semiotic continuity[20] is an understanding of the causal structure of nature that has much in common with Peirce's view. In its simpler form, Bohm presents his system as a chain much like Peirce's. In more extended treatments, he puts forward a view of the world comprising two ontological orders enfolded in each other without boundaries. These orders are the material, or "somatic," order and the order of meaning, or "signification." The two orders are in a continual process of enfolding into and unfolding out from each other. Enfolding renders one order implicit in the other, whilst the complementary process of unfolding makes the emerging order explicit. What appear to be material objects or events emerge from the order of signification while, in complementary fashion, what we take to be mental events emerge from and are inseparable from the somatic order that produces or supports them.[21] Bohm and Hiley refer to the "unbroken wholeness of nature," which moves from the chain-like slice to an interrelated plenum of semiotic causation and which is thus boundary free.[22] It might be possible to express Bohm's world picture in terms of Peirce's triadic ontology of first, second, and thirdness. The somatic order is a first: mere existence. The order of signification is a second, being intrinsically relational. The process of unfolding/enfolding is a third, since in it, relations are interpreted.

These ideas help to enrich our understanding of Whitehead's terminology. For example, in the excerpt from *Process and Reality* quoted above, we encounter the terms "superjective character" and "actual entity." The latter is a semiotic event in which a sign transmits activity from one level of reality to another. The former is transmission of aim from one semiotic event to another.

This re-shaping of metaphysics is more than just an academic exercise. It helps to promote a worldview that covers both scientific findings and normative human values, which is also one of the aims of integral ecology. A metaphysic of process and signification evades the boundary between "is" and "ought" that David Hume saw as unavoidable. Science has moved on from his time, and we now have richer conceptual tools with which to conduct research and to apply its results. If, as Whitehead's "big idea" suggests, the ultimate constituents of reality are *prehensive events*, they will by definition express some degree of intentionality. Even though this may be vestigial, it serves to repair the damaging exclusion of subjectivity from our world picture.

Proposing that the ultimate constituents of the universe are event-like, and that these events have some degree of intention about them, has to be done with caution. It is not a claim that these elementary events have the richness of intentionality found in human mental life. But it is to claim that there is always an intentional element to them, albeit one so small that it ceases to have any resemblance to intentionality as experienced. There is a precedent, or analogy, here with physical science. Popular accounts of contemporary physics, especially of quantum gravity, stress that the objective components of reality, matter, space, and time are minutely divisible, but not without limit.[23] Once physics had developed to the point of dealing with micro events at the Planck length, space, time, and matter cease to have much resemblance to the macro world of objects and events encountered in everyday experience. Nevertheless, the micro world must be the basis of the macro world. Given Whitehead's big idea about what the micro events really are, why shouldn't what goes for the objective aspects of reality also be true for the subjective ones? Vestigial elements of intentionality will have very little about them that resembles the sort of intentionality that concerned Husserl, but they will provide the basis for it nonetheless. Husserl's phenomenological methods depended on reflexive consciousness to investigate intentionality, but they would be irrelevant to the investigation of intentionality at the vestigial level. In a similar way, although one can learn a great deal about the physical world through careful observation and experiment with macro objects, much as Galileo did, those methods cannot by themselves show the deeper structure of reality.[24]

Intentionality and, with it, subjectivity, which is intrinsically value-laden, are in the cosmos. They do not need the human mind, or any form of mind, for that matter, to exist. The reflexive form of consciousness, which appears to be a human monopoly, is required for examining subjectivity, but, examined or not, it is there *a priori*. If we accept that value-laden subjectivity is ubiquitous, and if everything that exists is linked through networks of semiotic causation, then *values are as ubiquitous as subjectivity*. This is a very different worldview from that regnant at the end of the nineteenth century. Then, it seemed that mechanism had triumphed, and Ernst Haeckel declared "The great abstract law of mechanical causality rules the entire universe, as it does the mind of man."²⁵ This heroic expression of confidence in the universality of scientific understanding set an agenda that has lasted until today. It gives us a mechanistic world picture in which efficient causation is supreme, and in which subjective experience, Husserl's *Lebenswelt*, has no place. By and large, and despite the opposition of scholars like Whitehead and Peirce, that world picture persists, rendering the normative world of human values an alien anomaly in a world that is in reality nothing but a vast machine.

In fact, something akin to Haeckel's declaration can be accepted so long as the "nothing but" is fundamentally changed. Rather than dead matter and mechanical causality, it is organic patterns of biosemiotic causation that constitute the universe and all beings in it. This shift from mechanism to organism and to a biosemiotic view of causation is advanced here as a way of putting subjectivity, and especially human subjectivity, back into the natural order of things. It opens the way to tracing how the world of human values and norms arose within the prehuman world. It will re-establish some of the harmony expressed in Aristotle's geocentric universe that Donne feared to lose, but with a richer view of causation that includes Aristotle's unjustly overlooked category of formal causation. The world will no longer be "all in pieces, all coherence gone." It will also offer a more harmonious picture than the geocentric one, since in it there will be a qualitative continuity of cause rather than the variety of causes said to be at play in the Artistotelian universe.

This effort after a more harmonious picture is also a way to start on the task outlined above, namely, making process-relational metaphysics a more commonly understandable and hence applicable worldview that will have some traction in the geopolitics of our time. In effect, what is being attempted here is a recreation of the harmony of Donne's geocentric worldview, using Whitehead, Peirce, and biosemiotics to create a new worldview with a new center. For Donne, the earth was literally at the center of everything. Now we realize that this is not physically the case, but there is still a conceptual center; namely, subjectivity.

Putting the Pieces Back Together

One of the founders of contemporary Biosemiotics wrote: "The world is full of subjects and something must have created them.... Subjectivity has its roots in the cosmos and, at the end of the day, repression of this aspect of our world is not a viable proposition."[26] Indeed, tracing subjectivity to its roots might be one way to describe the projects of both Whitehead and Peirce. Accepting fully the statement that "something must have created them" points to some form of panpsychism, that is, a view that subjectivity is, and always has been, present at all levels of existence. This is a variety of speculative metaphysics that avoids both a homunculus like regress and a lapse into supernaturalism, and that also provides integral ecology with an accessible worldview that can help stop and hopefully repair the damage being done to the living systems of the world.

The causes of the damage emerge from a dense web of political, economic, and technological forces. But close to the center of the web, and in some sense driving it, is alienated human consciousness and the actions stemming from it. As Ernst Schumacher put it over fifty years ago: "It is no longer possible to believe that any political or economic reform, or scientific advance, or technological progress could solve the life-and-death problems of industrial society. They lie too deep, in the heart and soul of every one of us. It is there that the main work of reform has to be done."[27] Alienated, urbanized, technologized ways of living lead directly to over-consumptive flows in systems that link human beings, animals, and the living world. The results are all too clear: "Our data indicate that beyond global species extinctions Earth is experiencing a huge episode of population declines and extirpations … We describe this as 'biological annihilation.' … All signs point to ever more powerful assaults on biodiversity in the next two decades, painting a dismal picture of the future of life, including human life."[28]

This global impact arises from networks of local actions, too many of which are detached from the moral intelligence referred to at the start of this chapter. As a mundane example, consider the way in which pigs used to be and, sadly, may still be intensively reared in Europe. The animals were kept in steel pens with concrete floors, conditions that could hardly have been more alien from those of their evolutionary ancestors. When it was the cheapest feed, cassava was imported from the Far East, to which hormones and antibiotics were routinely added. Waste from the pigs was then exported back to the Far East as cassava fertilizer. The end result was neatly packaged bacon on supermarket shelves. The suffering, environmental damage, and health risks packaged with it were invisible to the people buying it. Most of them would probably never have seen a live pig or given much thought to where cheap bacon comes from. Various campaigns have improved things a bit, but their effects are small, given the gigantic force of global mass markets.

Metaphysics does not often figure in making bacon, but here the link is direct enough. If we lose awareness of the environment and the way our everyday lives relate to it, we are disconnected from the source of the moral intelligence which tells us that mistreating living beings is wrong. This sensitivity, which is practical rather than romantic, is still retained by peoples who live in a way that is more directly related to what the world around them can provide. They know what is valuable and hence what should not be destroyed.

Metaphysics, in the sense that has been advanced here, reconnects what David Hume disconnected, namely the investigation of what the world actually is and the values we come to adopt. The explicit values of the human world, those that can be critically examined and agreed on as norms within a community, are patent examples of what is meant by value. But there are implicit values, too, that come from a sense of connection to a more-than-human world. The indigenous rainforest dweller referred to at the start of the chapter exhibited just this sense when he wondered why the men destroying the forest didn't know what they were doing was wrong. This sense is also shown in the great nature writers such as John Muir and Aldo Leopold. As Leopold puts it "A thing is right when it tends to preserve the integrity, stability, and beauty of the biotic community. It is wrong when it tends otherwise."[29]

If we were to accept Hume's dictum, such value statements would have to be taken as just normative conventions with no other basis than human agreement. But we no longer need to do that in light of the metaphysic proposed here, since it holds that value is intrinsic to the causal continuity of the cosmos. It is a metaphysic that evades conventional boundaries, including those that have previously been taken to separate the mental from the physical and the factual from the normative. Semiotic causation, which is formal causation in the Aristotelian sense, thus helps to restore that part of the worldview that Donne feared was under attack. With this metaphysic, perhaps we are in a better position to recover something of the unity of the Aristotelian worldview, and to use it to address the urgent geopolitical issue of our time, which is the severe degradation of the prehuman parts of the living world.

But how is it to be done? Bringing together Whitehead, Peirce, and biosemiotics is a worthwhile intellectual project, but it will remain little more than that unless it is used outside the academic world to help reveal and address the environmental dangers that face us. One way to do this would be to connect with the work of environmental activists like David Abram, Arne Naess and Johanna Macy.[30] They, along with many others, presently fulfil the role Shelley gave to poets, namely, to be the "unacknowledged legislators of the world."[31] Indeed, it seems that the real causes of environmental degradation are more fully understood, and certainly more powerfully depicted, by poets than by politicians. The environmental activist and poet Gary Snyder writes: "The 'free world' has become economically dependent on a fantastic system of stimulation of greed which cannot be fulfilled... The soil, the forests and all animal life are being consumed."[32] This stimulation is pervasive. Increasing proportions of people now grow up and live in urbanized surroundings that are saturated with media technology whose only purpose is to promote consumption by creating artificial needs.

Globalization, which is Westernization by and large, means pervasive signification. This was clear over thirty years ago, when it was observed that "In technocratic societies there is overwhelming propaganda and advertising which encourages false needs and destructive desires... designed to foster increased production and consumption."[33] This is what creates the fake norms and distorted values of alienated consciousness. More than at any other time in human history, developing a sense of self is now bound up with powerful depictions of what to be, what to own, and what to aim for. If a metaphysic of process and relation, of the sort that's been outlined above, is to be of significance, it should be used to give a richer image of what selfhood actually consists in. A biosemiotic understanding of human selfhood will help recover norms with real ecological value. Such an understanding is that the essence of selfhood is a *semiotic process*, not the possession of something akin to the Cartesian soul.[34]

It has been suggested that the Western experience of people feeling that they are something exceptional, exisiting apart from the living world and hence entitled to use it for human ends, originated in Judeo-Christian teachings about the nature of the soul.[35] Changing this experience is seen by many environmentalists as a vital part of any response to the ecological crisis. Arne Naess, a philosopher whose position has come to be called the Deep Ecology movement, is sometimes identified with Eastern systems of thought, especially Buddhism. There we find a different view of selfhood. Naess puts it this way when discussing how to take more care not to harm the environment: "Care flows naturally if the 'self' is widened and deepened so that protection of free Nature is felt and conceived as protection of ourselves. Just as we need no morals to make us breathe ... (so) ... if your 'self' in the wide sense embraces another being, you need no moral exhortation to show care."[36]

Perhaps this broadening of the boundaries of the self is part of the reform of which Schumacher speaks. With care, it may be possible to approach Eastern traditions in this spirit, as helping human beings to experience their place in the world as part of a more inclusive and participatory cosmology.[37] These moves are towards a more modest image of the place of human experience in what Abram implied in the subtitle to his book *The Spell of the Sensuous;* namely, *Perception and Language in a More-Than-Human-World*. Some non-Western religions are occasionally cited as being environmentally sensitive in something like this sense. Hinduism, Jainism, and some native American traditions are examples here. They are said to allow human beings to experience themselves as a part of, rather than apart from the living world, especially by recognizing the sentience of other living things.[38] This implies that the boundary between self and world may be set more widely and felt to be more permeable. This connection is well brought out by Johanna Macy, who takes from Buddhism the view that: "To be interdependent and reciprocally affecting is to be a process. In this fluid state of affairs, the self is no exception."[39] From this view she concludes that: "If the self is a pattern ... or transformations of energy and information arising in interaction with the surrounding world, its nature is profoundly participatory in that of other beings. ... this [then] involves an extension of constructs of self-interest, in which the needs of other beings begin to emerge as covalent with one's own."[40] In a somewhat similar sense, Polly Yong-Eisendrath, a psychoanalyst strongly influenced by Buddhism, notes that this extension to our sense of self can be profoundly therapeutic: "If we conceive of the self as wholly interdependent and impermanent, as a function rather than as a thing, then we appreciate more deeply our true freedom in this world."[41] Interdependence and impermanence are intrinsic to a semiotic understanding of selfhood.[42]

This revision of our sense of self touches directly on environmental issues. There is presently deep concern at the loss of diversity of habitats and species.

Since human action is often a major cause of the loss itself, people may also feel that it is a human responsibility to do something about it. But such feelings depend on the degree to which people feel threatened and on how strongly they feel they belong to the natural order and have a duty of care towards it. Following Naess and Macy, it is clear that experiencing selfhood as a thing apart from, rather than a part of, the natural world leaves people more open to feelings of alienation and meaninglessness. It diminishes the sense of experiential continuity on which empathetic connection with the world depends. This is the internalized culmination of the "disenchantment of the world" that Max Weber saw as an experiential consequence of the shift from medieval to modern worldviews. Not only is the world divested of intrinsic meaning, but the self which encounters that world is also diminished.

However, shifts in the opposite direction, towards reenchantment, as it were, have been clear for decades now.[43] These shifts reflect the effort to repair a fundamental dislocation of our sense of belonging to the natural order and of kinship with other living beings, especially other animals.[44] Paradoxically, although globalization has meant the spread of manipulative media technology, it has also raised awareness of the interconnectedness of human cultures and of the natural systems on which they depend. As Michel Serres puts it, in setting out what he calls a "Natural Contract" between human beings and the world, this has "to do with the recent passage from local to global and with our renewed relationship to the world, which was long ago our master and of late our slave, always and in all cases our host, and now our symbiont."[45]

We are indeed symbionts, as are all living things. A metaphysics of process and relation, such as the one that has been sketched here, links all orders of existence into a living web of mutual, semiotic causation, which includes the human phenomenon. Whitehead and Peirce have created the foundations for it, and biosemiotics builds on them a conceptual structure that gives a fresh perspective on how the world of human values arises from the prehuman world. The task now is to use these ideas, in combination with the many thinkers and activists who are doing Schumacher's "main work." That work is to recover the moral intelligence that arises from being aware of our interdependence with the living world and, hence, of the damage being done to it. The more that work succeeds, the more we will be able to repair the damage and to re-establish the *coherence and just supply* that Donne feared to lose.

Endnotes

1. M. Heidegger, *The Question Concerning Technology and Other Essays*, trans. William Lovit (New York: Harper and Row, 1977). The original essay was published in 1954 as *Die Frage nach der Technik*.
2. A. N. Whitehead, *The Aims of Education and Other Essays* (New York: New American Library, [1929] 1949), 84.
3. D. Nicholson and J. Dupre, eds., *Everything Flows: Towards a Processual Philosophy of Biology* (Oxford: Oxford University Press, 2018), 7.
4. M. Merleau-Ponty, *The Phenomenology of Perception* (London: Routledge & Kegan Paul, 1962).
5. M. Merleau-Ponty, *Nature: Course Notes from the Collège de France*, trans. R. Vallier (Evanston, IL: Northwestern University Press, 2000).
6. P. Goff, *Galileo's Error: Foundations for a New Science of Consciousness* (New York: Pantheon Books, 2019).
7. A. N. Whitehead, *Science and the Modern World* (London: Pelican Books, 1926), ch. 4, 125.
8. G. Strawson, "Realistic Monism: Why Physicalism Entails Panpsychism," *Journal of Consciousness Studies* 13.10–11 (2006): 3–31; D. Skrbina, *Panpsychism in the West* (Massachusetts: MIT Press, 2005); D. Skrbina, ed., *Mind That Abides: Panpsychism in the New Millennium* (Amsterdam: John Benjamins, 2009).
9. D. Chalmers, "Panpsychism and Panprotopsychism," *The Amherst Lecture in Philosophy* 8 (2013): 1–35, http://www.amherstlecture.org/chalmers2013/.
10. A. N. Whitehead, *Essays in Science and Philosophy* (London: Philosophical Library, [1925] 1947), 64.
11. A.N. Whitehead, *Modes of Thought* (New York: The Free Press, 1938), 152.
12. A. N. Whitehead, *Process and Reality: An Essay in Cosmology* (New York: Cambridge University Press, 1929), 87.
13. See J. Buchler, ed., *The Philosophy of Peirce: Selected Writings* (London: Routledge and Kegan Paul, 1940), 99.
14. J. Deely, *Four Ages of Understanding: The First Postmodern Survey of Philosophy from Ancient Times to the Turn of the Twenty-First Century* (Toronto: University of Toronto Press, 2001).

15. T. von Uxeküll, "Jacob von Uexküll's Theory of Meaning," *Semiotica* 42 (1982): 1–88.

16. T. Sebeok and J. Umiker-Sebeok, eds., *Biosemiotics: The Semiotic Web* (Berlin: Mouton de Gruyter, 1992).

17. F. Rothschild, "Laws of Symbolic Mediation in the Dynamics of Self and Personality," *Annals of New York Academy of Sciences* 96 (1962): 774–84.

18. K. Kull, "An Introduction to Phytosemiotics: Semiotic Botany and Vegetative Sign Systems," *Sign Systems Studies* 28 (2000): 326–50; J. Hoffmeyer, *Biosemiotics: an Examination Into the Signs of Life and the Life of Signs* (University of Scranton Press, 2008).

19. W. James, *The Principles of Psychology, Volumes I and II* (Cambridge, MA: Harvard University Press, 1983), 288.

20. D. Bohm, *Unfolding Meaning* (London: Routledge, 1985), 72–99.

21. Bohm, *Unfolding Meaning*.

22. D. Bohm and B. Hiley, *The Undivided Universe* (London: Routledge, 1993), 381–88.

23. C. Rovelli, *Reality Is Not What It Seems: The Journey to Quantum Gravity*, trans. Simon Carnell and Erica Segre (New York: Penguin Books, 2017).

24. P. Goff, *Galileo's Error,* chaps. 1 & 4.

25. E. Haeckel, *The Riddle of the Universe at the Close of the Nineteenth Century*, trans. J. McCabe (New York: Harper Books, [1895] 1906). These words are attributed to Haeckel in O. Barfield, *History in English Words* (London: Faber & Faber, 1926), 188.

26. J. Hoffmeyer, *Signs of Meaning in the Universe* (Bloomington: Indiana University Press, 1996), 57–58.

27. E. F. Schumacher, *Good Work* (London: Jonathan Cape, 1979), 25.

28. G. Ceballos et al., "Biological Annihilation Via the Ongoing Sixth Mass Extinction Signaled by Vertebrate Population Losses and Declines," *Proceedings of the New York Academy of Sciences*, 10 July 2017: E6089–E6096, https://doi.org/10.1073/pnas.1704949114.

29. A. Leopold, "The Land Ethic," in *A Sand County Almanac* (New York: Oxford UP, 1949), 224–25.

30. D. Abram, *The Spell of the Sensuous: Perception and Language in a*

More-Than-Human World (New York: Vintage Books, 1997); J. Macy, *Mutual Causality in Buddhism and General Systems Theory* (Albany: SUNY, 1991); J. Macy, "The Greening of the Self," in A. H. Badiner, ed., *Dharma Gaia: A Harvest of Essays in Buddhism and Ecology* (Berkeley: Parallax Press, 1990, 53–63), eBook: https://www.goodreads.com/book/show/19237630-greening-of-the-self); A. Naess in M. Fox, *Toward a Transpersonal Ecology: Developing New Foundations for Environmentalism* (Boston and London: Shambhala Publications, 1995. Originally published in 1990 by State University of New York Press.

31. Percy Bysshe Shelley, *Essays, Letters from Abroad, Translations and Fragments,* in two volumes, ed. Mary Shelley (London: Edward Moxon, [1839] 1840).

32. G. Snyder, *Earth House Hold.* (New York: New Directions Publishing, 1969). This quotation comes from the section "Buddhism and the Coming Revolution." It is also available online at http://www.bopsecrets.org/CF/garysnyder.htm.

33. B. Devall and G. Sessions, *Deep Ecology: Living as if Nature Mattered* (Salt Lake City, UT: Peregrine Smith, 1985), 68.

34. J. Pickering, "Selfhood is a Semiotic Process," *Journal of Consciousness Studies* 6/4 (1999): 31–47; also in J. Pickering, *The Authority of Experience* (London: Curzon Press, 1997), 149–69.

35. L. White, "The Historical Roots of Our Ecological Crisis," *Science* 155 (1967): 1203–07.

36. A. Naess in M. Fox, *Toward a Transpersonal Ecology*, 217.

37. See, for example, I. Harris, "Buddhist Environmental Ethics and Detraditionalization: The Case of EcoBuddhism," *Religion* 25/3 (1995): 199–211; S. James, *Zen Buddhism and Environmental Ethics* (Aldershot: Ashgate, 2004).

38. R. Gottlieb, ed., *This Sacred Earth: Religion, Nature, Environment*, 2nd Ed. (New York: Routledge, 2004).

39. Macy, *Mutual Causality*, 107.

40. Macy, *Mutual Causality*, 194.

41. P. Young-Eisendrath, "The Transformation of Human Suffering: A Perspective from Psychotherapy and Buddhism," *Psychoanalytic Inquiry* 28/5 (2008): 541–49.

42. J. Pickering, "Selfhood is a Semiotic Process": 45, footnote 32.

43. See, for example, D. R. Griffin, ed., *The Reenchantment of Science: Postmodern Proposals* (Albany: SUNY, 1988); D. R. Griffin, *Unsnarling the World Knot* (Berkeley: University of California Press, 1998), Introduction.

44. F. Matthews, *The Ecological Self* (London: Routledge, 1991); F. Matthews, *Without Animals Life is not Worth Living* (Adelaide: Ginninderra Press, 2016).

45. M. Serres, *The Natural Contract*, trans. Elizabeth MacArthur & William Paulson (Ann Arbor: University of Michigan Press, 1995), 38.

TWO

Nature and Experience: Between Process Philosophy and Phenomenology

Luca Vanzago

WHAT IS NATURE? This philosophical question is often conceded to the perspective of natural scientists. Even philosopher Edmond Husserl, who criticizes the natural sciences for commonly objectifying nature, never completely overcomes the scientific view of nature, in that Husserl describes phenomenology as the structures of consciousness seen through a transcendental perspective.[1]

Maurice Merleau-Ponty offers a different approach. He starts from a phenomenology of the embodied subjectivity, thus posing a problem to Husserl, insofar as his transcendental approach must account for the embodiment of the transcendental subject. In doing this, Merleau-Ponty paves the way for further inquiry into nature—an inquiry he explored primarily in his courses at the Collège de France, where he encountered Whitehead's philosophy. Merleau-Ponty developed a processual conception of nature, influenced by his reading of Whitehead, which provides the means for renovating phenomenological ontology.

When the notion of nature is approached through a phenomenological perspective, the meaning of nature is always conceived in terms of its experience. Nature, in other words, is a notion that depends on the constitution of its status, as affected by transcendental subjectivity. An example of this is found in Husserl's famous discussion in the second book of his *Ideas Pertaining to a Pure Phenomenology and a Phenomenological Philosophy*. Nature is, in the first place, the correlate of the natural-scientific attitude, understood as a kind of theoretical attitude. Husserl writes "nature is there for the theoretical subject."[2] He immediately adds that:

> Of course, that does not mean simply that nature is already completely determined considered as the correlate of a possible theoretical, cognitive, subject. Nature is an object of possible knowledge, but it does not exhaust the total realm of such objects. *Nature, as mere nature, contains no values, no works of art*, etc., though these are indeed objects of possible knowledge and science.[3]

This approach to nature leads to the well-known concept of "mere things" (*blosse Sachen*).[4] This is the realm of "material nature." Husserl remarks very clearly that this is only the lowest level of the constitution of reality, underlining that there is a "striking" difference between material nature and animal nature. The latter is the realm of nature in a "second, broadened sense, i.e., things that have a soul, in the genuine sense of 'living', animal nature."[5] The difference between the two realms consists in introducing a non-extensional property that qualifies the second realm and differentiates between things devoid of it and things that possess it. In other words, within the wider realm of material things, what Husserl calls material thinghood, a difference can be drawn between things that are only extensional things and extensional things that also possess a non-extensional property.[6]

Thus Husserl can say that every "thingly being" is temporally extended and has its place in world-space. Among these "things," there are some that differ in possessing something that is to be qualified differently. Husserl writes:

> The thing is moveable in space, in virtue of the corporeal extension which belongs to it by essence and is exclusively proper to it, and which can constantly alter its location in space. These propositions can be understood so universally that they hold in fact and apriori for *every thingly being whatever*.[7]

However, an important distinction arises with respect to corporeal extension between material thinghood and thinghood in the sense of animal nature. It was not without reason that Descartes designated *extensio* as the essential attribute of the material thing, which is also called "corporeal"—over against psychic or spiritual being which excludes it. In fact, *extensio* rightly understood should distinguish between nature in the first sense from nature in the second sense, such that the essential attribute of material being is not mere extension, but materiality—which requires temporal as well as spatial extension. What matters most here is to know the distinctive manner in which everything else that belongs to a material thing is yet related *a priori* (that always means essentially) to its extension. Spiritual nature, understood as animal nature, is a complex composition of a lower stratum of material nature, whose essential feature is *extensio*, and an inseparable upper stratum, which is of a fundamentally different essence and which, above all, excludes extension. Thus, even if the comprehensive essential feature of the material thing is materiality, it is at once understandable how extension can be taken as the essential feature differentiating the material from the psychic or spiritual.[8]

Is Husserl's *a priori* account of nature (matter as extension) the best explanation? Perhaps not. In fact, this view could be challenged along several different philosophical lines. I think the most interesting way of dealing with this issue is to deepen it, following Merleau-Ponty's account of Husserl's position. Merleau-Ponty is at once close to Husserl in stressing the role of corporeality, and worlds apart in proposing a different understanding of corporeality itself.

Like Husserl, Merleau-Ponty emphasizes the interconnection between matter and experience. But Merleau-Ponty is convinced that this account of "material thinghood" is not to be seen as the lowest level of constitution. It is to be conceived as quite an abstract conception of matter with respect to what is effectively experienced. Husserl follows here, according to Merleau-Ponty, a (openly admitted by Husserl, after all) Cartesian line of thought that could be disputed for many reasons, the most important of which being the very way in which matter and experience are to be linked. True, Husserl goes further than Descartes in attributing a nonmaterial layer to some material objects, called for that purpose *animalia* in the etymological sense of this word. But if the subject that constitutes the meaning of reality is related to matter, then this Cartesian account of material thinghood needs to be revised for intrinsic reasons. Since Husserl himself admits that transcendental subjectivity is incarnate (in a sense to be specified), then the main problem consists in understanding in what sense a phenomenological approach to nature can take into account the fact that nature is at once constituted and constituting, that is, it cannot simply be conceived as an object.

Matter and material objects understood as mere things are concepts deriving, according to Merleau-Ponty, from an intellectual account of experience that cuts off the living bonds between the incarnated subject and the world. But if perception is taken into account, then quite a different outlook comes to the fore. Before constituting the objects of experience in terms of material things, the process of perception involves the body, which entertains a network of relations with the world as such, and with what lies within it, such that it requires a wholly different account of nature—in particular, a revision of the ontological categories governing the conception of nature and matter.

The question concerning us here is: where do the notions of sheer matter and mere material object come from? Merleau-Ponty's answer resides in showing that they come from an account of experience that programmatically excludes what is most peculiar to perception as such and reduces perception to a lower intellectual form. Perception, then, does not grant an adequate access to the objects of the world, for it consists in a vague and indeterminate apprehension of sense-data that are constantly varying and never persistent enough so as to constitute the basis for a stable and reliable approach to what exists. Such an approach is to be sought in intellection, reasoning, calculation, and the like. Merleau-Ponty holds, on the contrary, that this account of perception is unfaithful to its task, and, in fact, it represents a camouflage of what perception actually is when considered as such; that is, when investigated in a properly phenomenological perspective.

Such an investigation is performed throughout his *Phenomenology of Perception*. After having criticized the realist and intellectualist accounts as being united in describing sense-perception along the lines quickly sketched above and, in particular, in being at unison in eliminating any affective and qualitative aspect from the relationship between the subject and the material object, Merleau-Ponty shows that, in fact, both approaches conceive of sense-data in terms of atoms placed within space seen as a container that is indifferent to what it contains. The same can be said for time. The material thing is thus the outcome of a synthesis performed on these data, consisting in a collection and a configuration that unite what is in itself separated. The only difference between the two accounts is represented by the nature of the synthesis: the realist approach understands it in terms of a passive recollection of a real multiplicity, while the intellectualist approach attributes the synthesis to the unifying power of a transcendental subject. According to the former perspective, there is no actual role for subjectivity, while, according to the latter, there is indeed one, but it is excessive and does not enter into a real contact with what is being unified. The subject limits itself to an external perception of its content, according to the well-known metaphor of the *kosmotheoros*—that is, unengaged by what it contemplates.

The bonds between the material object and the incarnated subject are therefore to be understood in different terms. A useful way of accounting for Merleau-Ponty's most advanced achievements in this respect is to take a look at his lectures on nature. In these lectures, Merleau-Ponty develops his conception of perception in the direction of a phenomenological ontology of nature that further discusses the ontological presuppositions already criticized in the major work, while providing a somewhat more accomplished positive standpoint from which to evaluate the concept of matter and nature.

In the section devoted to Husserl, Merleau-Ponty individuates two opposite attitudes entertained by Husserl with respect to nature and matter. One has been described above, in relation to *Ideas* volume 2, while the other will be discussed in what follows. Merleau-Ponty in particular emphasizes Husserl's later thought as offering valuable and fecund insights into the primordial bond between nature and experience. There are the three main features of this alternative philosophy of the body and its material nature (the *Subjektleib*, as Husserl calls it): 1) it is an organ of the "I can" (*Ich kann*); 2) it is "excitable" insofar as it possesses a capacity to sense and, therefore, is to be understood as "subject-object"; and 3) it is the "zero of orientation," that is, it is the standard for the constitution of each thing. These three aspects of the lived body deserve some qualification, at least as far as the notion of sheer matter is concerned.

With respect to the first question, Merleau-Ponty writes that:

> When I perceive an object, I am aware of the motor possibilities that are implied in the perception of the thing. The thing appears to me as a function of the movements of my body.... I am aware of my body as an undivided and systematic potency to organize certain unfoldings of perceptual appearance. My body is that

> which is capable of passing from one such appearance to another, as the organizer of a "transitional synthesis." .... The body appears not only as the exterior accompaniment of things, but also as the field where my sensations are localized.[9]

This means that the lived body functions as a sort of incarnated transcendental field of experience. There is properly no material thing unless it is encountered through the openness warranted by the lived body, which is therefore no usual body at all. Accordingly, in this perspective:

> I organize with my body an understanding of the world, and the relation with my body is not that of a pure I, which would successively have two objects, my body and the thing, but rather I live in my body, and by means of it I live in the thing. The thing appears to me in this way as a moment of the carnal unity of my body, as enclosed in its functioning.[10]

If, therefore, the body is not a pure I, then the thing is not sheer matter, either. In fact, the two determinations are interconnected, and they stand and fall together.

The lived, experiencing body should not, however, be seen as some sort of substitute for the pure I, only endowed with more fleshy features. The peculiarity of the *Leib* is that it is double-faced; that is, it is at once passive and active, and this is the ground for granting to it the function of opening the field of experience. In other words, it is important to stress that the body is not without incarnation, not immaterial in any sense. Rather, it is the notion of matter that is in need of revision, for if there is at least some matter that cannot in any way be accounted for in terms of sheer thing, then a whole different ontology is opened for investigation. This can be done by discussing, as Merleau-Ponty does, the famous §36 of *Ideas* 2 that is concerned with the peculiar structure of touching. Touch is undoubtedly a material performance, for, without something material to be touched, there would be no tactile experience at all. Husserl stresses the localization involved in this kind of experience. As Merleau-Ponty remarks:

> The sensing of my body is not found in the soul, but rather it is localized in my body, which is its field of localization. In order to understand this relation of sensation and my body, Husserl appeals to an experience of touching. When I touch my left hand with my right, my touching grasps my touched hand as a thing. But

suddenly, I perceive that my left hand becomes the sensing. The relation is reversed. We have the experience of a recovery between the contribution of the left hand and that of the right, and of a reversal of their function. This variation shows that it is always a question of the same hand. As a physical thing, it remains always what it is, yet it is different according to whether it be the touched or the touching. In this way I touch myself touching. I realize a sort of reflection, of cogito, of a grasping of the self by itself. In other words, my body becomes subject, it senses itself. But the concern is for a subject who occupies space, who communicates with itself interiorly, as if space had taken to knowing itself interiorly. ... My body appears ... as a "thing that senses."[11]

This emphasis on the reversibility of touch, as any subject can experience it, is justified by its ontological relevance. Merleau-Ponty rightly remarks that if we conceive of the body as a spatial thing, then it is space itself that communicates with itself. There is indeed some sort of interiority at play here, but it is an interiority of exteriority, so to speak. One can also speak of a material *cogito*, or of space grasping itself.

There is an image that can help with understanding what Merleau-Ponty is trying to convey through Husserl's own analysis; namely, the fold. If the subject is an incarnated I, then it is spatial. Spatiality is the mark of extension, and, accordingly, it should be opposed to mind or *res cogitans*. But Merleau-Ponty rejects this dualism precisely because he thinks it possible to show, by means of this analysis of touch, that extension itself possesses features that cannot be properly understood without abandoning the underlying Cartesian ontology. Extension possesses the capacity of folding itself upon itself, thus carving out an interiority of exteriority, without necessarily attributing this sort of interiority to a mental activity of sorts.

This approach poses a problem: if the approach remains on the level of human experience, it is always possible to say that the approach presupposes what it wants to demonstrate, namely, that exteriority thinks. For one could object that, in fact, this is not pure exteriority, but only the instrument of mind, which, accordingly, is already there from the beginning. As a matter of fact, the latter—that the mind is already presupposed—is one of the possible interpretations of the final meaning of Husserl's work. Merleau-Ponty, on the other hand, is clearly interested in a different understanding of nature, that is, an account of nature that can encompass experience and indeed take experience itself as one of its defining characteristics. Thus Merleau-Ponty's approach could be accounted for in terms of nonmaterialistic materialism, or nonnaturalistic naturalism. But this approach must at least provide some clues as to how to account for the emergence of experiencing things. Otherwise, it would end up unearthing what, in his opinion, was the corpse of panpsychism, which is exactly what Merleau-Ponty openly wants to avoid.

This is the reason that leads Merleau-Ponty to scrutinize some of the most relevant biological and ethological doctrines of life: to understand consciousness as a feature of nature, and hence to conceive of matter differently. Life is self-enjoying and self-producing nature. In discussing living forms, therefore, Merleau-Ponty wants to show how exteriority can achieve its own interiority without presupposing an external principle.

Living forms are eminently structures of becoming. Life is marked by transience, birth, and death. There is a facticity intrinsic to nature that is not due to the finitude of the knowing subject—which, on the contrary, must be understood as but a particular possible example of a living being. In emphasizing this aspect, Merleau-Ponty is criticizing the existentialist conception of truth as grounded in the human subject. This also means, for him, that life is marked by indetermination. The deterministic model of science, which was undermined by the revolutions that occurred in twentieth-century physics, is clearly even less tenable when biology is taken into consideration.

Merleau-Ponty finds in Whitehead the philosophical means to treat nature as a whole, with an ontological approach different from the Cartesian one that underlies Husserl's approach. Accordingly, I will now synthetically discuss Merleau-Ponty's appropriation of Whitehead's conception of nature.

Merleau-Ponty's aim is to conceive of nature in terms of autoproduction, and the purpose of his courses on nature is to find out in what way this autoproduction can be understood. The autoproductivity of nature requires a philosophical perspective that is not subsumable under either one of the two opposed views synthetically sketched above. But nature is not to be conceived in terms of finalism either. As Merleau-Ponty writes:

> There is nature wherever there is a life that has meaning, but where, however, there is not thought; hence the kinship with the vegetative. Nature is what has a meaning, without this meaning being posed by thought: it is the autoproduction of a meaning.

> Nature is thus different from a simple thing. It has an interior, is determined from within; hence the difference of "natural" to "accidental". Yet nature is different from man: it is not instituted by him and is opposed to custom, to discourse. Nature is the primordial—that is, the nonconstructed, the noninstituted; hence the idea of an eternity of nature (the eternal return), of a solidity. Nature is an enigmatic object, an object that is not an object at all; it is not really set out in front of us. It is our soil [*sol*]—not what is in front of us, facing us, but rather, that which carries us.[12]

Thus the autoproduction of nature that Merleau-Ponty describes is seen as the self-production of a form of meaning neither deriving from, nor comparable to, human meaning. Nature, as Merleau-Ponty adds, is an enigmatic object, an object not totally object, because it is not completely before us. Rather, it is our soil—not what stays in front of us (the *gegenstand*), but what supports and sustains us.

To talk about a support, in turn, means that nature is not the foundation of meaning, either. The connection between the sense of nature (in the subjective of this genitive) and the meaning proper to humankind is thus not directly or linearly derivable. There is a kind of fracture between the two, and we human beings are placed somewhere after the fracture has taken place, and unable to recover it. Nature is not the primordial paradise to be somehow recovered. The recovery is not possible anymore. To talk about a recovery would mean to betray genuine thinking about nature, for nature is precisely that which "has taken place" and is constantly taking place at every moment, accompanying human existence like its shadow. It is the barbaric principle discussed above.

Whitehead's position is investigated after an evaluation of Laplace's cosmology, followed by an important discussion of the philosophical meaning of quantum mechanics. Then Merleau-Ponty turns to an examination of the notions of space and time, an examination that brings Bergson into the picture and shows in what measure and to what extent the discoveries of scientists (Einstein included) are in need of philosophical discussion. The purpose behind this discourse is not so much to correct and put in a proper way what is naïvely stated by the scientists themselves, but to correct their naïve philosophy, which is more often than not outdated by their discoveries (Einstein's case is the most instructive). Philosophy is neither the tutor nor the pupil of the sciences. It retains a specificity of its own, due to its own different approach to reality. The sciences, in turn,—says Merleau-Ponty—are, in themselves, philosophically relevant only negatively. That is, they afford the means to exclude untenable philosophical positions, but cannot provide positive ones. A clear example of this is the problem that the discoveries of the relativity theory and quantum mechanics raise for the concept of time. Merleau-Ponty writes that:

> Einsteinian theory must be followed by a critique of continuity in the measure of time. It is the conception of a "cellular space," of an atomic time, the "chronon," below which we cannot descend. We end up evidencing, as a milieu, a milieu of which we would know to say only that it is neither temporal nor spatial into evidence. In the eyes of [these] physicists, the critique of the dogmatism of unique time appears as a particular element within a general critique of these notions.[13]

What is most important for the purpose of the present investigation is Merleau-Ponty's emphasis on a "cellular" notion of space and on the atomicity of time, which are necessary consequences of the scientific discoveries and not philosophical speculations. Thus Merleau-Ponty shows that the criticism of the classical conception of the uniqueness of time (Laplace's doctrine) implies the need to devise a general critique of the operational concepts of physical science. What is crucial here, however, is that the notions of cellular space and time (the epochal theory of time) are precisely that which can be found in Whitehead's reflection.

Merleau-Ponty starts with Whitehead's criticism of the instantaneousness and extensionlessness of time as it is conceived in classical physics.[14] Once again, Laplace's model is here the reference. He then connects this criticism to Whitehead's criticism of another classical conception, namely, what Whitehead calls the "fallacy of simple location." Merleau-Ponty seems to consider the two criticisms as equivalent. In fact, Whitehead distinguishes between the two arguments, but as they are also related to one another, perhaps it is this relatedness that Merleau-Ponty is aiming at, for he stresses the importance of conceiving punctual spatiotemporal existence as something that does not exist in nature, but only in the well-polished notions of scientific procedures. What is important in this case is that, for Whitehead, this criticism derives from a strictly logical and epistemological discussion. In other words, it is physical science itself that is in need of different notions of time and space, or, to put it more correctly, the development of science has shown that the notion of dimensionless points of time and of space is an abstraction that has no relation to physical reality. Merleau-Ponty, on his part, emphasizes Whitehead's notion (similar in this respect to Bergson's, James's, and Husserl's) of time as extended and without clear-cut boundaries. Accordingly, Merleau-Ponty concludes that nature, in this conception, is not a sum of unrelated elements, but a whole that can be legitimately subdivided, for the sake of measurement and knowledge, into smaller parts (events), but it is not in itself actually constituted by these parts. Whitehead shows the derivability of the extensionless points of space and instants of time from this wider whole through a mathematical procedure, that Whitehead calls the "method of abstractive extension."

Merleau-Ponty also insists on the processuality and dynamicity of Whitehead's conception of nature. This consideration is directly opposed to Newton's and Laplace's conceptions (and, in this respect, also Kant's). It is instructive to see that Leibniz (as Deleuze correctly remarks) put forth the same criticism to Newton. It could be said that this static conception of nature is a consequence of Descartes's geometrical ontology. Thus, what in Descartes, and then in Newton and Kant, is attributed to a mind or a subject, must be rather found on the part of nature itself. The processuality of nature is lost because of an abusive fragmentation of its structure into extensionless parts, which, inevitably, lose their dynamicity too. The process is a given, and it is not the outcome of a synthesis (be it objective or subjective).[15] Whitehead draws these conclusions from his interpretation of the physical notion of field of forces, which allows physical science to overcome the dilemma between causality through contact and action at a distance. This consideration has a scarcely negligible importance for the problem of the nature of subjectivity, as well, as is seen in Whitehead's treatment of the problem.

The processual conception of nature is thus also, and at the same time, a structural concept. Nature is a whole, and it is a dynamic whole. The process of nature manifests itself, but gets lost in its (physical) mathematical treatment. This means that classical physics was founded on a fruitful (for its epoch) but ontologically non-grounded abstraction. Only static extension was considered to pertain to objective reality, while movement, acceleration, and tendency (all the aspects that come back into the picture when adopting the field theory of vectors) were attributed to something external. Whitehead's approach thus is closer to everyday experience than Newton's physics. The new conception of nature also entails, as Merleau-Ponty remarks, a criticism of the classical concepts of matter and substance. Here again, Whitehead became aware of this implication very early in his career. But what Whitehead adds to this is the parallel recognition that the criticism of the notion of substance is twofold. Both physics and logic, while being separated, concur in this overcoming.

Merleau-Ponty at this point remarks that Whitehead's conception of nature makes room for an "internal activity," which, however, remains a problem and does not consist in a passage from nature to mind or spirit (*esprit*).[16] While it is true that for Whitehead the mind is not separated from nature, in his speculative philosophy he tries to show in what way a mind can be seen to emerge from nature. This is the problem that is already present in Leibniz's criticism of Descartes (and, for different reasons, of Spinoza). Deleuze, in turn, poses this question especially with respect to Leibniz, while not ignoring Whitehead. This is precisely the whole problem, for the issue is how to account for the emergence of a mind—soul, interiority, subjectivity—from that which seems deprived of it. Either: (1) one finds that spirit is already present from the beginning, but then misses the problem of the exteriority of nature turning upon itself, that is, the "fold," as was seen in the chapters of the second section, or; (2) one must face the problem of accounting for something that, while not totally separated from nature, is no longer simply nature. In other words, this is the problem of a natural negativity.

This is Merleau-Ponty's problem and the most important reason for him to investigate Whitehead's philosophy, as can be seen from his account of Whitehead's notion of event. Merleau-Ponty stresses, in particular, Whitehead's awareness of the non-serial nature of time. Matter and substance are concepts closely related to the treatment of time and space in terms of uniformity. Once the latter are recognized as more complex structures, showing features that span from nonuniformity to nonlinearity and mutual overlapping, an account of natural reality in terms of bits of matter substantially and univocally identified and separated from one another is no longer tenable. Merleau-Ponty once again refers this antiquated picture to Descartes, but Whitehead, already in *The Concept of Nature*, shows that Descartes's ontology is, in this respect, the evolution of Aristotle's substantialism translated into the new physics.

Thus the real problem is constituted by the relation between the ontology of substances and a logical account of reality in terms of subjects/substances that possess attributes. Merleau-Ponty, however, makes another, very relevant remark, stressing the importance of a return to sensible experience that is able to overcome the unnatural and unjustified division between primary and secondary qualities, as Whitehead, too, recommends. There is an implicit, or hidden, phenomenology of perception in Whitehead that is decisive in order to understand Whitehead's notion of experience as "natural." Merleau-Ponty himself, however, quite surprisingly does not link this hint to the philosophical generalization accomplished by Whitehead in *Process and Reality* and in *Adventures of Ideas*. Merleau-Ponty remarks that:

> This process of Nature which assures the interiority of events in relation to one another, our inherence in the Whole, links observers together. It is what joins. The process of Nature is represented here as making progress, as being annexed to the body of subjects. In other words, the process of Nature, which corresponds to the unity of the sensing body, and since the body is itself an event, makes the unity of the body, [and] also makes the unity of different observers, it is also a Nature for many. There is a sort of reciprocity between Nature and me as a sensing being. I am a part of Nature and function as any event of Nature: I am by my body a part of Nature and the parts of Nature allow for them relations of the same type as those of my body with Nature.[17]

Nature is characterized by an intrinsic activity which, however, is not understandable in terms of consciousness. Merleau-Ponty here states that Whitehead opposes his own conception to a long tradition, initiated by St. Augustine and ending with Bergson but also with Sartre, which opposes nature and spirit or mind. For Merleau-Ponty, Whitehead's conception of nature means that nature is the memory of the world, a nonconscious form of permanence which affects the process of nature itself.[18] The past, then, is not operated by a subject on the otherwise indifferent issue of nature, for the present event is what it is only insofar as it is somehow dependent on nature's previous states. The very same future is implied in the present state of the passage of nature. These are but consequences of a dynamic notion of nature, but they entail enormous consequences for the problem of the relation between body and soul, matter and spirit, nature and culture, as well as for the problem of distinguishing between natural and human sciences, *Natur-* and *Geisteswissenschaften*. This latter distinction is of no use here, not because of a generalization of the notion of culture, but rather through a revision of the notion of nature.

Memory and expectation, past and future, are thus found in nature and are not only proper to an anti-natural spirit. Time, in particular, plays a decisive role, for it is neither serial and cyclical, as with the Greeks; nor linear and historical, as in the Christian tradition. Once again, it is the non-linearity of time that Merleau-Ponty emphasizes, and this means the presence of a folding, the structural process of a relational and non-univocal bond.[19]

It is at this point that Merleau-Ponty mentions (but it is a *hapax*) the Whiteheadian notion of concrescence, which is a synonym of actual entity.[20] Merleau-Ponty's hint at this term is connected more with Wahl's reading of Whitehead's philosophy than with Whitehead's texts themselves, but it represents in any case a decisive passage. To link the notion of concrescence to the complex of themes delineated thus far and, in particular, to the nonlinear nature of time, on the one hand, and to the processuality of nature, on the other, means to see that nature possesses a generativity of its own, capable of explaining the emergence of (at least) some form of subjectivity, while avoiding panpsychism. Merleau-Ponty adds that Whitehead does not develop this perspective, but Whitehead's texts allow us to refute this latter statement.[21]

Before proceeding with the analysis of Merleau-Ponty's reading of Whitehead, it is worth pausing here to evaluate the meaning of the attention devoted by Merleau-Ponty to the connection between the nonlinear temporality of natural events and the question of subjectivity. Merleau-Ponty, in relation to Whitehead's notion of concrescence, writes that

> Whitehead always supported the idea of a "concrescence" of Nature in itself which is taken up again by life. Time realizes the "joy of itself" in the organism. The movement by which a morsel of matter folds back on itself prolongs the "process of Nature."[22]

In Whitehead, Merleau-Ponty finds what in other philosophers is only sketched, at best: the notion of nature as that which communicates with itself, and which, in this doing, is neither pure object (the correlate of thought) nor pure subject (the transparent contact of the self with itself).

The words that Merleau-Ponty uses in order to account for Whitehead's notion of nature are very instructive. Merleau-Ponty writes:

> If Whitehead says that Nature is not accidental, he does not mean thereby that it is necessary: it does not have internal necessity. What he means in speaking of the "subject-object" is that Nature "communes with itself," without this self-communion allowing Nature to be conceived as a creative principle. It is this outside of which is nothing, that from which is taken all spatiality and temporality. It is what always appears as already containing all that appears. In it, creature and creator are inseparable. It is with this reservation in mind that we must call Nature an "operating presence."[23]

Nature is thus the whole that exists only in its parts, always at the same time producer and product and, in this sense, both exterior and interior to itself. Time, understood as passage and becoming, is in this respect essential to nature. Nature would not be nature were it not for this becoming, this passage, which explains the unsurpassable opacity that characterizes its comprehension. Every attempt at understanding nature and grasping it as a whole takes place from within nature itself and is affected by this passage, while the attempt itself affects the passage as well. Nothing that happens is, in this sense, without some effect. Thought must be able to take this self-perturbation into account. This is one of the meanings of hyper-reflection (although Merleau-Ponty speaks of *surréflexion*, giving it a surrealistic overtone that the English translation inevitably misses).

When Merleau-Ponty attributes those very temporal features to nature, which in his *Phenomenology of Perception* were assigned to the bodily subject, a shift occurs. This shift does not consist in a denial of the earlier account, but a deepening that presents Merleau-Ponty with two questions: (1) the ontological status of nature, and (2) the phenomenological/methodological status of the investigation itself of nature. On the one hand, what Merleau-Ponty had earlier assigned to the subject, although incarnated and in this sense already in contact with Being, he now sees as an attribute of existence—which is a more consistent view. Merleau-Ponty is not reifying what in *Phenomenology of Perception* was conceived in terms of phenomena. On the contrary, he is now building a coherent ontology of manifestation (a counterpart can be found in Whitehead): an ontology that entails the fuller immersion of the (incarnated) subject within nature.

On the other hand, the co-determination of nature and spirit, subject and object, or rather the overcoming of the opposition between these determinations for something "in between," implies that the very notion of manifestation is transformed. Therefore, the science of manifestation, phenomenology, must be erected "from within," in this peculiar sense of interiority. It is the science that must be able to account for the particular event that folds exteriority into its own interiority. Since the subject performing this scientific (phenomenological) investigation is in its turn the outcome of this fold, access to the fold itself cannot take place in a direct way. Retrieval of the original event cannot be produced through a reduction that can truly imagine bracketing everything and going back to the things themselves, for in this case the "thing" is the reduction itself. Or, better, it is the particular event that produces a "meaning," which then originates the very question about meaning which the reduction is. Hence, either phenomenology is (1) a hyper-reflection that reflects on its own opaque origin, with this unsurpassable, unattainable origin having always already taken place; or (2) it is a phenomenology that sees phenomena not in terms of a direct, but rather an indirect emergence, one that resembles the emergence of symptoms. Phenomenology then becomes the psychoanalysis of nature, as Merleau-Ponty writes in his The *Visible and the Invisible*.[24]

Endnotes

1. See E. Husserl, *The Crisis of European Sciences and Transcendental Phenomenology*, ed. and trans. D. Carr (Evanston, IL: Northwestern University Press, 1970).

2. E. Husserl, *Ideas Pertaining to a Pure Phenomenology and a Phenomenological Philosophy, Second Book: Studies in the Phenomenology of Constitution*, trans. R. Rojcewicz and A. Schuwer (Dordrecht: Kluwer, 1989), 4.

3. Husserl, *Ideas, Second Book*, 4.

4. Husserl, *Ideas, Second Book*, 18.

5. Husserl, *Ideas, Second Book*, 30.

6. Cf. Husserl, *Ideas, Second Book*, 30–32.

7. Husserl, *Ideas, Second Book*, 31.

8. Husserl, *Ideas, Second Book*, 32.

9. M. Merleau-Ponty, *Nature: Course Notes from the Collège de France,* ed. D. Séglard and trans. R. Vallier (Evanston: Northwestern University Press, 2003), 74.
10. Merleau-Ponty, *Nature,* 74.
11. Merleau-Ponty, *Nature,* 74-75, emphasis mine.
12. Merleau-Ponty, *Nature,* 3-4.
13. Merleau-Ponty, *Nature,* 110.
14. Cf. Merleau-Ponty, *Nature,* 113–114.
15. Cf. Merleau-Ponty, *Nature,* 114.
16. Merleau-Ponty, *Nature,* 114.
17. Merleau-Ponty, *Nature,* 117.
18. Merleau-Ponty, *Nature,* 120.
19. Cf. Merleau-Ponty, *Nature,* 119.
20. Merleau-Ponty, *Nature,* 119.
21. Merleau-Ponty, *Nature,* 120.
22. Merleau-Ponty, *Nature,* 119. The translation is not totally faithful to the French original. Merleau-Ponty, once again following Whitehead, says "enjoyment" [*jouissance*] and not joy; and he speaks of a *passage* [*passage*] of Nature. Cf. the French original: "Whitehead a toujours soutenu l'idée d'une 'concrescence' de la Nature en soi qui est reprise par la vie. Le temps réalise "la jouissance de lui-même" dans l'organisme. Le mouvement par lequel un morceau de la matière se replie sur soi prolonge le 'passage de la Nature.'"
23. Merleau-Ponty, *Nature,* 120.
24. Merleau-Ponty, *The Visible and the Invisible: Followed by Working Notes,* ed. C. Lefort and trans. A. Lingis (Evanston: Northwestern University Press, 1968), 267.

THREE

Memory and Thought

Jason Brown

There is no essential reason why memory should not be raised to the vividness of the present fact. *-Alfred North Whitehead*[1]

THIS CHAPTER ON THOUGHT and memory has several goals: (1) to discuss some of the complexities of memory that are glossed over in cognitive theory, particularly the continuity of thought and perception; (2) to argue that the endogenous substrate of perception is memorial, with conscious thought occurring as an enhancement (by retardation or neoteny of process) at preterminal phases in revival; (3) to show that the memory trace cannot refer to a localized store but repeats the trajectory of the actualization process in the original perceptual experience; and (4) to further the idea that forgetting is incomplete revival, not decay.

The distinction between thought and memory depends not only on novelty and a departure from reproduction, but on a feeling of presentness for thought, even for an idea that is revived, and on a feeling of pastness for memory. A thought image felt in the present has some feeling of agency, which occurs primarily with a lack of resolution and/or a direction to the future, while the pastness of memory deprives the image of volition, though a sense of effort can accompany attempts to revive a past experience. The analysis of *déjà vu* is relevant to this distinction.

Introduction

If thought is thinking about the possible, memory is for the irrevocable. Memory is fidelity to experience or replication; thought includes dream, daydream, fantasy, imagination, planning, problem-solving, contemplation, rational and irrational ideation; basically, almost anything in the mind apart from feeling that is a departure from memory. Inaccurate recall becomes thought in bringing forth new content. As memory is judged by exactness to experience, thought is mental activity that is not reproductive. Memory becomes thought on branching to novelty; thought reverts to memory when it is forgotten or revived. Since we recollect ideas and can, to some extent, revive feelings, memory does not solely depend on external experience. Nor does it require consciousness of mental content, for behavior is dominated by the recurrent or habitual, which approximates memory to the extent novelty is excluded. This is captured in the distinction of representational and procedural memory. Memory as conscious (or unconscious, e.g., dream) representation is close to thinking; thought that is unconscious or implicit relies on memory but differs in the novelty of outcome. Further, what begins as thought inevitably becomes memory, as in learning a skill or the automaticity of habit. Thought must be replaced by memory or we would be overwhelmed on every occasion by the slightest decision.

Novelty in thought or imagination rests on the expansion or recombination of learned content, but even if the material of thought is given—say, words for Shakespeare, notes for Beethoven—thought is not mere rearrangement but a novel pattern or perspective on what is available. Creative thinking results in truly novel forms. A favorite example is Coleridge's "the clock has gone mad, it has struck 1 four times." The remark may be a reformulation of learned elements but is a wholly unpredictable outcome. The intersection of differing lines of thought—insanity in a mechanical object—exposes the process within a frozen metaphor, such as a *friendly* bank, or a simile such as "crazy like a fox." Poetry, especially, is propagated by metaphor, in which disparate items come together on the basis of shared attributes. Thought and memory, the productive and reproductive, are closely aligned but seem opposing spheres separated by imagination, by effort and voluntariness, degree of novelty, and a sense of past or present. There is also a difference in feeling. A new idea may be thrilling; an old memory can be painful or pleasurable. Nostalgia pertains to memory, not thought. A sustained memory may give pleasure while sustained thought is difficult, even tiresome. In one, there is a struggle for precision, in the other, for originality. Ideas can be recollected while feelings, though remembered, are difficult to reproduce. With memory one struggles for precise replication; with thought, for originality.

Thinking cannot be readily studied in animals except as problem-solving where failures tend to be discarded and successes rewarded. Thought is difficult to study in humans as well, for it is sporadic, variable, and, unlike memory, cannot, except as deviation from the rote, be compared to a template. There is a good deal of experimental work on memory with division into components and their attribution to brain areas. Methods of research also influence the way we interpret thought and memory. The interval or delay in recall, the duration from exposure, distraction, accuracy, repetition, the nature of what is recalled, e.g., whether physical features or meaning, motivate the division of memory into a variety of components and set it apart from thought. In the study of memory, as in so many other areas of cognition and language, deconstruction into components replaces thoughtful understanding of the faculty itself. As to the reduction of memory or its constituents to brain or to gene, the road down is one thing, the road up (to cognition) another.

The highest reaches of thought are, arguably, in artistic, philosophical, and mathematical genius; the lowest in those developmentally disabled or of dull routine. In the former, creative thought triumphs over memory; in dullness or habit it is the reverse. Yet a prodigious memory may not be conducive to original thought, and thinking suffers when thought retreats to the habitual or over-learned. Indeed, an excessive memory can interfere with the reception, isolation, and formulation of novel concepts. A photographic memory may be exhaustive but it is essentially replicative and may prevent the synthesis, propagation, and pattern recognition necessary for productive thinking. This was described in a case study by Luria and by Borges in his short story, *Funes the Memorious*. Exceptional memory occurs in autistic savants, mnemonists, chanting monks, or those, as in the recitation of lengthy biblical or Sanskrit texts, who have devoted many years to memorization. Forgetting and the suppression of irrelevancy are essential to selective recall and concept formation. In some fields, such as chess or music, accomplished masters can recall lengthy games or scores on a single exposure, but such performances (in chess) are largely reconstructions based on strategy and patterns of attack or defense, not rote learning. Recently, in a drowsy state, I heard much of the Brahms piano trio #1 in my mind several months after attending a performance, an experience not possible for me to play or hum. Such an occurrence is not unusual in the artistically gifted, for example, Wagner's composition of the Prelude to *Das Rheingold*, or the *Kublai Khan* of Coleridge in a dream or transitional state. This shows that memory is not easily fractured into components or interpreted as storage in a computer file, but is more complex than most imagine.

Perception is largely memory constrained and externalized by sensibility, though vivid memory can achieve actuality as a mode of perceptual experience. Hallucination and eidetic phenomena are transitional from the image to the object and the reverse. Veridical perception depends on the memorial as antecedent process to afford meaning and recognition to a changing object world. When perception deviates from the norm, as in psychosis and other pathologies, memory becomes thought-like, and the reality of objects is altered. We are not aware of memory as a substrate of perception—indeed, it is viewed as post-perceptual. The passage of forming objects from experiential to "working" memory to external perceptions, which is recaptured in forgetting, remains invisible because the memorial process is pre-empted by the object development and only reappears, in reverse, when the perception is incompletely revived. It is not memory but the substrate of the memorial that transforms to perception. Once the memory image becomes a conscious actuality, it no longer figures in perception. This is true of thought, which is conceived as largely conscious, though unconscious thinking occurs in dream, in spontaneous decision, insight, and in artistic or other work where the emphasis is on invention. Unlike memory, which is essential to recognition and the application of learning to sensory experience, unconscious thought remains submerged, and only its outcome reaches perceptual clarity. Moreover, memory as instinct is the earlier capacity on which thought develops as an improvisation that is inexplicable on the basis of inherited routines. Animals lacking an inner life do not have a thought process similar to that of humans; rather, it is closer to spontaneous invention, tacit decision, or trial and error, when instinct fails to provide a solution.

In animals, instinctual drive governs behavior with a small window of originality in which thought, as innovation or the unanticipated, intrudes according to the vicissitudes of circumstance. Instinct is the inheritance of memory and its implementation, with some deviation attributable to learning and/or implicit thought. Drive-categories shape object recognition and behavior in humans as well as in animals; every act of cognition begins with instinctual drive. Wittgenstein made a similar observation. In animals, the relative fixity of repertoires reflects the deposit of drive as memory into action. In humans, the memorial is also the larger part of behavior; life is mostly habit penetrated by imagination. Most decisions are unsurprising. Thinking "out of the box" is a creative act. For most, and for most of the time, decisions follow well-worn habitual paths even if not exactly repetitive. It would be a strange world indeed if decisions were constantly unpredictable.

The immediately preceding and the deep experiential are revived in what for conventional theory is a naked object. Personal knowledge and experience form the foundation of the object, infusing it with meaning and relevance. The transition to actuality is from before to after but, once complete, and over a series of states, a present is created in the disparity of the memorial with the perceptual—the past and the present—in relation to the incompleteness of revival. The state develops over the still-incomplete prior state, allowing for preservation (continuous revival) of early segments of self, character, core beliefs, and values. When the developing configuration or gestalt reaches a penultimate phase, it is analyzed into its featural detail and detaches as the object world, with antecedent segments constituting its memorial infrastructure. The implicit revival of antecedents in the present is largely intuited as an unconscious legacy in each perception. The overlap of the following before the actualization of the occurrent preserves early formative segments across state-succession.

Unlike objects, which externalize, actions do not detach from the mind of the actor. This conserves the sense of an action belonging to the self and contributes to the feeling of agency. The perceptual quality of hallucination and its memorial origins confirm that memory underlies perception with an application of sensory constraints on endogenous process. That is, the endogenous revival of memorial content, beginning with instinctual drive categories, forms a substrate that is shaped to perception by sensibility. Perception unfolds over a memorial infrastructure that is uncovered in forgetting. The sense of ownership and personal value of the intra-psychic pass to the impersonality of the external and the varieties of intrinsic worth.

Sensibility carves adaptation out of memory. The metaphoric extension and sensory parsing of memory lead to an improvisation of the familiar. The memorial passes to the perceptual by way of sensory constraints at multiple levels. Sensibility at the final phase leaves behind the personal history and world knowledge that form the corpus of every object-experience.

We tend to interpret dream as a play of memories, but fusion, displacement, and condensation of images (Freud's dreamwork) occur as well in the waking imagination, especially in creative thought, which taps certain aspects of dream cognition. The novelty of dream usually surpasses that of wakefulness, but what is lost in the free range of dream is regained in the adaptation and publicity of thought. Dreams are symbolic and thematic representations, rarely copies of prior experience. In this, they reveal the rudiments of productive thinking. They are not wishes but embodiments of feeling, as much what is feared as what is desired, as much thought as memory, as much what is possible as what is sheer fantasy. Freud's concept of wish-fulfillment derives from the actualization of dream at an intrapsychic phase close to drive and desire. The involuntary nature of dream, or spontaneous recollection, nulls the selectivity of volition and opens the door to contingency.

Past and Present, Receptiveness and Agency

Apart from documentation, photographs, and witnesses, which we do not rely on for personal memory, how do we know that what we remember really happened? Put differently, how do we distinguish a memory of an event from a thought, a dream, or an imaginary occurrence? I have had occasions of uncertainty as to whether a memory was a dream or an actual experience, as well as whether a thought was original, a prior idea, or something read or heard. These confusions point to subtle continuities between these phenomena. The piecemeal approach of cognitive science attempts to sequester what only continuity can explain. A related question is how we know memory is true to experience, or is incomplete or inaccurate. If details are forgotten, clearly memory or its narration is incomplete, but how do we know events and their sequence are accurately remembered?

Since the experience in waking memory depends on the content recalled, such as taking a walk to the park, what besides the recollection attests to its actuality? Does the feeling of a match of recall and the actual events reflect a background potential in relation to what is elicited? In all aspects of cognition, only a fraction of potential is realized. Warren McCullough described a mason who, under hypnosis, could recall every brick in a wall laid decades before. Even in recalling a walk, we do not remember every step, tree, leaf, or branch. Or do we? Is a limited, often fragmentary, remembrance compared to an undischarged potential for exhaustive recall to determine whether the remembrance is accurate? Is the intuition of unsatisfied potential the basis for knowing a memory is incomplete, or even that there is a memory—the potential to remember—that cannot be realized? Is this what is lost in those who do not even know they have forgotten?

The illiterate native who can enter a Brazilian rain forest and circle about for two hours returning to the same point, without relying on moss or lichen and unable to see above the canopy, has a capacity to form a mental map that may well be a potential in all individuals but is lost in literacy and education. Similarly, the fact that incidental or unnoticed events reappear in dream implies a greater potential for recall than what is consciously remembered. Presumably, the withdrawal in dream (or hypnotic trance) to a pre-perceptual phase allows the elicitation of otherwise unremembered items from the potential in the configural precursors of conscious recall. This raises the question, if dreams are memories, what happens to the dream content once it is forgotten? Does it persist like a memory in wakefulness, never to be realized again, or does it fade forever into the shadows?

On the materialist account, an experience that is encoded in the brain distinct from its conscious "retrieval" is stored like a computer file that persists after each occasion of access. The existence of the file might then account for the sense of having a memory in the absence of recall. An experience exists for the individual when it is recalled or, indirectly, when it influences other thoughts or behaviors, yet we presume that memory persists long after it has been forgotten, no less than before it is recalled. This supports the idea of consolidation, storage, or a lasting physical trace that, to date, has eluded localization. Stimulation of the brain may arouse a memory or an epileptic aura, but the aura or memory recurs after the stimulated area is excised. Holographic theory postulates the generation of memory throughout the brain. Is the trace localized or everywhere? What is a neural memory if not a latent configuration or potential for recall that rests in the relative strengths of innumerable synapses? The configuration has the potential for activation if one segment is aroused. The trace is modeled on the original perception. That is, the process of perception constitutes the trace, the distal portions of which perish or are erased by the oncoming state. The trace must be nonlocal, for it is doubtful that the sounds, sights, conversations, and feelings on a walk, that is, the entire perceptual experience, is "stored" in the same place. One can say that the memory trace is a distributed pattern of synaptic relations recruited over the same path as the original experience.

Presumably, the derivation from one configuration to another in the sequence of recall or perception entails a figural prominence that privileges the elicitation of one subset over another. An ingredient of the experience, a tree, a bench, can revive the memory, just as the memory can elicit the ingredient. Put differently, the whole gives the parts, but a part can refresh the whole. A memory cannot be recalled all at once; portions become active or conscious before others. An effort can be made to evoke events selectively or in order of occurrence, usually generating one item to reconstitute the experience. The more emphatic the memory for one event, the less pronounced for others. As a single word can be unpacked to a book, the totality of an experience can be collapsed to an event. Initially, recall approximates experience; then it fades so only the salient events are revived. It is difficult to imagine a fragmentation of the trace over time such that what is recalled is what is left in the trace, especially when long forgotten events are later recalled, some as habit, some spontaneously, others in daytime reverie, or symbolically in dream, or in a trancelike state. More likely, events "drop out" or are revived in relation to personal meaning or affective tone.

The transmission from one configuration to the next in recall, as in perception, is like a travelling wave, with the pattern of derivation comparable to that of a category/member relation. A neural configuration can be said to correspond to a category if subsets individuate as members. Presumably, the affective tonality or the relevance to a context or situation is apportioned to virtual items so as to bias the arousal of the subset, with a falling-away of less salient constituents by an inhibitory surround. The subset is then the next configuration (subcategory) to undergo partition. Initial partitions are determined by affective and meaning-relations, such as those that deposit in dream; subsequent partitions reflect "physical" relations to the original percept.

The relation of memory to *a* memory, a capacity or competence to a performance, is similar to that of *la memoire* to *le souvenir* in French, memory as potential and a memory as an actuality. The potential for total recall in near-death or trance-state experience (*Lebensfilm*, picture strip theory) is a mark of the coherence and pictorial quality of initial renewal, while the categorical nature of revival incorporates the multimodality and serial unfolding of memorial content. On the other hand, the concept of a static trace that is looked up and retrieved, as Lashley famously noted, has too many problems to be seriously considered, including his emphasis on a mechanism that scans serial order, but also plasticity, decay, continuity with the before and after of the recollected event as well as with other phenomena, the often fragile nature of recall, recurrence in dream or trance, integration with cognition more generally, how the trace is found or selected, and so on.

When I remember walking to the park yesterday, what provides the assurance that my recollection is for an actual experience, that is, a faithful representation of what happened, and that it occurred yesterday and not last week? Can we know a memory is inaccurate without supplementary access to the events on which it is based? Is incompleteness or inaccuracy felt in a way that is independent of the experience to which it is compared? Does memory just feel right or accurate, and if so how? How is the memory of an experience compared to the experience if the experience gives the memory, or if the memory—"memory trace"—is all we have of the experience? Does partial recall reflect a partial trace, and if not, what determines what part of the trace recurs? If the memory is felt as more or less adequate to the experience, or if nothing essential is left out in recall, how does this occur since all there is in consciousness is what is recollected? Does a present memory realize another deeper memory that is an implicit record of what occurred?

As noted, what survives is a fraction of what transpired, since in the parsing to precision the elicitation of one item requires the suppression of others, so that much is lost in each instance of recall, or remains as potential for later visitation. Likely, it is the potential to generate a memory that permits one to know the memory is "there" but unavailable. In pathologic memory, the person is usually unaware of having forgotten. In the amnesia of Korsakoff syndrome, or confabulation, or in the megalomania and exaggeration of syphilitic dementia, the person is usually not aware that remembrance is inaccurate, even false; embellishments often have a grain of plausibility. Typically, in Alzheimer's disease, the family, not the patient, is concerned about failing memory. If the patient is unaware of memory loss, what has been lost? the memory, the revival, or the unconscious record?

These questions go to the problem of an occasional confusion of dream and thought. How do I know a false memory was not implanted in my brain, or developed spontaneously, or is mixed with imagination or thought, or arose in therapy or suggestion? Is the difference between a false memory and delusion the belief in its veracity? Is delusion a false belief or does it entail a strong belief in a false memory or thought? When is the problem that of belief or judgment? Fixed delusional beliefs often accompany a loss of memory. The person does not know if the memory or idea is true to experience, as the failure in recall permits only a rudimentary revival to a level of dream cognition where novel contents arise without critical judgment in relation to affective needs. The delusion of thought-transference, that one sends or receives thoughts to and from others, is common in psychosis; mind-reading and telepathy are the popular correlates.

We can recall an event many times and it still remains a memory, but if the event recurs many times, it loses its temporal locus and becomes part of experience. Once the episodic relation of memory is lost, that is, the temporal tagging of an event, as in learning a word, a skill, a route, general knowledge, or after many repetitions, the content is no longer felt as a memory but a part of one's personal or world knowledge. In this way, memory passes into thought. Events that are redundant, good or bad, or cannot be recalled, especially for early life, go into the formation of personality. This is why memories of early childhood are often misrepresented. They are in a more superficial relation to the personality. In a very real sense, what is forgotten is what one becomes. I often have the feeling that parts of my life not witnessed might as well never have occurred. Such reflections raise a still deeper question. What is the difference between a real and a fictitious life?

One distinction of thought and memory hinges on the fact that thought is felt in the present, while there is a feeling of pastness for memorial experience. The quality of pastness in the memorial bridges into the present with the feeling of partial agency for image-production. If I recall a walk and consider what other events might have occurred, or did not occur, there is a mix of memory and thought as well as a feeling of some intent and digression in the present. Even with digression, the reproductive portion is felt as past and the digression is felt as present. When I recall a tree I passed on the walk, it is a memory and felt as pointing to the past, but when I wonder at the beauty or age of the tree or imagine resting for a while beneath its shade, it is a thought that is in the present. The term reflection applies to thought and memory. Thought is deviation in recall, or the revival of the memorial when it is unhinged from experience. This shift to a sampling of world knowledge is accompanied by a shift from the past to the present, from a backward look to a forward glance, from spontaneity or passivity to agency and purposefulness. Knowledge is termed semantic memory, but actually memory becomes knowledge when it is unmoored from a point of acquisition. This liberation of memory from experience leaves the past for the present and shifts passive recollection to volitional thought.

Agency is not confined to action, presentness is not restricted to thought or perception; both are prominent in thought imagery, as in picturing a mouse crawling on the back of an elephant. The images are learned and, in that sense, reproductive, but the experience is that of thought, thus it is felt in the present. The image can be "manipulated" at will. Agency is an intrapsychic experience that is lost when images externalize, but retained in actions—speech, motion—that engage the body and are partially intrapsychic. The relation of self to an intrapsychic image is critical. Agency for the body depends on the "body image," which, unlike objects, remains partly interior. We lift the hand volitionally, but the hand lifting the cup is an outcome. Memory may occur with a feeling of effort in recall, though volition and exertion do not seem to appreciably aid recall, as when searching for a name is unsuccessful until attention is diverted. The involuntariness of imagery in memory is parsed to necessity in perception. In volition, the image must be directed to the future as agency cannot effect the past. The involuntary precedes detachment; agency is lost for ordinary objects that act on us causally but not as a result of personal volition.

The simple response to the question of why memory carries a feeling of the past, and thinking is felt in the present, is that the sense of pastness relates to the awareness of prior experience, or that the object-experience is not happening now, or that it represents an absence of presentness, or the content is felt as familiar or reproductive. How then do we know that what we take for a present experience is not a recurrence of a previous thought? This does not require forgetting the prior thought, so thinking will not be apprehended as recall since we can revisit a thought many times but do not feel the thought is a memory, even if thinking on a problem requires constant revival. Perhaps for a recurrent thought to be felt as a memory, or to convey a feeling of pastness, it first has to be a perception. Once the memory is elaborated as thought, it loses its experiential ground and thus its relation to re-perception (memory).

Perception is the realization of memory sculpted by sensation with a sense of increasing passivity until the image detaches as an independent object. The passivity relates to pastness and lack of agency for present experience. The final outcome of the pastness and passivity of memory is the detachment, immediacy, and presentness of objects. The present becomes the past in forgetting; the past becomes the present in perceiving. Different phenomena occur at successive planes in the passage of memory to perception or past to present. In one such phenomena, *déjà vu*, past and present are confused, so a present occasion is felt as past or having previously occurred. A recurrent event in thought or imagination that is experienced as novel is not necessarily felt as past, nor are the daily repetitions of life, while in *déjà vu* a unique experience is felt as a memory. The problem of how we know an experience that we remember has actually happened is the opposite of the problem of how we have (the feeling of) a memory for an experience that has not occurred.

Agency or volition entails an arc from self to act, to object or image (e.g., proposition). The feeling of volition is primed in passing through an implicit phase of choice or a delay in spontaneity. Commonly, the active and passive are merged. My writing is an active and agentive performance, but the words arise passively without conscious control. The process of word production is involuntary with a feeling of agency only in the final act of writing or in revision. In fact, revision is felt as more volitional than original writing, which is largely a passive experience. Memory rises to perception as the actualization of past in present, while action carries a feeling of volition outward into the present occasion. Agency requires a forward surge in the isolation of part out of whole. This is the intentional quality of feeling in the subjective aim. Choice heightens agency in the selection of content, in the resolution of potential, and in the conscious accentuation of partition.

We may have an experience of uncertainty as to whether a dream is a remembrance, but the ongoing dream is felt as a present occasion. There is no past or future. A waking recollection of a past event is a present experience, though memory carries a feeling of pastness into the present. Dream may be about a past event but, when it happens, it is felt in the present. Memory and dream both actualize in the present: memory in perception, dream as hallucination, but the former is transformed by sensibility. That is, memory achieves a present immediacy on becoming a perception, and perception takes on a memorial quality in the incompleteness of revival to an object. Dream content arises passively and involuntarily as an elaboration of thought and memory felt in the present of the dream. The self of dream is passive to the imagery with a contracted present and without a past or future. The transience of the present is due to the truncation of the state, the absence of revival, the lack of disparity between perception and forgetting—there is no sense of forgetting *within* the dream—and the presentness of all dream experience. Memorial experience in dream is often based on actual occurrences, particularly fragments of daytime perception. Ordinary memory is for—or about—an actual experience; dream is an elaboration or symbolic representation that is itself apprehended as an experience. We say, I remember a walk and I remember a dream. Why should a dream, even one that is relatively veridical, be felt as an experience and not as the memory or thought of an experience? On waking, a lucid or realistic dream may be felt as faithful to a past experience but the dream—within the dream—is not felt as recollection. There may be confusion as to whether dreams are thoughts received from others or are one's own. William James wondered if he was getting mixed up in other people's dreams.

Memory develops through unconscious phases to appear in conscious recall, while the unconscious origin of dream impacts the assessment of its unreality. If the unconscious origin of dream heightens the feeling of unreality, does the lack of awareness for unconscious segments of memory support the sense of its realness? Certainly, a dream that veers from waking reality implies a psychological distance from actual experience, but dreams that revive an experience are not confused with the memory of that experience. If I dream of walking to the park, I do not confuse the ongoing dream content with a waking memory. In one instance, I remember the walk; in the other, I remember a dream of the walk. Is this the main difference? Unlike dream, memory is contextually real, that is, there is a before and after that supports the reality of the memory, even if recall is incomplete or erroneous. Dream is unconscious and recollected in consciousness; it is the conscious reconstruction or narrative of the imagery, not necessarily the actual dream that is recalled. The order of dream events is often uncertain in the dream, which consists of a replacement of one image by another without immediate memory. Likely, serial order is imposed on the waking narration.

Memory, Thought, and Existence

Existence is more than being; it is the recurrence of an epoch of becoming over successive states such that the process of recurrence—the actualization or becoming of entities—together with the categories that actualize, constitute a world-becoming as a moment of existence of all constituents. Recurrence in a primitive entity is more or less replication with minimal novelty. Rocks and elementary particles do not merely persist but undergo continuous iteration to be what they are. A single becoming is insufficient to establish existence. A thing does not appear out of nothing; there is a before and an after. The shift from before to after could be a causal sequence or iteration, a boxcar of change or a fountain of recurrence. On causal theory, one state is carried into the next. The transmission that preserves the cause in the effect or carries the past into the future can be interpreted as the revival of an antecedent state in a consequent one. In this respect, in the assimilation of the consequent to the antecedent, the effect "remembers" the cause. In recurrence theory, the after is not a direct resultant of the before but develops over its residue. The prior state can be said to be a memory in the current state. Put differently, the after unfolds as a near-replication of the before with some degree of novelty in the replacement. On a causal account, the origin of change is uncertain. The effect incorporates much of the cause but the transmission is uncertain. With recurrence there is a transition from potential to actual. Change is not from state to state or cause to effect but within the state itself, as the just-after is derived over the just-before.

Memory is recurrence. The revolution of an electron in a hypothetical atom is a mode of physical memory that reinstates the being of the atom. So, too, are the physical forces that govern the process. Becoming is a recurrence of the memory of being, while being is the substance (category) realized in becoming. In the example above, the category—the atom—is a complete revolution that enfolds all phases in the orbit of an electron. In human mind, being refers to a fully-derived mental state that actualizes on completion. Being is not a product or output of becoming, since it is an indivisible compilation of all phases in its realization. Put differently, an entity becomes what it is when all phases actualize one cycle of becoming.

From a lowly origin in physical entities, the pattern of continuous replication passes to plants and primitive organic forms. The concealed replication of organism is secreted in the DNA for auto-replication and the reproduction of like others. Memory is transmitted to progeny in the self-replication of individual becoming. That is, reproduction is an overt manifestation of the implicit replication of individual organism, and *the revival of perception as memory is an extension into mentation of the reproductive nature of existence.* The evolutionary series is a continuous reinstatement of organism in a nonconscious resurgence of form until finally the cycles of replication develop to human mind as unconscious revival is revealed in conscious imagery. This constitutes an endpoint in the transformation of memory to perception, or the uncovering, in memory, of the process of recurrence that underlies life and change.

Once memory becomes perception, or the reverse, the arousal of imagery—as an embedded pre-object—permits consciousness of memorial content as a preliminary to thought. Nonconscious entities, and the worlds in which they are ingredient, are precursors to conscious mind as an iteration of instinctual memory, primarily in auto-recurrence, secondarily in progeny, with all instances of recurrence as modes of organic recall. Every act of memory is forged to a world of perception that re-creates itself to exist, whether as a conceptual or mind-independent entity. An organism is not just what it is; it is remembered into existence.

Creativity in perception is attributed to the world as a source of beauty, innovation, and surprise, not the inner process of reproduction which gives a novel world and organism in each iteration. Inexactness in renewal is the starting point of thought and the creative imagination. In recurrence, the past of memory becomes the present of perception, perishing in the ensuing revival. The before and after have no fixed present, the illusion of which is essential to past and future. In the revival of memory, the transition is from the distant past of animal inheritance, to a more recent past of personal experience, to a final phase of recall that approximates the objective, at which point it ceases to be memorial and transforms, through sensibility, to perception. In this objectification, a present moment and an external world are created. The past, in relation to memory, experience, feeling, and knowledge, gives thought as a branching to novelty at submerged phases. The direction is from an evolutionary and experiential past to the immediacy of the now, with an intuition of the future in the forward surge to the present. In this way, the replication of the past gives way to innovation in the future.

Individuals with a great capacity for thought, or the ability to use memory in the service of the creative, may have ideas that change the world. The world of the ordinary is the surface toward which it is striving. The evolutionary outcome of memory is not conscious revival but its loss in the growth of thought, as the fading of the present prepares for the state that follows. That is, while perception occurs as an endpoint in the development of memory, thought arises in its infrastructure. If the perceptible world is created out of the adaptation of memory to sensibility, thought arises as incompleteness in the realization of memorial content. As memory disappears in perception, thought is a replacement of its penultimate phases. The perceptual exists in a confrontation of adaptation with recurrence. We exist in the evolution of memory to thought. The creativity that begins in the world shifts to mind-internal as imagery takes the place of objects as the vehicle of originality. The genius creates a subjective world as companion to a world of silent objectivity.

An escape from repetition is a goal of thought. Other goals are solutions or useful actions. In most organisms, this amounts to little more than feeding, avoiding predators, nesting, care of young, and navigating in a habitat. Thought appears in the cracks of contingency when memory no longer assures survival. The pragmatics of thought adapt to the environment, that is, to the world that memory creates, to which thought, however abstract, eventually yields.

Thought is a capacity to think, but the organism is not thought up in the same way it is reinstated by memory. Thinking is predicated on memory; thinking something exists is predicated on its existence. Memory is a "knowing what"; thinking is a "knowing that." Memory reinstates its object, while the object of thought is distinct from the act of thinking. The only existence created by thought is the thought itself. If thinking were the equivalent of existing, existence would depend on an act of thought or its content. An organism lacking or deprived of thought still exists, no less than one that thinks. Consciousness of existence as a class of thought implies existence as something that consciousness is about. The paradox is that thinking as a creative act depends on implicit memory to create the organism that thinks.

Endnotes

1. A. N. Whitehead, *The Concept of Nature* (Cambridge: Cambridge University Press, [1920] 2015), 45

FOUR

The Anthropocene, Ecozoic Era, and Organic Philosopnhy:
A Provocative Trio in Hamilton, Berry, and Whitehead

Herman Greene

MUCH OF THE EARLY MODERN VISION captured in the famous epigram of Descartes has been realized: that humans would become the "masters and possessors of nature"[1] by developing a mathematical science that would give a true understanding of natural processes along with the ability to control them. And yet science, together with other aspects of modernity, including the industrial mode of development, has also brought human mastery into the Anthropocene, where nature has now reasserted itself in a new guise beyond our possession and control.

The Anthropocene now judges us and all of our institutions and all of our ways of understanding. It is the context for the future, and it is in this context, as presented by Clive Hamilton, that I want to examine the work of Thomas Berry and Alfred North Whitehead. Clive Hamilton's Anthropocene, Thomas Berry's Ecozoic era, and Alfred North Whitehead's organic philosophy create a provocative trio for understanding the challenges and possibilities of the future.

The Anthropocene

The term "Anthropocene" was coined by Paul Crutzen and Eugene Stoermer, in an article published in 2000,[2] as the proposed name for a new geological epoch, which they claimed had now succeeded the Holocene epoch.[3] Crutzen and Stoermer identified large-scale changes humans have made on Earth and in its atmosphere, arguing that, in light of these still growing impacts, the role of humans should be recognized by naming the current epoch the Anthropocene. As to when to date the beginning of the epoch, they proposed the latter part of the eighteenth century, which was the time the Industrial Revolution began.[4] Though the term has not yet been recognized by the International Commission on Stratigraphy or the International Union of Geological Sciences, the Working Group on the Anthropocene presented a recommendation for recognition to the International Geological Congress on August 29, 2016.[5]

The scientific meaning of the term changed dramatically between the 2000 proposal of Crutzen and Stoermer to the 2016 recommendation of the Working Group on the Anthropocene, and in a way that is only beginning to be appreciated by the humanities. Clive Hamilton, in *Defiant Earth*,[6] gives a lucid account of the meaning for the humanities of the Anthropocene as currently understood by science.

Hamilton explains, "The idea of the Anthropocene was conceived by Earth System scientists to capture the very recent rupture in Earth history arising from the impact of human activity on the Earth System as a whole."[7] Then he asks his readers to read the preceding sentence again with an emphasis on "very recent rupture" and "Earth System as a whole." Instead of dating the Anthropocene back to the late eighteenth century or, as some have, to the entire Holocene epoch, Hamilton, in agreement with the current scientific view, dates the Anthropocene as beginning around 1945. This period he calls, as others have, "the Great Acceleration."[8]

According to Hamilton, the principal reason for recognizing a new epoch is the buildup of carbon dioxide in the atmosphere and its cascading effects on the Earth System. Ocean acidification, species loss, disruption of the nitrogen cycle, and other matters also support the naming of a new epoch.[9] The effects may, however, be so great that we are entering not just a new epoch but a new era.[10] Hamilton observes,

> The planet will not settle into a state that looks anything like the Holocene—the 10,000-year epoch of mild and constant climate that permitted civilization to flourish. It has been diverted into a different trajectory. Experts are already suggesting that the changes caused by humans in recent decades are so profound

and long-lasting that we have entered not a new epoch but a new era—the Anthropocene era—on a par with the break in Earth history brought by the arrival of multicellular life.[11]

In explaining the significance of the transformation that has occurred, Hamilton states:

> The entire history of Earth [has been] split irrevocably into two halves—the first 4.5 billion years in which Earth history was determined by blind natural forces alone, and the remaining five billion years in which it will be influenced by a conscious power long after that power is spent.[12]

If humans now compete

> with the forces of nature in its impact on the way the planet as a whole functions, the human imprint is the effect of a force fundamentally unlike physical ones such as weathering, volcanism, asteroid strike, subduction, and solar fluxes. This new "force of nature" contains something radically different—the element of volition.[13]

It was only when science understood that Earth had a history that humans were seen as having a history independent of Earth. Now, however, "human history and geological history have converged."[14]

This represents an "ontological shift in the deep history of the planet.... We are entering a geological episode whose designation depends not only on gathering and evaluating the available data, but also on human impacts on the Earth System that *have not yet occurred*."[15] Science, with the industrial development it made possible, brought humans and Earth into the Anthropocene and also provided the knowledge, through Earth System science, that enabled humans to understand they had entered a new epoch. The study of Earth as a system only began in the latter part of the twentieth century. For example, the notion of global climate was not accepted until after World War II. Until that time, climate was understood to be the result of local variations. Donella Meadows's modeling of Earth's resources, Lovelock's Gaia theory, the view of Earth from the moon, the results of Antarctic ice-core drilling, and many other scientific developments ultimately led to the understanding of Earth as a system.

> The new Earth System thinking...is the integrative meta-science of the whole planet understood as a unified, complex, evolving system beyond the sum of its parts. It is a transdisciplinary and holistic approach assimilating earth sciences and life sciences, as well as the "industrial metabolism" of humankind, all within a systems way of thinking with special focus on the non-linear dynamics of a system. It represents a markedly novel way of thinking about the Earth that supersedes ecological thinking.[16]

Hamilton then goes into a substantial analysis of the many misunderstandings of the Anthropocene—such as that it is the increasing gradual influence of humans; or that it is simply a measure of the human footprint on Earth; or that it is the continuation of a natural process; or even that it is evolution to higher consciousness and the fulfillment of modernity. All the while, Hamilton returns to his key notions that the Anthropocene is a rupture in the functioning of the Earth System, and that understanding Earth as a system is a fundamentally new meta-science, a paradigmatic shift in knowledge. He laments that the Anthropocene is misinterpreted by the use of conventional categories, such as archaeology, social geography, ecology, and landscape geography, as a continuation rather than a rupture. Thus it is deprived of its dangerous quality and rendered benign.

The danger arises from the counter-power of Earth now awakened from its slumber, enraged by human activity. Both humans and nature are more powerful in the Anthropocene. As much as Hamilton wishes to call attention to the activity of humans, he wishes to make clear the "Anthropocene antinomy" of Gaia fighting back. Both are necessary for the "new anthropocentrism." His goal is to redefine the human role and relationship in Earth.

Whereas environmental literature from the 1960s onward has seen Earth as victim of human neglect and abuse, now we are confronted with Earth's more than equal power. Hamilton proceeds to develop a philosophical anthropocentrism that differs not only from the old anthropocentrism, but also from

> virtually all philosophical understandings of modern environmentalism and post-humanism. Attempts to counter anthropocentric stances by adopting a non-human-centered standpoint (that of nature, or ecosystems, or of other creatures) or by spreading agency

around without regard to the human exception, cannot resist the evidence of Earth System science.[17]

Hamilton cites Vaclav Smil's stunning calculation that if one were to divide all of the land-based vertebrates on Earth into the three classes of humans, domesticated animals, and other, then, of the total, by body mass, humans would constitute 30%, domesticated animals 67%, and other 3%.[18] This being the case, there is no way we can leave Earth alone, or that Earth in response will leave us alone. The old anthropocentrism sees human mastery of Earth as a moral right; the new anthropocentrism recognizes human mastery of Earth as a fact that puts humans in a place of responsibility *and peril* not heretofore imagined.

> We may have acquired it foolishly, but we now have a responsibility for the Earth as a whole and pretending otherwise is itself irresponsible. So, the question is not whether human beings stand at the center of the world, but what *kind* of human being stands at the center of the world and what is the nature of that world. . . .
>
> Contrary to the comforting expectations that in the Anthropocene we can have "the kind of nature we wish to have," as we enter the new epoch, we will meet an Earth that is further and further from the Earth we might want. And against the belief that "the world we will inhabit is the one we have made," the world we will have to live with is the Earth we have turned against us.[19]

This breaks down modern philosophy's foundational, Kantian division "between the realm of necessity [nature and its laws] and the realm of freedom [occupied by humans]."[20] The new anthropocentrism acknowledges that humans are agents more powerful than ever, yet confirms our ultimate inseparability from the forces of the natural world we inhabit. "The new anthropocentric self does not float free like the modern subject, but is always woven into nature, *a knot in the fabric of nature.*"[21]

The cosmology of the Anthropocene must be based on the concept of agency that extends beyond humans to the freedom that is woven into nature itself. In this view, nature is a "self-organizing dynamic system characterized by *emergent properties*. . . . Emergent properties belong to the system but cannot be found in any individual element of it and evade all cause-and-effect explanations. In such systems . . . the future always evades full predictability and inevitably holds surprises."[22] Humans in a unique way manifest the spontaneous creativity of nature. Their "creative powers embody the possibility that they be used to *enhance* the life-enriching potential of the Earth as well as to improve the human condition. Nature therefore contains within it the possibility of mutually harmonious human-Earth enhancement."[23]

But if freedom is woven into nature, so is responsibility. In the Anthropocene, "our inescapable responsibility for the Earth defines us as moral beings," even more than "our own welfare, our virtues, and our duties to one another."[24] We cannot even let "nature take its course," which is realistically impossible with the still increasing impacts of humans on Earth. We must become involved as agents in a new way. "For humankind, how to create worlds while remaining within nature's limits . . . is the supreme challenge."[25]

Reconsidering Thomas Berry and Alfred North Whitehead in Light of the Anthropocene

So what do Thomas Berry and Alfred North Whitehead have to offer of relevance to the Anthropocene? Do they provide guidance? How does the works of Hamilton, Berry, and Whitehead relate to each other?

Thomas Berry (1914–2009)

Arguably, Thomas Berry can be credited with having developed the concept of the Anthropocene *avant la lettre* (before the term was coined). In 1988 he wrote:

> The anthropogenic shock that is overwhelming the earth is of an order of magnitude beyond anything previously known in human historical or cultural development. . . . We are acting on a geological and biological order of magnitude. . . . We are changing the chemistry of the planet . . . . We are upsetting the entire earth system.[26]

Anticipating that—due to the role of humans—we may be entering a new geological era and not just a new epoch, he wrote, "All of this disturbance of the planet is leading to the terminal phase of the Cenozoic era."[27] Emphasizing the centrality of human influence in this new period, he wrote:

"Natural selection can no longer function as it has functioned in the past. Cultural selection is now a decisive force in determining the future of the biosystems of the Earth."[28] And more emphatically, he wrote:

> The entire pattern of functioning of Earth is altered in the transition from the Cenozoic to the Ecozoic era. The major developments of the Cenozoic took place entirely apart from any human intervention. In the Ecozoic, the human will have a comprehensive influence on almost everything that happens. While the human cannot make a blade of grass, there is liable not to be a blade of grass unless it is accepted, protected and fostered by the human.[29]

Like Hamilton, he understood the inadequacy of past ethical frameworks in the new period:

> We find ourselves as ethically destitute just when, for the first time, we are faced with ultimacy, the irreversible closing down of the Earth's functioning in its major life systems. Our ethical traditions know how to deal with suicide, homicide, and even genocide; but these traditions collapse entirely when confronted with biocide, the extinction of the vulnerable life systems of the Earth, and geocide, the devastation of the Earth itself.[30]

He wrote of the unity of humans and Earth—"In reality there is a single integral community of the Earth that includes all its component members whether human or other than human"[31]—and that the destinies of humans and Earth were linked—

> In the twentieth century, the glory of the human has become the desolation of the Earth; the desolation of the Earth is becoming the destiny of the human; and all human institutions, professions, programs and activities must now be judged primarily by the extent to which they inhibit, ignore, or foster a mutually enhancing human-Earth relationship.[32]

Berry described the coming period as the "Ecozoic era," rather than the Anthropocene. The Ecozoic era was an ideal, a time of mutually enhancing human-Earth relations. He chose to speak of the future as promise, but he also said that achieving this future involved a "Great Work" that was epic in its dimensions, beyond anything previously conceived under this term and exceeding in its complexity all other great works. It involved not simply adjustment to disturbances of human life patterns, as, for example, that occasioned by a great depression or even a world war, but to disruption of the life systems that have governed the functioning of Earth in the 67 million years of the Cenozoic era.

Anne Marie Dalton wrote an insightful paper on Thomas Berry where she addressed the style of his writing. She first distinguished between descriptive and explanatory language and said that Berry's writings were primarily of the descriptive type. Then she drew attention to the ecopoetic[33] nature of much of Berry's work. For example,

> Berry does not write merely "the inspiration from my life work arose from the destruction of the natural world by the rise of industry." No—he wandered (one pauses to dwell on this word) into the field (or meadow), saw not flowers or plants in general, but lilies arising above the thick grass—; and he heard not just insects but crickets. It was not merely a clear day—, there was a blue sky with drifting white clouds.[34]

Throughout his work, Berry uses memorable poetic phrases, such as "Our quest for wonderworld is making waste world. Our quest for energy is creating entropy."[35] He calls the Cenozoic era the "lyric period of life development on the Earth."[36] And "our hope for the future is for a new dawn, an Ecozoic Era, when humans will be present to the Earth in a mutually-enhancing manner."[37]

Though highly erudite, Berry did not write in an academic style. He rarely gave citations. He imaginatively described the dangerous quality of the Anthropocene and the possibility of mutually harmonious human-Earth enhancement. This is his gift to an explanatory writer like Hamilton. In Berry, Hamilton's ideas become grounded in human experience and the living Earth.

Berry, however, preceded Hamilton. As noted above, the current understanding of the Anthropocene was based on science of the twenty-first century, much of which was not available to Berry. Hamilton, from the perspective of his interpretation of the Anthropocene, offers criticisms of Berry's work and how it has been applied by his followers.

Hamilton sees the origin of the Anthropocene in the characteristics of humans as a species. He notes that throughout the history of humans they are "world-making" creatures. Hamilton discusses how there has been much criticism of the term "the Anthropocene" because it seems to place collective guilt on all humans without identifying the West or capitalism or industrial development or other factors as the real culprits, as different authors would have it. Hamilton argues that this is a category mistake. The Anthropocene is not a socioeconomic or human historical category; it is a geological category. Further, even if the origins of the industrial revolution were in the West and were propelled by capitalism, today this has been adopted by people around the world and the leading actors are Sino-Americo-Eurocentric, soon to be Indo-Sino-Americo-Eurocentric. Consequently, Hamilton approves the attaching of the new epoch to an undifferentiated *Anthropos*.[38]

In this new epoch, in Hamilton's view, "the problem is not that humans are not anthropocentric, but that *we are not anthropocentric enough.*"[39] Rather than biocentrism, ecocentrism, or post-humanism, which stress human immersion in nature, the multiplicity of natural agents, and a leveling of human agencies with these other agencies, Hamilton emphasizes the need to pay attention to ourselves as the exceptional agent in relation to a powerful Gaia. Further, we need to exercise the powers of Western thought, science, and technology in exercising our agency. While there are elements of Berry's thought that seem to predate Hamilton's, Berry falls within those types of environmental philosophy and philosophical anthropology that Hamilton criticizes. Berry's historical analysis places the blame on the West and industrialism for the terminal Cenozoic era. Humans are to be reinvented at the species level, but within the community of life systems.[40] We are to be ecocentric, yielding ourselves to the guidance of a nearly always benevolent Earth.

This quote captures Berry's orientation:

> The task of renewing Earth belongs to Earth, as the renewal of any organism takes place from within. Yet we humans have our own special role, a leading role in the renewal, just as we had the dominant role in the devastation. We can fulfill this role, however, only if we move our basic life orientation from a dominant anthropocentrism to a dominant ecocentrism. In effecting this change we need to listen to the voices of Earth and its multitude of living and non-living modes of expression.
>
> We should be listening to the stars in the heavens and the sun

and the moon, to the mountains and the plains, to the forests and rivers and seas that surround us, to the meadows and the flowering grasses, to the songbirds and the insects and to their music, especially in the evening and the early hours of the night. We need to experience, to feel, and to see these myriad creatures all caught up in the celebration of life.[41]

While praising science for the knowledge it has given us of the epic of evolution, Berry cannot assign a role in the emerging Ecozoic era to advanced technology. He saw the "opposition between the industrial-commercial entrepreneur and the ecologist [as] the central Earth issue of the twenty-first century."[42] He saw the future as a struggle between the technozoic and the ecozoic.[43]

Berry was heavily influenced by Teilhard de Chardin. Hamilton criticizes Teilhard for his mystical holism:

> Teilhardian holism may seem consistent with the broad vision of the Earth System, but as philosophy it eviscerates its scientific content by attempting to levitate above it, into that ethereal layer of consciousness that ... he names the noösphere. ... This kind of transcendent holism exalts humankind to a unique place, but detaches us from the actual world, and does so just at the time we realize how inescapably rooted we are in the Earth itself.[44]

While, to my knowledge, Berry never carried forward the idea of the noösphere in his writing, there is an element of mystical consciousness in a pervasive dream of the universe and Earth accessible in our visionary experiences and creative moments as insight and guidance.[45]

Hamilton also criticizes attempts to adopt or adapt non-Western philosophies of nature as a political answer to the ecological crisis of the Anthropocene.[46] With specific reference to Indigenous cultures, he wrote, "looking upon [them] with awe and regarding them as having magical potency is to fetishize them, a tendency now taken so far by some as to attribute to them the power to fix the climate and reverse the geological destabilization of the planet."[47] While respecting insights of ancient cultures and acknowledging that they offer elements to build on, he observes that in daily life Indigenous people are as taken aback by the Anthropocene as people anywhere, and to cope with the world of the Anthropocene they have to go back and forth between their ancient ways of being and knowing and the Western scientific ways of knowing. Hamilton says Indigenous people know that the answers to the Anthropocene are not in their ancient ways of knowing,[48]

While approving of associating the Anthropocene with an undifferentiated Anthropos, Hamilton acknowledges the concern of Andreas Malm and Alf Hornborg that species thinking "will see analysis descend into 'mystification and political paralysis.'"[49] Drawing on Lisa Sideris, Hamilton then gives, as an example of such mystification, Berry's universe story as presented in the *Journey of the Universe* book and film of Brian Thomas Swimme and Mary Evelyn Tucker. This work purportedly offers a wondrous view of cosmic evolution as "a process based on immense creative, connection, and interdependence," one in which humans are the "mind and heart of the vast evolving universe."[50] According to Hamilion,

> Sideris points to the affinity of this kind of cosmic thinking with the "good Anthropocene" stories of ecomodernism, ones that gloss over the actual causes and dangers of ecological destruction to focus on the marvelous ability of the human species to transcend any obstacle and continue its inexorable rise to a golden future.[51]

Hamilton's final criticism of Berry is for his alleged cosmic utopianism:

> If Nietzschean nihilism is unfazed by the end of humans on the planet, the obverse mistake is to deny that the end of humans is possible.... Such is the stance of... Teilhard de Chardin and Thomas Berry, according to which God or the Universe has a higher plan, one in which the dark side of the human relationship to nature, and so the depredations of the Anthropocene, become a mere phase to be transcended as the plan unfolds.[52]

I think Hamilton was wrong in lumping together Teilhard and Berry in the quote above. Berry was not naïve about the human or Earth prospect. He did not adopt Chardin's idea of the noösphere or of the inevitable movement to the "Omega Point." There is an aspect of Berry's writing, however, that suggests movement to the Ecozoic era will happen. This is probably what Sideris meant when she spoke of *The Journey of the Universe* adopting the "good Anthropocene" view, and what Hamilton meant when he spoke of cosmic utopianism.

I would, however, say that if Berry, and Tucker and Swimme, adopted the good Anthropocene view it was not that of ecomodernists. In Berry's, Tucker's, and Swimme's work, this is a good Anthropocene in the sense that it is a good time to be human and take responsibility for Earth and thus realize the promise of the Ecozoic era. If this Great Work does not occur, however, the Ecozoic era will not occur. It is not foreordained.

In light of the hard truths that Hamilton sought to impart about human dominance, Earth's reaction, and the need for human agency in being responsible for a fractious Earth, the criticisms he gives above of Berry and his followers are understandable. Yet I believe it is wrong to see Berry as being in opposition to Hamilton's project. Both call for recognition of the disruption of the Earth system. Both call for human agency. I can't think of a greater call to human agency than Berry's call for humans to do the Great Work. Both call for a new cosmology and for a recognition of the agency of both humans and nature that are woven into the fabric of the universe, though they express this very differently. Hamilton calls for a global meta-narrative of the Anthropocene. Berry calls for a global meta-narrative of the universe story. Both see the role of the human as being significant in the story of the universe and both interestingly agree that without the human, there would be no universe and no Earth, because there would be no being that comprehends them. It is also interesting that Berry and Hamilton agree that the universe is self-referential (in other words, the answers to the universe must be found within the universe) and that ultimately significant action is in care for Earth.

The biggest differences I see in the two positions are that Berry does attempt to articulate an ecocentric position and to locate humans in a broad, benevolent Earth community. Further, Berry could not take a position on advanced science and technology and tended to overlook the globalized, urbanized, energy- and technology-dependent reality of human existence in the twenty-first century and the complex issues that raises. Hamilton acknowledges this state of affairs, but in *Defiant Earth* offers only, but importantly, a philosophical basis for acting in the Anthropocene and for human agency as the answer.

In truth, there is much to be gained by Berry's call for humans to learn from Earth. This is a needed outcome of recognizing that we are embedded in Earth's processes. Berry's view that the future needs primarily to be ecozoic, rather than technozoic, also deserves important consideration. Hamilton acknowledges the need to live within limits, but encourages a human agency that builds on Western thought and technology. I understand what Hamilton is trying to accomplish with human agency, and it is needed. I also understand the importance of an ecozoic vision. It is a vision of learning from Earth and becoming coherent with the functioning of Earth. Perhaps the Berry folk need to take into account Hamilton's view that Earth is both mother *and other*. Berry's call for intimacy with Earth community is mythical. That has a good side, but in a way, it fails to respect that this mother is full of passion.

Alfred North Whitehead (1861–1947)

Alfred North Whitehead ended his work before the beginning of the modern environmental movement. There were people, such as George Perkins Marsh and John Muir, who had awakened to environmental issues, but sensitivity to them was not widespread. I am not aware that Whitehead ever wrote explicitly about environmental issues, yet I believe he provided the undergirding philosophy for an ecological worldview.

That Whitehead did not address environmental issues in his writing is consistent with his avoidance of political commentary or practical advice for living. He seldom told stories to illustrate aspects of his philosophy. This was because his overall aim was to develop understandings that would be applicable in every situation and at all times.

Concerning the aim of philosophy, he wrote:

> Philosophy is the attempt to manifest the fundamental evidence as to the nature of things. Upon the presupposition of this evidence, all understanding rests. A correctly verbalized philosophy mobilizes this basic experience which all premises presuppose. It makes the content of the human mind manageable; it adds meaning to fragmentary details; it discloses disjunctions and conjunctions, consistencies and inconsistencies. Philosophy is the criticism of abstractions which govern special modes of thought.[53]

In his magnum opus, *Process and Reality,* he offered a speculative philosophy, which, he said, is

> the endeavor to frame a coherent, logical, necessary system of general ideas in terms of which every element of our experience can be interpreted. By this notion of 'interpretation' I mean that everything of which we are conscious, as enjoyed, perceived, willed

or thought, shall have the character or a particular instance of the general scheme.[54]

With such a broad undertaking, it is difficult to give a summary of Whitehead's thought. Every aspect of his thought has to be interpreted in relation to some other aspect, and his scheme can never be completely understood. Whitehead admits his own inability to develop a closed and encompassing set of ideas, and he emphasizes that he did not intend to do so. His work, as reflected in the title of one of his books, was truly an "adventure of ideas."[55] He declared "how shallow, puny and imperfect are efforts to sound the depths in the nature of things. In philosophical discussion, the merest hint of dogmatic certainty as to finality of statement is an exhibition of folly."[56]

Given this, and considering the urgency of the Anthropocene, why bring up Whitehead at all? I bring up Whitehead because of the importance of philosophy to the Anthropocene.[57] Ideas are what make the existing state of things seem obvious and necessary, and therefore resistant to change. Our ideas are abstractions from our environment and call our attention to certain aspects and relations in our environment. Just as Hamilton attacked habits of thought in the contemporary academy that disempowered human agency, Whitehead, in perhaps a more profound way, did the same.

Whitehead explains in *Modes of Thought* that our environment comes to us with infinite complexity. While we have private, primary, bodily experience, conscious reflection arises in relation to an outer world. The "first principle of epistemology is that the changeable, shifting aspects of our relations to nature are the primary topics for conscious observation."[58] Language is an abstraction from actual experience and identifies only certain aspects of the underlying reality.

> [Language] utilizes those elements in experience most easily abstracted for conscious entertainment, and most easily reproduced in experience.... Each language is the civilization of expression in the social systems which use it.
>
> Apart from language, the retention of thought, the easy recall of thought, the interweaving of thought into higher complexity, are all gravely limited. Human civilization is an outgrowth of language, and language is the product of an advancing civilization.[59]

In humans, Whitehead observes, nature burst through a boundary.

> The conceptual entertainment of unrealized possibility becomes a major factor in human mentality. . . . The definition of mankind is that in this genus of animals the central activity has been developed on the side of its relationship to novelty. . . . There is the novelty received from the aggregate diversities of bodily expressions. Such novelty requires decision as to its reduction to coherence of expression.
>
> [And] there is the introduction of novelty of feeling by the entertainment of unexpressed possibilities. This second side is the enlargement of the conceptual experience of [hu]mankind.[60]

Beginning in the sixteenth century, modern science liberated humans from ancient ills and showed great power to manipulate nature. But this science, and the philosophies that gave rise to it and followed from it, saw the world as consisting of independent bits of inert matter in motion, existing in empty space. Empirical knowledge obtained through the senses was given primacy in epistemology. Mind was excluded from nature as well as feeling, emotion, purpose, and value. The elemental, non-perceptual experiences of the body were ignored. The world was reduced to bare facts, subject to universal laws of nature, to be connected and manipulated.

These modern understandings could not take away from humans their outrageous capacity for novelty, but they restricted the ability of humans to be aware of those aspects of existence that give rise to life and motion, and, derivatively, to morality, religion, and power. In *Modes of Thought*, Whitehead writes about morality as the maximization of the intensity of feelings of importance in a particular occasion. It is "the aim at greatness of experience in the various dimensions belonging to it."[61] "Morality," he says, "is always the aim at that unity of harmony, intensity, and vividness which involves the perfection of importance for that occasion."[62] "Religion emphasizes the unity of ideal inherent in the universe."[63] Morality and religion are the disrupting and energizing forces in civilization.[64] "Power is the compulsion of composition. . . . The essence of power is the drive towards aesthetic worth for its own sake. . . . It constitutes the drive of the universe. It is efficient cause, maintaining its power of survival. It is final cause, maintaining in the creature its appetite for creation."[65]

Nothing is ever simply a fact being just what it is where it is. It is an aspect of a universe in process, composed of subjects apprehending each other, engaging stubborn fact and creative advance into novelty. The "energetic activity considered in physics is the emotional intensity entertained in life."[66]

Whitehead is often explained with reference to *concresence, prehensions*, and the many other novel terms he coined in *Process and Reality*, and to his technical ideas in that book. This is all well and good, though rarely comprehensible to the casual reader or listener. I have been reading Whitehead's technical philosophy for over 50 years and am still working to understand it; or, perhaps better, I should say, I am still gaining new insights from it. His system is a fascinating collection of ideas that discloses the nature of reality in new ways and opens up vistas of exploration and communication across disciplines and traditions, and with other-than-human nature.

His technical work in *Process and Reality* is worthy of exposition. The important point for the purposes of this chapter, though, is what was behind his drive to develop his speculative philosophy, and what can be learned from his less technical works, such as *Modes of Thought*. Why is Whitehead important for the Anthropocene? The answer I would give is that Whitehead energized and empowered the human project; he released human agency stifled by the abstractions of modernity.

Hamilton does mention one of Whitehead's major contributions: "Posthumanism has taught us to blur the hard-and-fast division between subject and object by accepting our inescapable physical entanglements. It has made us understand, thanks to ecology and Whitehead, that nothing exists outside of its relationships."[67] Hamilton doesn't recognize Whitehead's contribution to human agency. Hamilton's own call for human agency is devoid of that sense of importance and greatness of experience and aesthetic achievement, found in Whitehead, on which a new civilization must be built. On the other hand, Whitehead's call for greatness lacks the historical urgency of Hamilton's. Whitehead views the long march of civilization occurring without the immediacy of the existential threat of ecological catastrophe.

Berry, in his work, mentions Whitehead on many occasions. When a person with a Whiteheadian background reads Berry, it is hard to avoid reading Whitehead into Berry's work. An obvious example relates to perhaps the most important and famous of Berry's statements: "The universe is a communion of subjects, not a collection of objects."[68] Whitehead, in his "ontological principle," put it this way: "Apart from the experience of subjects there is nothing, nothing, nothing, bare nothingness."[69] I do not know whether Berry came up with his statement on the basis of Whitehead.

Berry did read Whitehead. He told me so, and it is evident in his references to Whitehead. But he objected to Whitehead because, in Berry's view, Whitehead's philosophy didn't go anywhere. Berry was taken with the story of evolution as given in Teilhard de Chardin's work, and in the accumulation of scientific knowledge of the evolution of the universe and of life on Earth. Berry, like Hamilton, was focused on the urgency of human action in the Anthropocene, and by the historical context given to the human project by the Anthropocene.

Whitehead, however, provides one outstanding service to Berry, specifically in regard to Hamilton's criticisms of Berry's mystification and cosmic utopianism. Hamilton thinks this floats over concrete reality and misleads as to what is important. Whitehead clarifies that "the characterization of importance is that it is that aspect of feeling whereby a perspective is imposed upon the universe of things felt."[70] Concentration on discrete fact, logical theory, and minute detail fails to disclose the connectedness that is the "essence of all things of all types."[71] "Nothing is fully understood until its reference to process has been made evident."[72] Conscious understanding is never complete. "Deeper truths must be adumbrated by myths."[73] Hamilton's meta-narrative of the Anthropocene appeals to "universal reason—the logic of Earth System science that has been painstakingly put together over the last three or four decades and continues to evolve."[74] Berry's, Swimme's, and Tucker's universe story is mythic in a classical sense. It reveals a deeper truth. And Berry's ecopoetics lends emotional intensity to what is important. Whitehead helps in understanding Berry's contribution to Hamilton's call for human agency.

A Provocative Trio

To me the work of Hamilton, Berry, and Whitehead are mutually enhancing. But, so as not to confuse this with sameness, I will say that this trio is highly provocative.

Hamilton is the *explainer*. He explains the current scientific understanding of the Anthropocene, that it is a rupture in the Earth system. This gives rise to questions of what kind of human caused this rupture and what kind of Earth are we dealing with now? He issues a passionate call for human agency in relation to a fractious Earth. He emphasizes that the Anthropocene is a geological category, not a sociohistorical category. The Anthropocene nonetheless offers a new vantage point for understanding the sociohistorical past and future. Hamilton deconstructs philosophical positions that he believes disempower humans in relation to their task in the Anthropocene. He offers a realistic perspective: It is not outside the globalized Western, technological, consumerist culture that the Anthropocene must be faced, but inside it.

Berry is the *describer* and the *ecological poet*. He offers a mythic vision of a transition from the terminal Cenozoic era to an emerging Ecozoic era. If carefully read, he is as vigilant of the perils of the Anthropocene as Hamilton. Like Hamilton, he issues a call for human agency in the Great Work of moving into a period of mutually enhancing human-Earth relations. Hamilton says the supreme challenge for humankind is how to create worlds while remaining within nature's limits. Hamilton emphasizes that Western thought and technology must be used in doing this, but I think Berry's insight that a future within limits is more ecozoic than technozoic is probably right. I don't know if Hamilton would say Berry was nostalgic for an unrecoverable agrarian, 'organic' past. Berry's work and the application of his work by his followers is open to this criticism. In my view Hamilton's work may bring a needed realism to the Berry community. The re-invention of the human that Berry calls for cannot be repetition of a past human mode of being, it must be creation of a future form of humanity in the midst of the givenness of our complex world.

Whitehead is the *grand philosopher*, both explainer and describer. If I had to place him on one pole more than the other, I would call him a describer, and also a poet. Whitehead is wrongly characterized as hopelessly complex and technical, dry as toast. Whitehead turns a world of dead objects in motion into a world of emotion, intensity, purpose, and value. He discloses a world of high adventure where all is put at risk in the creative advance into novelty. He wrote, "The teleology of the Universe is directed to the production of Beauty."[75] This dominant element of poetic empowerment in Whitehead must be understood. If this were all he offered, however, there would have been no empowerment because modern habits of thought would remain in place and disempower that very agency. Whitehead's technical philosophy was an accomplishment of the highest degree. It did not just reconcile science and the humanities;

it transformed the potential of science while embracing the accumulated scientific knowledge of modernity. In my view, Whitehead provides the philosophy that is needed for the Anthropocene. I would even say that it is necessary globally, but would hasten to add that elements of Whitehead's philosophy are articulated by others who have never studied him and do not know his name, but they absorb and make use of the understandings given in Whitehead's philosophy. These understandings are present in Berry's writings, whether he obtained them from Whitehead or not, and they are present in Hamilton when he wrote that Earth operates as a unified, relational system, and the history of humans and nature have converged.

Clive Hamilton's Anthropocene, Thomas Berry's Ecozoic era, and Alfred North Whitehead's organic philosophy...a provocative trio indeed!

Endnotes

1. R. Descartes, *Discourse on Method for Reasoning Well and for Seeking Truth in the Sciences*, trans. Ian Johnston (1637) pt. 6, available at: http://www.faculty.umb.edu/gary_zabel/Courses/Bodies,%20Souls,%20and%20Robots/Texts/descartes1.htm#:~:text=Rene%20Descartes%20(1596%2D1650),optics%2C%20geometry%2C%20and%20meteorology.&text=He%20later%20(in%201641)%20published,in%20Meditations%20on%20First%20Philosophy.
2. P. J. Crutzen and E. F. Stoermer, "The Anthropocene," *IGBP Newsletter* 41 (May 2000): 17–18.
3. In geological terminology, an "epoch" is a time span of many thousands of years, indicated by the suffix "cene." The current epoch, which began around 10,000 years ago, is called the Holocene epoch. See A. Kiplinger, "Naming a New Geological Era: The Ecozoic Era and Its Historical Antecedents," *The Ecozoic Journal* 3 (2013): 13.
4. Crutzen and Stoermer, "The Anthropocene," 17.
5. D. Carrington, "The Anthropocene Epoch: Scientists Declare Dawn of Human-Influenced age," *The Guardian*, August 29, 2016, accessed July 16, 2017, https://www.theguardian.com/environment/2016/aug/29/declare-anthropocene-epoch-experts-urge-geological-congress-human-impact-earth.

    In May 2019, the Anthropocene Working Group (AWG) of the International Commission on Stratigraphy (ICS) voted to recognize the new epoch as beginning around 1950. The AWG identified the

Anthropocene epoch by phenomena related to it, as follows:

> An order-of-magnitude increase in erosion and sediment transport associated with urbanization and agriculture; marked and abrupt anthropogenic perturbations of the cycles of elements such as carbon, nitrogen, phosphorus and various metals together with new chemical compounds; environmental changes generated by these perturbations, including global warming, sea-level rise, ocean acidification and spreading oceanic 'dead zones'; rapid changes in the biosphere both on land and in the sea, as a result of habitat loss, predation, explosion of domestic animal populations and species invasions; and the proliferation and global dispersion of many new 'minerals' and 'rocks' including concrete, fly ash and plastics, and the myriad 'technofossils' produced from these and other materials (Anthropocene Working Group of the International Commission on Stratigraphy, Results of Binding Vote, http://quaternary.stratigraphy.org/working-groups/anthropocene/.

The ICS itself, however, has not yet recognized the new epoch

6. C. Hamilton, *Defiant Earth: The Fate of Humans in the Anthropocene* (Cambridge, UK: Polity Press, 2017).

7. Hamilton, *Defiant Earth*, 9.

8. Hamilton, *Defiant Earth*, 2. Explaining the term, the "Great Acceleration," the International Geosphere-Biosphere Programme states:

> The second half of the 20th Century is unique in the history of human existence. Many human activities reached take-off points sometime in the 20th Century and sharply accelerated towards the end of the century. The last 60 years have without doubt seen the most profound transformation of the human relationship with the natural world in the history of humankind. (International Geosphere-Biosphere Programme, "Great Acceleration," Global Change, accessed July 16, 2017,_http://www.igbp.net/globalchange/greatacceleration.4.1b8ae20512db692f2a680001630.html).

See generally, J. R. McNeill and P. Engelke, *The Great Acceleration: An Environmental History of the Anthropocene since 1945* (Cambridge,

MA: Belknap Press of Harvard University Press, 2014).

9. Hamilton, *Defiant Earth*, 1. There must be geological evidence for the naming of a new geological period. Markers for the Anthropocene beginning after World War II may include radionuclides from atom bomb tests; unburned carbon spheres emitted by power stations; wide dispersion of plastic, aluminum, and concrete debris; phosphates from fertilizers; and rapid spread of domestic animals.

10. A geological era is a unit of time spanning dozens of millions of years, for example, the Cenozoic era (Kiplinger, "Naming a New Geological Era," 13).

11. Hamilton, *Defiant Earth*, 4. Hamilton's argument is that the changes wrought during the Great Acceleration are irreversible and hence the conditions of life on Earth have changed irrevocably.

12. Hamilton, *Defiant Earth*, 5. The "remaining five billion years" refers to the remaining expected life of the Sun.

13. Hamilton, *Defiant Earth*, 5–6.

14. Hamilton, *Defiant Earth*, 8.

15. Hamilton, *Defiant Earth*, 7.

16. Hamilton, *Defiant Earth*, 11–12. "Ecology studies the local and regional; Earth System science studies the Earth as a total system" (11–12). The Earth System involves the coevolution of its spheres: the atmosphere, the hydrosphere, the cryosphere (ice), biosphere, and the lithosphere (Earth's crust) (14). Earth is not a collection of ecosystems, rather it is "a single, total functioning system" (34).

17. Hamilton, *Defiant Earth*, 49.

18. Hamilton, *Defiant Earth*, 42.

19. Hamilton, *Defiant Earth*, 43, 47–48.

20. Hamilton, *Defiant Earth*, 51. Hamilton ascribes this division to Kant, (139).

21. Hamilton, *Defiant Earth*, 52.

22. Hamilton, *Defiant Earth*, 137–38.

23. Hamilton, *Defiant Earth*, 144.

24. Hamilton, *Defiant Earth*, 52.

25. Hamilton, *Defiant Earth*, 152.

26. T. Berry, *The Dream of the Earth* (San Francisco: Sierra Club Books, 1988), 211, 206.
27. Berry, *The Dream of the Earth*, 6.
28. T. Berry, *The Great Work: Our Way into the Future* (New York: Crown, 1999), 4.
29. T. Berry, "The Determining Features of the Ecozoic Era," in *Selected Writings on the Earth Community*, selected by M. E. Tucker and J. Grim (Maryknoll, NY: Orbis Books, 2014), 142.
30. Berry, *The Great Work*, 104.
31. Berry, *The Great Work*, 4.
32. Berry, *Selected Writings*, 164–65 (numbering of sentences omitted).
33. Ecopoetics is poetics that concerns humans and ecology.
34. A. M. Dalton, "The Intellectual Legacy of Thomas Berry," *The Ecozoic Journal* 4 (2017), 21–22.
35. Berry, *The Great Work*, 68.
36. Berry, *The Great Work*, 49.
37. Berry, *The Great Work*, 55.
38. Hamilton, *Defiant Earth*, 30–31.
39. Hamilton, *Defiant Earth*, 43.
40. Berry, *The Great Work*, 159.
41. T. Berry, *The Christian Future and the Fate of Earth*, ed. Mary Evelyn Tucker (New York: Columbia University Press, 2009), 73.
42. Berry, *The Great Work*, 59.
43. B. Swimme and T. Berry, *The Universe Story: From the Primordial Flaring Forth to the Beginning of the Ecozoic Era—A Celebration of the Unfolding Cosmos* (New York: HarperCollins, 1994), 14–15.
44. Hamilton, *Defiant Earth*, 57.
45. See Berry, *Dream of the Earth*, 197.
46. Hamilton, *Defiant Earth*, 57.
47. Hamilton, *Defiant Earth*, 106.
48. For example, if an Indigenous community is disrupted by a palm oil plantation or by a gold mine, knowledge that trees are sacred or that the Earth is living, or convening a communal council, does not

provide a means to address or cope with the occupation of land by the plantation or the pollution of a river by the gold mine. Even more so, traditional knowledge does not have resources to address non-local emissions of carbon dioxide and global warming, which have very local effects.

While Hamilton does not mention Berry in this criticism, it could apply to an aspect of Berry's work as he advises that a key wisdom for the future is that of Indigenous people. See, e.g., "The Historical Role of the American Indian," in Berry, *Dream of the Earth*, 180–93; and "The Fourfold Wisdom" with specific reference to Indigenous wisdom in Berry, *The Great Work*, 177–80. Berry does not attend to the limitations of that wisdom in the way that Hamilton does; provided, however that along with the wisdom of indigenous people, Berry advises that another key wisdom for the future is the wisdom of science. While not making the same point as Hamilton, Berry does emphasize that more than one type of wisdom is needed for the future.

49. Hamilton, *Defiant Earth*, 59, is here quoting from A. Malm and A. Hornborg, "The Geology of Mankind? A Critique of the Anthropocene Narrative," *The Anthropocene Review* 1.1 (January 2014).

50. Swimme and M. E. Tucker, *Journey of the Universe* (New Haven and London: Yale University Press, 2011); *Journey of the Universe: An Epic Story of Cosmic, Earth and Human Transformation*, directed by David Kennard and Patsy Northcutt, written by Brian Thomas Swimme and Mary Evelyn Tucke, DVD (Shelter Island, 2013).

51. Hamilton, *Defiant Earth*, 59.

52. Hamilton, *Defiant Earth*, 114.

53. A. N. Whitehead, *Modes of Thought* (New York: The Free Press, 1938), 48–49.

54. A. N. Whitehead, *Process and Reality: An Essay in Cosmology*, Corrected Edition, ed. D. R. Griffin and D. W. Sherburne (New York: Free Press, [1929] 1978), 3.

55. A. N. Whitehead, *Adventures of Ideas* (New York: Free Press, [1933] 1967). "The true method of discovery is like the flight of an aeroplane. It starts from imaginative generalization; and it again lands for renewed observation rendered acute by rational interpretation" (Whitehead, *Process and Reality*, 5).

56. Whitehead, *Process and Reality*, xiv.
57. Hamilton also emphasized the importance of philosophy. He wrote, "Earth System science is the first science to arise from the merging of the realm of necessity and the realm of freedom. It can give us knowledge of the Earth System but it cannot, taken alone, give us knowledge of the larger implications of the Anthropocene. For that we need philosophy" (Hamilton, *Defiant Earth*, 129).
58. Whitehead, *Modes of Thought*, 29.
59. Whitehead, *Modes of Thought*, 34–35.
60. Whitehead, *Modes of Thought*, 26.
61. Whitehead, *Modes of Thought*, 14.
62. Whitehead, *Modes of Thought*, 14.
63. Whitehead, Modes of Thought, 28.
64. Whitehead, *Modes of Thought*, 19.
65. Whitehead, *Modes of Thought*, 119.
66. Whitehead, *Modes of Thought*, 168.
67. Hamilton, *Defiant Earth*, 110.
68. T. Berry, *Evening Thoughts: Reflecting on Earth as Sacred Community*, ed. Mary Evelyn Tucker (San Francisco: Sierra Club, 2006), 149.
69. Whitehead, *Process and Reality*, 167.
70. Whitehead, *Modes of Thought*, 11.
71. Whitehead, *Modes of Thought*, 9.
72. Whitehead, *Modes of Thought*, 46.
73. Whitehead, *Modes of Thought*, 10.
74. Hamilton, *Defiant Earth*, 79.
75. Alfred North Whitehead, *Adventures of Ideas*, 265.

FIVE

Cause and Influence in Whitehead

John B. Cobb, Jr.

WHITEHEADIANS OFTEN CRITICIZE economists, political theorists, and even sociologists for being too individualistic. We often affirm that Whitehead frees us to understand ourselves as social beings; that our welfare is bound up with the welfare of others. We talk much about the common good. It turns out, however, that some of Whitehead's language cuts in a different direction, and that this has limited the contributions of Whiteheadians to important issues in social thought. Several Whiteheadians have modified Whitehead to overcome the tendency toward individualism that they think they find in his writings.

First, Whitehead's announcement that he is an atomist tends to shock the reader. Our picture of atomistic thinking is one that separates everything from everything else in order to study it in its individuality. This has led to an individualism that has done great psychological and social harm and to a fragmentation of thinking that prevents the world from viewing itself and its needs realistically.

But, of course, this is just one kind of atomism. For a philosophy to be an atomism, it is required only that it affirm that there are real individuals and that more complex entities can ultimately be analyzed into these. It leaves open the question of whether the societies of individuals have characteristics lacking in the strict individuals that make them up. It does not tell us what the individuals are like. Whitehead's individuals are socially constituted, so it is meaningless to analyze them in separation from the world out of which they come, a world largely constituted by societies. The world is made up of social individuals, individuals that are the becoming of one out of many. The implications are profoundly different.

Herman Daly and I thought that this allowed us to envision an "economics for community." This gives priority to the societies in which individuals find themselves. The editor changed our title to "For the Common Good," and we accepted that. But that phrase does not appear anywhere in the text.[1] The priority of societies was our point, and we considered the goal of politics and economics to be the development of the kind of societies that have the characteristics we associate with the word "community." I am just learning that the social character of individuals by itself does not sufficiently ground the belief that economics and also politics should work to improve communities. We made a jump that needs defense and explanation.

I have been surprised since then to find that some students of Whitehead think that his atomism blocks an adequate understanding of the role of societies. I was particularly impressed by Joseph Bracken's work, designed among other things to recognize the full reality and importance of the church. But I have tended to feel that Whitehead already offered what was needed.

Cliff Cobb's writings finally broke through to me that there is an important issue on which many of Whitehead's followers have sided against what I have assumed is his actual position. With Andrew Schwartz, I recently edited a book composed largely of the section plenaries delivered at the Tenth International Whitehead conference in June 2015.[2] Since the paper by William Connolly for the section on social thought was committed to publication elsewhere, I asked Cliff to write a paper on this topic for the book. It is a careful assessment of the potentials and limitations of Whitehead's thought for a creative breakthrough in social and political theory.[3] Cliff rightly believes that we need political, economic, and social theories that emphasize the central role of society. This cannot be done if society is understood as simply a togetherness of individuals. Indeed, the evidence that social patterns affect individuals is simply ignored by most social and political philosophers because it cannot be explained by their individualistic theories.

Cliff gives the example of the distribution of income in a society as having effects on its individual members. This distribution cannot be found in the effect of any one individual on another. That distribution of wealth within a society affects its individual members is empirically demonstrated, but it is not given attention because of the all-controlling individualist theory. As I was working on this chapter, I received in an email an essay explaining why, for the first time in some years, life expectancy in the United States declined in 2016. The author, Alan Grayson, holds that extreme differences of income are the only available explanation. He provides convincing evidence, just as Cliff had.

My reaction has been that Whitehead would expect just such effects. However, Cliff showed that those Whiteheadians who have worked on social and political theory have in fact held back from recognizing the actual effects of the characteristics of societies as such on their members. And I finally realized that the deeper problem is not what Whitehead says about atomism but what he says about causality.

Showing the role of causal feelings in all occasions is one of Whitehead's greatest accomplishments. It has the potential of transforming modern philosophy. Hume had argued that we have no experience of causal relations and cannot discern them in the outside world. For him, our supposition that they exist is simply a matter of habitual expectations. Kant recognized that we cannot help but organize our world in terms of causal relations, but that this must be because of the way our minds are structured. It tells us nothing about the real world.

Most subsequent philosophy has accepted either Hume or Kant as a starting point. In my view, the results have been uniformly damaging. Whitehead has shown that the conclusions of Hume and Kant follow from their prior assumption that sense experience is the foundation of all human knowledge. I would like to add that the sense experience on which philosophical attention has been based has almost always been vision. A philosophy written by someone who had been blind from birth would not have supported the mistakes on which modern philosophy has been based.

In any case, Whitehead rejected the assumption of the primacy of sense experience. He followed William James, who showed that, if we are truly empirical, we will recognize that much more is going on in experience and that the "more" is actually fundamental to it. Whitehead showed that this "more" includes "causal feelings."

But, finally, I realized that Whitehead's own statements have led to a problem, one that has seriously distorted the use of Whitehead's philosophy in social thought. On the one hand, Whitehead describes the process of concrescence as involving many features of the given world. On the other hand, he associates "causality" with only one set of these features. "Causal feelings" are "simple pure physical feelings." That is, they are feelings of the pure physical feelings of individual past occasions. No other feelings are called "causal." If these past pure physical feelings are the only features of the past world that exercise "causality" in the present, then it seems that hybrid feelings, transmuted feelings, conceptual feelings, propositional feelings, and intellectual feelings have no causal role. They must be creative developments in the concrescence rather than descriptive of how the past informs the present. With this conclusion, Whitehead's followers have too often supported the dominant individualist assumptions in political and social theory.

I was shocked to learn that although Douglas Sturm had clearly intended to develop a communitarian political theory, since he did not make clear how societies affect individuals, he did not, however, succeed. Other writers make explicit reference to Whitehead's limiting causal relations to individuals and develop their theories accordingly. This places their contributions on the side of what is now the overwhelming majority, whereas Whitehead certainly intended something quite different.

Once we state matters clearly, we can see that the implications drawn from Whitehead's definition of "causal feelings" by some of his followers cannot correspond with his own intentions. Hybrid physical feelings have as their data conceptual feelings of antecedent occasions. These are a real aspect of the real past that really affects the present concrescence. They certainly participate in the constitution of an actual occasion. The fact that Whitehead does not call them "causal" should not lead us to ignore that for Whitehead an occasion is a creative synthesis of many kinds of prehensions and that every prehension has a datum in the given world. Clearly the data of all its prehensions play a role in the constitution of every occasion. The extraordinarily detailed and rich discussion of concrescence in *Process and Reality* is all about this. It cannot be that his restriction of a "causal" feeling to a simple pure physical feeling is intended to contradict everything else he has written.

The question is, then, what distinguishes these simple pure physical feelings from all the other feelings that together constitute the new occasion? I believe the answer is that these feelings are the only ones not subject to modification by the other prehensions, by the subjective aim, or the decision. Physicists are able to predict much of the behavior of physical objects with remarkable exactitude. This is true of heavenly bodies and of billiard balls. But it is true of much else besides. The laws of the conservation of energy and matter indicate that these are transmitted from the past to the present deterministically. In short, the mechanical model gives us correct information about much of what happens in the physical world.

Although Whitehead calls his thinking a "philosophy of organism," he goes on to describe the world in most exact terms as composed of "organic mechanisms."[4] He was impressed by the extensive determinism identified and elaborated by physics. The deterministic features of reality are the ones in which what he calls "causality" is operative. His proposal is that simple pure physical feelings are responsible for the mechanistic features of the world. If A causes B, then one can deduce from the occurrence of A the occurrence of B. Whitehead intends this by what he calls "causality."

We disciples have tended to underplay the mechanistic aspects of reality and of Whitehead's description of it. For him, it was important to distinguish what in the past strictly necessitates elements in the present and what does not. For Whitehead a "cause" is determinative of its effect. Only simple pure physical feelings play this role.

But what about the other feelings that Whitehead deals with at length? Whitehead does not call them "causal" because they do not operate deterministically. I wish he had dealt with this question explicitly so as to have avoided the misunderstandings that have inhibited his disciples from giving full importance to societies and even to ideas. That these do not function deterministically does not mean they make no difference. In my less rigorous use of "causal," they also play a "causal" role, specifically, in introducing an element of unpredictability into each occasion, especially living ones. Although it is important to Whitehead to insist on the detailed predictability of much of the future based on knowledge of the present and past, it is also important to him to show that the exact nature of future events in their entirety is never exhausted by the deterministic aspects.

Since Whitehead does not provide an alternative term to describe the way other elements of the past affect the present, I suggest "influence." The past flows into the present. Societies and ideas of all sorts influence actual occasions, especially the actual occasions that are final percipient ones in animals like us.

Much of what Whitehead describes in the concrescence of an occasion applies only to rare ones, some perhaps only to human experiences. These are the ones of major importance in social and political theory. In addition to being physically determined by the past in certain respects, the present occasion of human experience is profoundly affected by other features of the past that flow into it.

What I think, in one moment, flows into, or influences, the next moment. Much of this results in repetition or reenactment of much of the past without change. But sometimes the later moment is affected by a subjective aim that subtly changes it. Or one may be newly encountering ideas that interact with that of the previous moment in unpredictable ways. Or one may be in the process of critical thinking that independently connects what the occasion receives from the past with previously unrealized potentials of some kind. What comes to be in the later moment is not strictly determined by what it derives from the past. So the conceptual feeling of the preceding occasion is not the "cause" of what wins out in the new occasion, but that certainly does not mean that it is not influential in the outcome. In my language, it plays a causal role, but to avoid this imposition of the term on Whitehead, we can just say that it is an influence.

The societies into which most of the relevant past is organized unquestionably affect the new occasion. Whitehead describes the way this occurs as transmuted feelings. The prehensions of individual occasions, such as the "causal" feelings, rarely, if ever, are conscious. In memory, or in vision, or in bodily feelings, the many individual feelings are organized into feelings of societies. The way the felt occasions are actually related to one another to constitute societies profoundly influences, but does not exactly determine, how they are felt. This may be affected by the subjective aim, for example, or by propositional feelings that are not directly derived from the society. Memories of earlier experiences influence the process of transmutation. So, finally, does the new occasion's decision. Thus, the influence of the society on the occasion is not "causal" in Whitehead's sense.

Societies shape the sensory experience that plays so large a role in conscious experience. Vision gives us a world organized into societies. What these societies are is strongly influenced by the actual relationships among the members. But the language and sensitivities with which we approach them also affect the way they influence our experience. The societies do not have the deterministic consequences that Whitehead associates with "causality." But it would be sheer nonsense to interpret Whitehead as saying that what we see is not influenced by what is there in the external world, or that it has no effect on our behavior. And for Whitehead, what is there are societies of actual occasions.

Physicists can, for the most part, ignore these noncausal influences. Their success in doing this has unfortunately led to efforts in the whole range of sciences to follow suit. Biologists also tend to neglect those aspects of what they study that they cannot explain deterministically, but in fact their efforts to predict exactly what will happen with living things fail. On the other hand, statistical probabilities work better. This is explainable if, in addition to the deterministic causes, there are other influences that express themselves in tendencies, sometimes very strong, sometimes almost undetectable.

When we deal with human beings, influences play a very large role. Of course, we are bodies in which the deterministic causal laws of physics operate. But we are living bodies that respond to environmental stimuli in often unpredictable ways. Our nervous systems and brains lead to our being influenced by a vast array of circumstances.

A very important set of issues in actual human societies is whether we can change the condition and behavior of individual human beings by restructuring society. Do characteristics of society such as relative equality of income affect the individual members of the society? If one thinks that only what Whitehead calls "causal" feelings are important, then it would not. There are no "causal" feelings of the differences of income among individuals. If the bundling of the many simple physical feelings involved in transmutation does not lead to additional effects in the resulting experiences, then improving the society will be simply improving the lot of individual participants. Relational aspects, such as relative income, will not be considered relevant. But if the result of transmutation is to bring into effect many characteristics of societies that are not characteristics of any individual member, then one may expect that individual members of society are benefited by improving the society and harmed by its decay. There is no doubt that Whitehead is on this side.

It is important to recognize, however, that changing social structures will affect different members of the society differently. These changes are not deterministic. They will be influences that are expressed in tendencies, such that one cannot predict the behavior of individuals. The effects will appear in statistical studies.

The same will apply to the effect of beliefs. Whiteheadians will expect that a Mormon community will show some differences in the psychological health of children in comparison with a secular community. We will be unlikely to find a one-to-one deterministic relation between any particular difference of belief and health in the two communities, but we are likely to find tendencies that show up statistically.

Since what a Whiteheadian proposes is largely common sense, one might judge that there is little importance in clarifying Whitehead's views. However, this is to misunderstand the relation of theory and common sense. Societies often appeal to "experts" to guide them in policy development. These "experts" are specialists in particular fields of study. They are shaped in their thinking by the theories that dominate their specialties. Since these theories are often shaped by assumptions about the primacy of physical causation, the advice of experts is often informed more by reductionist theories than by real life experience.

Whiteheadian thinkers should free themselves from the confusion about causality that has led to failing to consider in their social theorizing the great importance for human beings of multiple types of influence. The acceptance of a theory that leads to expectation of many types of influence can open us to evidence and enable us to promote wise policies.

In Whiteheadian terms, the issue discussed in this chapter boils down to the question of whether transmuted feelings, that is, the feeling of many individuals as a single whole, have an effect on their subjects. Asked in this way, the answer is unquestionably YES! So, what difference does this make, in economics, for example?

I have given an example. Income distribution is an important aspect of the economy. It affects life expectancy. That this is the case is clearly understood when we understand the role of transmuted feelings, since they allow us to feel characteristics of societies that do not exist in their individual members.

There are many other features of society that affect their members. A family or a larger society in which individuals are respected and cared for by others has a profoundly different effect on its members from one in which each is expected to compete with all the others for personal advantage. We call the former a community. For the sake of those who participate in them, Whiteheadians believe that economic practice should encourage caring communities. Even if purely competitive relations ended up producing more goods and services, there is no question for a Whiteheadian that individual members will be healthier and happier if they live in healthy communities. Sadly, the dominant economic theories do not consider mutual relationships other than exchange. They focus on what individuals want for themselves. The application to third world "development" of the dominant theories has led, all over the world, to the destruction of relatively healthy village communities and the creation of vast, unhealthy urban slums. If this increases market activity, many economists think they have benefited the people.

Development based on an economics for community would, of course, have an opposite effect. Economists committed to this would have little interest in increasing market activity, although they would want all to have what they need and much that they want beside. Such economists would celebrate an increase of mutual concern and responsibility and the fuller inclusion of all within the communities. They would also celebrate improvements in the soil and in plant and animal life, and an increase of the sense of community with the environment. In general, they would encourage the development of ecovillages, given considerable freedom by the wider society, and enjoying extensive participation by its members in deciding how to strengthen the community and make it more prosperous. They would work toward producing what is needed as near to consumers as possible so as to avoid excessive dependence on those who do not share concern for the community's well-being.

Clearly an economics oriented to serving communities would not be separate from political and social factors. Whereas economics as now practiced demands the service of political, educational, cultural, and social institutions, economics for community would serve all of these. All together they would seek to embody "ecological civilization."

Endnotes

1. H. E. Daly and J. B. Cobb Jr., *For The Common Good: Redirecting the Economy toward Community, the Environment, and a Sustainable Future*, 2nd edn. (Boston: Beacon Press, 1994).

2. J. B. Cobb, Jr. and W. A. Schwartz, eds., *Putting Philosophy to Work:*

Toward an Ecological Civilization (Anoka, MN: Process Century Press, 2018).

3. See C. Cobb, "Overcoming the Impasse in Political and Social Theory," in Cobb and Schwartz, *Putting Philosophy to Work*, Ch. 10.

4. See A. N. Whitehead, *Science and the Modern World* (New York: The Free Press, 1967), 80 and 107.

PART TWO
Organic Society

SIX

Growth, Commodification, and Property Rights

Maria Teresa Teixeira

For many years, growth has been one of the main tenets of Western social and economic order. Growth-based development has also been preached and implemented in the so-called Global South. In the West, growth is evolving into sustainable growth in an attempt to reconcile the need to protect ecological systems with the need to boost the economy. Consumerism emerges both as the natural outcome and the fuelling element of growth.

The need for growth led to the attribution of economic value to things that were not previously considered in economic terms. Commodification devastated world societies and ancient cultures, monetizing and undermining valuable, traditional livelihoods. It permitted communal rights over the use of land by the people to be transformed and regarded as yet another object of trade.

For more than two centuries, property rights have been based on individualism. The old Christian communitarian worldviews were replaced by the capitalist/collectivistic ideologies, both propounding a fragmented view of society and its economic organization.

In this chapter, we will take a Whiteheadian perspective that can overcome both growth economies and commodification; we will search for new models for property rights, based on a holistic, interrelational, integral standpoint.

In times of economic, financial, political, cultural, and moral crises, the belief in growth presents itself as the only remedy to overcome the unsustainable, perilous situation in which societies find themselves. Politicians and economists alike envisage growth as the only way out for the civilization crisis.

The endless growth delusion is based on the belief that production is an endless process, and that resources are unlimited. It bases itself on the belief we can simply ignore the cycles of nature and the temporal rhythms of living creatures. Endless growth is the obvious and necessary model for the preservation of the global economic system, and for the imposition of the predatory paradigm that consists in the belief that natural resources are inexhaustible and can be endlessly appropriated.

Commodification, i.e., the possibility of trading anything for a profit, undermines life as well as inorganic existence; it is an inevitable consequence of the growth myth. The outcome of growth is a fragmented society that attributes value to things not previously considered in economic terms. Commodification thus leads to the destruction of our societies, erasing values and valuable livelihoods.

Commodification is not only centered on the transaction of goods and services for a profit. It also envisages the conversion of independent workers, like farmers or artisans, into wageworkers who sell their labor in exchange for money with which to buy commodified goods. They stop producing their own food, making their own clothes and shoes, or building their own houses, in order to earn a wage that can be exchanged for fungible goods.

The belief that endless growth is possible under different variations of the same theme, whether it is the economy, financial speculation, or new technologies, is currently accepted without further questioning. Everyone seems to overlook the obvious fact that growth created poverty in prosperous, so-called third world societies, social and generational inequality in Western societies, and, above all, ecological devastation all over the world. Commodification thus relates directly to the consequences of growth on the environment.

As the need to resolve isolated environmental issues, like climate change, becomes too obvious, growth has changed its status and become sustainable growth. But rampant consumerism keeps doing well, as societies replace carbon energy by greener alternatives. These transitional efforts to more acceptable forms of producing energy keep growth as the main tenet of social and economic order. They preserve the usual, neoliberal or Keynesian mentalities, both requiring growth for the success of their teachings.

The endless growth fantasy is founded on the assumption that the output of goods and services can always be increased so that natural and temporal cycles can be simply disregarded. Infinite growth is needed to keep up huge scale business and maintain the global economic system. But large-scale business erodes time; it does not respect the rhythmic nature of beings, and it shows no consideration for the temporal needs of living creatures. As more and more resources are needed to produce more and more goods and services, an increasing desire for growth also becomes patent. Increasing the scale of business and the speed of the economy are thus mandatory for the swelling of global growth.

Limitless economic power and limitless growth challenge the ontological constitution of being, institutionalizing new ways of enduring and endurance. Growth proponents disregard the rhythms of enduring of different beings. But the rhythm of duration enables the coming into existence of different creatures. According to Bergson, these different durations are differences in interior tensions. Inner rhythms thus signal that all inner constitutions have their particular importance emerging from different durations, i.e., from different temporalities and modes of enduring.[1] Beings carry with them their own duration: they coincide with it. Duration is thus the grand element in the constitution of beings. In this sense, beings have worth.

Economic growth, in reducing qualitative time to spatial time and artificially shortening time lapses for economic purposes only, reduces life to anemic matter and instrumentalizes sentient and organic beings alike. Also, as economic growth necessarily extracts economic benefits from the future, destroying natural resources relentlessly, future temporality is grossly anticipated and revoked. Deferring the consequences of growth to the future leads inevitably to the denial of future life.

The growth theorists push dualisms to their limits, confusing quality with quantity, freedom with necessity, and creativity with brutish reinstatement. They decompose and recompose reality, breaking it into separate parts and adding up the different bits back again, all to get a more convenient unit—as if real beings were interchangeable and fungible. In this way, they destroy the integrity of communities, as well as the integrity of their environment. Duration, which is the qualitative element in reality, is left out. And time is taken as sheer quantity and as a vacuous condition.

But the flux of time is creative. It expresses a certain order of development of events that reflects the very nature of things. As time advances, novel creatures emerge and creation is realized. "The whole antecedent world conspires to produce a new occasion."[2] Time is a living reality, and its advance is indomitable. The "creative advance" cannot be stopped or suspended; neither can it be reversed. Time has its own rationale; in effect, the laws of logic or mechanics do not seem to rule time.

Time has its own ways. These ways have been known since the dawning of humanity. When we consider time from our own experience, we know waiting is very important. Bergson's famous example of the sugared water that needs time for the sugar to be dissolved in the water illustrates how very important the wait is. In the same way, natural processes of maturing, growing, and development all need time as the essential factor for their success. But growth theorists ignore this need for natural wait and maturing and apply what Bergson called spacialized time to any production process. There is no time anymore to wait for vegetables to grow or fruit to get ripe. Seasons and ripening cycles are simply ignored.

Growth thus challenges natural processes and temporality itself. Time can be shortened, stopped, or inverted, depending on our conveniences. Frequently, the natural rhythm of existence is shortened. Economic cycles are ever more abbreviated. We have to produce more in less time, so that economic activity remains profitable. There is no question of respecting the natural cycles, let alone supplying the market with products grown in accordance with those cycles.

Commodification is a very important tool for growth. It is a devious way of transforming what is valuable and used in accordance with its purpose into something whose value is determined simply as an object of trade. Only commodified goods or commodified labor are of any relevance to growth. If you are a teacher or a carer in an elder care home, you are a contributor to growth, but if you are homeschooling your child or taking care of your old mother, you are not in the labor market and as such contribute nothing to the growth of your economy. If you grow your own fruit and vegetables and serve them to your family, you are not generating any growth, you are not producing any taxable goods, and your fruit and vegetables can actually be said to be worthless. Intrinsic value and societal value are thus dissociated from growth and relegated to an unproductive role.

Commodification can thus lead to ascribing value to worthless things, to increasing the value of ordinary things, to turning them into sheer speculative tools, or to making intrinsically valuable things worthless.

Whitehead's notion of actual entities can help us with the question of value. The process of constitution of actual entities enhances value. They are valuable creatures just because they come into existence. Actual entities thus have intrinsic value from an ontological point of view. Moreover, they all have the same ontological dignity. "God is an actual entity, and so is the most trivial puff of existence in far-off empty space."[3] Valueless existence is impossible. The stubborn fact of existence is the attainment of an end. Every actual entity goes through a process of self-constitution that is in accordance with its subjective aim. "This is the doctrine that each actuality is an occasion of experience, the outcome of its purposes."[4] The self-determination of an actual entity is a self-defining process. Any self-determining entity, i.e., any actual entity, is a novel entity. Its way of coming into being brings novelty and, consequently, it introduces value. "The novelty is introduced conceptually and disturbs the inherited 'responsive' adjustment of subjective forms. It alters the 'values' in the artist's sense of the term."[5] Constitution thus implies self-causation and purpose, which ultimately generates value. Worth is thus the basis of our very existence. Our first experience has some sort of value. It is not a clear, definite perception, but its haziness allows for some kind of individualization and thus for some kind of ontological worth. Whitehead writes: "Here the notion of worth is not to be construed in a purely eulogistic sense. It is the sense of existence for its own sake, of existence which is its own justification, of existence with its own character."[6] Value is thus at the bottom of every existence, of every being that dared come into being. Value has an ontological beginning. Primordial vagueness already carries some kind of importance, some worth. In *Science and the Modern World*, Whitehead writes: "the element of value, of being valuable, of having value, of being an end in itself, of being something that is for its own sake, must not be omitted in any account of an event as the most concrete actual something. 'Value' is the word I use for the intrinsic reality of an event."[7]

Commodification in erasing true value is a way of denying our ontological worthiness and our condition of being an end in itself.

Denying true value leads to the creation of artificial advantages and entitlements. Identity, dignity, and values all disappear under the rule of commodification. Cutting the relationship with nature leads necessarily to considering nature as a hindrance to social living. Commodified goods provide for our needs usually in an artificial, inhumane context, because most of them are standardized goods, which we wouldn't require if we were given the chance to have a free choice. Growth, on the other hand, requires the creation of ever more needs and goods; most of them are mere decontextualized products. Usually, our most basic human needs are met through these inadequate goods transforming, sometimes dramatically, our livelihoods.

The commodification of land and other real estate, like urban buildings, has led to a radical change in human livelihoods and lifestyles. Commodification is the direct result of individualistic law systems proposing to take private property as an absolute right. This is a fairly recent ideology going back to nineteenth century liberalism ideas. It is also an important foundation of capitalist societies.

Marxist theories also took property as an absolute, as they failed to present alternatives to the commodification of property in establishing the collectivistic paradigm. They simply transferred property held in the private sphere to the public sphere, keeping and enhancing all the commodified features that property, in general, had gained after the Industrial Revolution. Moreover, property was always considered to have its origin in the state. These doctrines ended up absorbing capitalism and consumerism into their socialistic structure, thus creating state capitalism.

The Christian tradition, on the other hand, never upheld property rights as absolute. And it never envisaged property as a commodity. Property rights are subordinated to the right of common use; the goods of creation are meant for everyone. This line of thought is confirmed in Pope Francis's encyclical on *Care for Our Common Home*: "The principle of the subordination of private property to the universal destination of goods, and thus the right of everyone to their use, is a golden rule of social conduct and the first principle of the whole ethical and social order."[8] The Christian tradition has never recognized the right to private property as absolute or inviolable, and has stressed the social purpose of all forms of private property."[9] Possession comes with stewardship; we are not the owners of nature, not even of our intellectual talents. We are but the stewards of

God's creation.[10] We are also cooperators in God's creation.[11] Creativity emerges as the source of all existence.

If we consider process philosophy, we may find a similar foundation, one we can use for a property rights theory. As Whitehead emphasized, creativity introduces novelty into the world.[12] He also underlined that the world is made up of relationships, and that actual entities emerge from those relationships. There is no absolute dominance of the subject over its object, because "the subject emerges from the world."[13]

Bergson, at the end of *Two Sources,* pictured human beings as *adjutores Dei,* as collaborators of God, as the makers of creativity. Again, creativity is the origination of all existence and subjects emerge from their commerce with the world. There is no strict separation between subject and object. We are part of the world and also its custodians. We cannot thus base property rights, or any rights, on the dominance of the subject over its object, because that kind of disconnection is not acceptable in process philosophy. We would be violating what we might call the ontological sacredness of all beings. Our condition as stewards of God's creation does not give us any right to an absolute appropriation of any part of God's creation; least of all, it does not give us the right to reduce the value of what is intrinsically valuable, or to induce artificial value in some worthless object.

In this light, the appropriation and commodification of land, or of any kind of property, would be illegitimate. It is no wonder indigenous peoples resist the Western property laws imposed on them: These laws mean the appropriation and commodification of their land. Ancient cultures do not consider land to be a tradable commodity on the marketplace, which can be converted into cash, regardless of its function or origination. Land is heritage; it is the means through which life is received. We are part of it, as much as it is part of us, because it is part of our temporality.

Once land is turned into a commodity and sold as a bundle of property rights, it no longer serves its purpose and is robbed of its ontological dignity. The new owners, which have bought it as a commodity, will in all probability use it as usurpers do, with no respect for its intrinsic value, temporal cycles, natural destination, or purpose. After the enclosure of land, environmental devastation follows. Land is also bounded in a juridical sense, for it can be disposed of at will; for instance, property developers will turn a beautiful city garden into a high-rise condo, or fields along fertile flood plains will become monoculture eucalyptus plantations.

In many indigenous cultures, land is communally owned. Families and individuals have the right to use certain plots of land, but they cannot dispose of these plots by selling them or abusing them in any way, thus ensuring that the land is there for use by future generations, as well. Custodial responsibility is the basis of communal property. Land is a common heritage, integrated into the right to life of future generations. Legitimacy in land use emerges from communal ownership and communal stewardship; individuals use the land and collect its fruits, which are also the result of their labor.

The use of land is also regarded as very important in Western cultures. For instance, in continental legal systems, land use is a means to legitimate appropriation of property. In usucapion, ownership is gained through possession, which requires continuous use of property for a certain length of time. The rightful and appropriate use of property leads to its legal acquisition. Use, primarily regulated by custom and tradition, leads to a legitimate right of ownership. Property rights emerge from the rightful exercise of possession and use of land, or any other kind of property. In other words, the flow of time as constitutive of property rights establishes the foundations of property acquisition. This is a very processual idea that can be developed further.

But acquisition of property rarely results from legitimate and genuine possession and use. Property is usually bought on the market; frequently, it is viewed as, and bought as, a commodity. It may serve its inherent purpose, like a house that is bought to serve as a dwelling. However, property may be used for sheer speculation. For example, one can buy a house in order to sell it later for a profit, without ever using it as a home; or it may be used as a financial vehicle to obtain credit through mortgages.

In continental law systems, subordinate real rights, such as the usufruct, also recognise use as the main advantage to be gained from property. The right to usufruct gives someone the right to enjoy someone else's property, provided its form and substance are never impaired or altered. The holder of the usufruct has the right to the use (*usus*) and to derive profit (*fructus*) from the thing possessed. This can be consistent with the natural purpose and destination of land. Such property rights can in some way limit commodification. Ultimately, usufruct has some remote similarity with indigenous rights over land. Land is considered as something entrusted to those who use it and reap its fruits. They respect and take care of their land. They are its stewards. They have no absolute right over land and cannot dispose of it as they please; they respect its natural purpose and destination.

Property rights raise other problems mainly connected with cultural and scientific knowledge, such as the appropriation of knowledge through patents and intellectual property. This kind of appropriation includes industrial and commercial activities, as well as any creations of the mind such as literary and artistic works. There is one important difference between intellectual property and ordinary property rights: the latter grant the holders of ownership the power to object to someone else's use, possession, and disposal of their property, whereas industrial and intellectual property grant the right to control the use of the registered patent or knowledge in any circumstance whatsoever. In other words, industrial and intellectual properties have a much wider range than physical property. They affect every usage of the patent or knowledge for as long as the patent or copyright is valid. It is not a question of controlling a certain object; it is the possibility of appropriating the knowledge of humanity, as well as God's creation.

Farmers who are compelled to buy seeds every year and held back from saving their own seeds do not have a right over the seeds they have produced, because the right they have over seeds is not considered physical property—these people don't even own the seeds that come from their own farming. If they use them without paying any royalties to whoever is entitled to receive them, they will be held accountable by the patent proprietors. Patent rights include and many times end up as a sovereign right to sue.

Seed patents thus lead to the appropriation of life and also to the appropriation of the sacred. Patenting seeds challenges the moral and ontological aspects of property rights. It commodifies life, transforming it into a sheer tradable good; moreover, patents are generally held as absolute rights. Commodification of life also destroys the cultural heritage of humanity.

Process philosophy, in rejecting subject/object dualism, avoids the correlative idea of a subject that dominates its object. Accordingly, property rights cannot be seen as a form of dominion. In process philosophy, subjects and objects are not opposites; they fuse together and emerge from one another. Whitehead's idea of a superject that results from the world leads to another idea, that of an object which is "a potentiality for being."[14] Interconnectedness rejects the fragmentation of the world and emphasises the temporal rhythms of every being that comes into existence.

Commodification leads to fragmentation and also to huge accumulation of parts resulting from the partition of a whole. Land that is entrusted to common use can be divided into different parts. And those different new properties can be reassembled into a bigger property to maximize economic efficacy. However, as Whitehead says in *Process and Reality*: "If you abolish the whole, you abolish its parts; and if you abolish any part, than *that* whole is abolished."[15] The integrity of land is lost and also the integrity of those who care for it. Fragmentation leads to a huge loss. It is not only the wholeness that is lost; the parts are also lost. Reassemblage creates a different reality and completely destroys the original existents. It erases temporality and ignores the rhythms of nature and beings.

To sum up: Growth is temporally demanding; it goes against the rhythmic nature of beings, disregarding the temporal requisites of every entity that comes into existence. Erasing temporal rhythms leads to the denial of life and nullification. Human societies only prosper amongst diversity in accordance with their temporal nature.

Moreover, self-determining entities, i.e., any actual entities, are novel entities. Their diverse ways of coming into being have different rhythms bringing in novelty; they consequently introduce value into the world. Ontological worthiness is the outcome of sheer existence. Value emerges only from the different temporal natures of beings. Temporality thus is the true foundation of human societies and prosperous economic living.

As our economies head for growth, they increase the scale and speediness of the economic system. Rampant production and consumption are seen as producing the acceleration of the economy we need. Although some governments try to promote sustainable growth and mitigate climate change hazards, they also heavily subsidise industry and push for the expansion of global trade, thus welcoming all the nasty outcomes that come with growth.

It will be a hugely difficult effort to try and stop the relentless forces that preach and propagate unlimited growth, consumerism, and commodification of all aspects of life.

Reversing growth, or degrowth, can lead to prosperity. But this can only be achieved if we take temporality as the foundational aspect of existence, as the ontological pillar of values. We might then achieve what could be called an austere or frugal prosperity, focusing on an economic system in which consumption makes a parsimonious use of resources, natural cycles are respected, and the intrinsic value of things is enhanced. The process of coming into being carries value within itself. It is "the emergence of a world at once lucid, and intrinsically of immediate worth."[16]

If we apply these principles to property rights we might also get a novel system in which the respect for land and common heritage might prevail.

Endnotes

1. H. Bergson, *Matter and Memory* (Paris: Quadrige/PUF, 1998), 330–31.
2. A. N. Whitehead, *Modes of Thought* (New York: The Free Press, [1938] 1968), 154.
3. A. N. Whitehead, *Process and Reality: An Essay in Cosmology*, Corrected Edition, ed. D. R Griffin and D. W. Sherburne (New York: The Free Press, [1929] 1978), 18.
4. A. N. Whitehead, *The Function of Reason* (Boston: Beacon Press, [1929] 1958), 31.
5. Whitehead, *Process and Reality*, 104.
6. Whitehead, *Modes of Thought*, 109.
7. A. N. Whitehead, *Science and the Modern World* (New York: The Free Press, [1925] 1967), 93.
8. Francis, *Laudato Sí,* 93
9. Francis, *Laudato Sí,* 120.
10. Francis, *Laudato Sí,* 236.
11. Francis, *Laudato Sí,* 80, 117.
12. Whitehead, *Process and Reality*, 21.
13. Whitehead, *Process and Reality*, 88.
14. Whitehead, *Process and Reality*, 88.
15. Whitehead, *Process and Reality*, 288.
16. Whitehead, *Process and Reality*, 341.

SEVEN

Nature-Based Solutions and the Complex Relations between Society and Nature

Morika Reker

THE TERM "NATURE-BASED SOLUTIONS" (NBS) is a fairly new idea, following concepts such as "resilience," "sustainable development," or "ecosystem services." After being used by the International Union of Nature Conservation (IUCN) in a position paper for the United Nations Framework Convention on Climate Change (IUCN, 2009), the term made its way into reframing policy debates on biodiversity conservation, climate change adaptation and mitigation strategies, and the sustainable use of natural resources. It aims specifically to link "nature" with positive outcomes for society: "solutions." The concept also made its way into literature on industrial design, as a follow up of biomimicry.[1]

For the European Commission, NBS is understood as actions that intend to help communities address all sorts of environmental, economic, and social challenges in sustainable ways. They are "actions which are inspired by, supported by or copied from nature."[2]

The EU identifies four main goals that can be addressed through NBS:

1. Enhancing sustainable urbanization;[3]
2. Restoring degraded ecosystems;[4]
3. Developing climate change adaptation and mitigation;[5]
4. Improving risk management and resilience.[6]

While Ecosystem Services (ES) are often valued in terms of immediate benefits to human well-being and economy, NBS focuses on the benefits to people and the environment itself, to allow for sustainable solutions that are able to respond to environmental change and hazards in the long-term. But to what extent is NBS concerned with the conservation and well-being of biodiversity and ecosystems?

Experts define Nature-based Solutions as instruments that aid in research, management, and policy to highlight the contributions of nature and ecosystems for the quality of life of urban residents and their resilience to climate change. These can be, for instance, ensuring an appropriate functioning of urban green and blue infrastructure, such as parks, green walls and roofs, allotments, or different types of water bodies. This all seems, at first, rather interesting and even exciting: a novel way to finding solutions for our cities' problems, with the difference being that this time, one looks at nature for inspiration to design ways out of the problems we create. Or, as Janine Benyus framed it (when explaining her concept of Biomimicry), "an era based not on what we can *extract* from nature, but on what we can *learn* from her."[7]

But what is meant here by "nature"? What is the concept of nature to which NBS refers? In "The Science, Policy and Practice of Nature-based Solutions: An Interdisciplinary Perspective,"[8] a paper reflecting on the implications of NBS for science, policy, and practice, the authors define NBS as a "concept that aims to explicitly link positive outcomes for society ("solutions") with a notion of "nature" as something helpful for these aims."[9] Nature, which helps us find solutions, is in itself specifically what? Further in the paper, "natural capital" is defined as "the stock of living and nonliving parts of the natural system that directly and indirectly yield benefits to humans,"[10] so we may guess that "nature" refers to the range of living and nonliving parts of the natural system (thus, biotic and abiotic elements of ecosystems).

From my experience working within a practical approach to urban intervention through arts and architectural projects, the idea of a "nature-based solution" sounds spot-on: finally we are looking back to nature, mimicking its ways and processes instead of finding harsh engineering solutions that create even worse headaches—like the recent reports concluding that wind turbines might create greater environmental (and ultimately also energetic) problems than those they were developed to solve. The blades are nonrecyclable, and their end-of-life disposal amounts to tons of polluting garbage,[11] not to mention the number of birds and bats that, year in year out, crash into the turbine blades and die. The same holds true for solar panels and other forms of alternative energies. NBS is presented as the common ground or platform where experts from different fields can come together to work on solutions to common problems, which is something we urgently need. However, it might be useful—not to say crucial—to reflect on the underlying concepts (especially when experts from different fields are dialoguing with one another and use the same words to talk about different things) before we engage once more in blind belief in technological miracle solutions to our resource-exhausting way of life.

What is the problem, after all, of having nature as base? Isn't it a good turn? Well, the issue at stake is that the concept of nature that is taken as base for NBS determines the kind of interventions that are allowed, and before that, the kind/range of processes that are "copied" or serve as a model. But NBS still hasn't put forth a clear definition of what is meant by nature.

One must wonder: should NBS have as an underlying philosophy, say, a platonic concept of nature, or would the outcomes differ from a Cartesian view?

Robert Lenoble, in his history of the idea of nature,[12] shows that despite the widespread use of the term nature—an apparently simple word—for so many different topics, once we try to define it problems arise, as it is by no means an easy task to describe exactly what nature is, or what one means by nature or the natural. The concept of nature in antiquity was bound to the idea of birth, potency, and generation, that is, to the creative principle behind life.[13] Thus, although in classic antiquity nature was a unity—the cohesion of all things and species—the certainty of the unity of the world, or what came to be called *Cosmos*, has changed many times. We can see this in the *Oxford Dictionary of Philosophy*, where the definition put forth is, although earnest, rather vague and ultimately unhelpful: nature is "an indefinitely mutable term, changing as our scientific conception of the world changes." Today, if asked to say the first thing that comes to mind as a definition of nature, some would no doubt associate it with *green*, i.e., the vegetable kingdom. Maybe some wild animals would wander around somewhere in the background of that somewhat intuitive definition, but most likely the animal kingdom would be altogether forgotten. (When one is asked about landscape that is what typically occurs.)

However, given time to reflect on the subject, most would not object if we were to say that the *common* idea of nature is the set of all beings composing the universe (with the universe being defined as the cluster of the earth, the planets and the cosmic system); nature as the totality of things—all that would have to be listed if we were to make an inventory of the universe, or the set of things that constitutes an order; that complete types or are produced according to laws. But would it include Aristotle's unmoved mover, nature as the cause of movement and rest intrinsic to each being? Or, would it include the idea of nature as a system of mechanistic causes ruled by laws that can be defined in mathematical equations?

If our chosen definition of nature were to follow Whitehead's *Concept of Nature*, as that which we observe in perception through the senses,[14] it would probably not include bacteria and microscopic fungi (unless we count observation aided by microscopes as sense-perception). On the other hand, we perceive by our senses not only quite a few inorganic substances, like stones or water and metals, but also synthetic materials created by humans. Can those count as "nature"? On the other hand, could NBS, by "nature," mean biotic nature: all the living organisms present in an ecosystem, such as bacteria, fungi, plants and animals, and elements produced by them— thus all living components that interact with another organism and affect it in some way? Could it also consider abiotic components of ecosystems (such as water, soil, and temperature) including ecosystems that have been manipulated by humankind, possibly for centuries, or landscapes? If we were to take Whitehead's view that nature consists of moving patterns whose movement is essential to their being,[15] abiotic components would certainly count as nature.

Once more, what is natural? What is nature? Is it that which human beings cannot create, which has inner life and reproduces itself?

Again, what we consider nature to be may impact the degree of interventions that we allow. And, for instance, if our goal is to mitigate climate change, and our focus is on maintaining or improving life conditions for human societies, then we might be tempted to mimic natural process in ways that don't nurture nature. Also problematic, should the intervention at hand be a "cosmetic" form of biodiversity conservation, it could possibly generate even more pressure on natural systems.

As NBS strategies are strongly encouraged by the European Commission, and as NBS is viewed as a means to reaching Europe's sustainability goals,

NBS is a topic that has come to attract broad interest, and research on its uses has multiplied. The report from the BiodivERsA workshop[16] identifies three types of NBS:

1. Better use of existing (natural or weakly managed) ecosystems, delivering a range of ecosystem services while minimizing the intervention on the systems themselves (e.g., marine protective areas, networks, and fisheries).
2. Definition of management rules to develop sustainable and multifunctional ecosystems modifying existing (possible intensively managed) ones, to better deliver selected ecosystem services (e.g., innovative planning of agricultural landscapes).
3. Managing ecosystems in very intrusive ways, or creating completely new ecosystems (e.g., through ecological engineering, green roofs, etc.).

But could "creating new ecosystems" also mean creating new organisms? How broad or tight are the limits to engineering that NBS allows? The above-mentioned EU report guarantees that artificial nature (an oxymoron in itself, as many would put it) will not be part of the (EU-supported) NBS: "There has been much debate over the components of nature-based solutions and, within the current EU framework, nature-based solutions exclude methods that artificially alter nature, such as genetically modified organisms."[17] I would stress the framing above: "current EU framework," which leaves an open door for future changes.

The paper mentioned above on science, policy, and practice of nature-based solutions touches on the question of the lack of a specific concept of nature underlying NBS. However, the paper does not consider the existence of multiple ways of defining the concept, a problem if each case makes its particular interpretation of nature (and of NBS) explicit: "engaging in pluralistic reflection about alternative framings and conceptualizations can in itself be useful for identifying what is meant by NBS and the expectations for 'solutions' in any particular context."[18] However, for NBS to be both integrated in policy making and implemented in practice, there needs to be a common ground of understanding. It is both impractical and unwise to be constantly adapting the concept to different situations.

Nevertheless, it should be clear that there are great examples of solutions—permaculture is one—that draw their inspiration from nature and are based on a philosophy of care: care for the soil, care for the Earth, care for oneself. There are ways of cultivating fruits, vegetables, and grains that mimic forests and replicate processes that happen naturally, building soil instead of draining its nutrients, planting mixed crops that are mutually beneficial instead of monocultures, and so forth. (Notwithstanding, permaculture is intensely designed.) Masanobu Fukuoka's natural agriculture uses a different approach but is similar in outcome. Stated somewhat simplistically, this is more of a non-agriculture approach, one that seeks the least possible intervention in order to allow nature to work by itself, taking the human intellect out of the decision-making process. It seems plausible to call both permaculture and natural agriculture forms of NBS. Also, for example, the knowledge gained by studying how certain plants "naturally" improve the living conditions for fish by filtering the water can be applied in wastewater treatment plants. This can be considered a NBS.

Another example is green roofs, which are often recommended for reestablishing natural habitats for birds, bees, butterflies, etc., making cities biodiversity-friendly. However, Hilde Eggermont, et al, [19] warn against creating green roofs using only a few plant species, "regardless of their biogeographical distribution," which could end up not providing the proper habitat for birds or butterflies, who then cannot thrive. Also, as they add up to the total percentage of green areas in a city, they may (inadvertently?) lead to a smaller investment in the plantation of new—on the ground—gardens and forested areas or even stimulate the reduction in size of existing gardens. In other words, is it enough to have nature as "inspiration" (which would mean possibly taking only part of a process into account and ignoring fundamental parts)? Or does one need to obtain "full" understanding of the matter at hand prior to replicating it?

At the core of this argument is the suspicion that despite its *good intentions*, NBS focuses too much on the benefit that humans get from nature (the "services"; the outcomes), and this language influences the way we look at nature. This is a way that is still very anthropocentric: it's good to have nature around us because we can benefit from it; let's look at nature's way, nature's "methods," so that we can profit from them!

That much is patent in a recent pamphlet from the European Centre for Nature Conservation (*Nature Works for Regions!*),[20] where several projects are depicted to illustrate how biodiversity and ecosystem services inspire or work in local and regional situations. Consider these chapter headings: "Nature works for agriculture"; "Nature works for water management and quality"; Nature works for climate and energy"; Nature works to combat pollution"; Nature works for human well-being." There are many examples of "services" that nature provides *us*. For instance, in a project that is presented as an example of how nature works for agriculture ("Valuation of pollination spurs support for beekeepers"), one can read:

> Between 1997 and 2006, by providing pollination, Swiss bee colonies ensured an average yearly agricultural production worth about CHF 256 million. Remarkably, this 'hobby' generates an economic value five times that generated by the production of honey. The production of a single colony has an estimated worth of CHF 1,260 for pollinated fruits and berries.[21]

Thus, simply put, we'll save the bees not because they have intrinsic value, but because we need them to pollinate our vegetables and fruits, and because we make money from it. We'll invest in cleaning rivers not because rivers should be kept clean and are the habitat for a number of species, but because we need clean water in our cities, we need "green and blue infrastructure" because we've learned that in the long run those become cheaper than traditional grey infrastructure.

Yet, the final part of the brochure is devoted to examples of projects where "humans work for nature," and the introduction to that chapter alerts us: "with all the attention for ecosystem services and how they can benefit people, one could almost forget that nature has a value in its own right, and that people have a moral duty to take good care of nature because of its 'intrinsic' value."[22] Although initiatives inspired by nature are "too numerous to name," only five case studies are presented. Of these, only those initiatives implemented, managed, or coordinated by NGOs or communities can be said to fully address "nature for its own sake." These projects are in contrast to ones developed by companies that may promote biodiversity or ecosystem services, but have competititveness as their main goal, or improving the company's brand and income.

Ultimately, does this mean that we only value nature if we can directly benefit from it? What about *integral ecology* or an *integral approach to nature*? Does it have a place in current policy making?

One can say that NBS is a start, a good way to have people re-learn living near nature. But if the focus is kept on the benefits, uses, and services, of nature, then it might very well be that the message we so urgently need people everywhere to grasp—that of degrowth—will not be clear enough.

It could also be argued that our societies—all mainly capitalist, to some degree—are built upon economic concepts, so maybe, by using terms like "natural capital" and by attaching a price tag to "ecosystem services," people will finally understand that nature is not the infinite bounty our forebearers believed it to be, and that we so desperately still want to believe. Also, some see the stress on "solutions" as a form of clarification, an explicit focus on the actions and inputs needed to change our way of life.

The EU *Final Report of the Horizon2020 Expert Group on Nature-Based Solutions and Re-Naturing Cities* states that:

> There is a growing interest and awareness within the business community of the value of managing and maintaining biodiversity and ecosystem services, *as a business opportunity and as an essential means to reduce economic risks* by ensuring the continued supply of vital resources. The burgeoning number of international, national, regional and local policy initiatives for the conservation and sustainable use of the natural environment are evidence of the realisation by policy makers of the importance of nature to society. Civil society also is increasingly recognising the benefits derived from nature for enhancing well-being, as seen in the numerous bottom-up initiatives, particularly in community efforts to bring nature back into urban areas. Finally, the science and research community is currently focusing on 'people and nature', generating knowledge for resilient and adaptable socio-ecological systems.[23]

Again, is NBS just another umbrella term that provides a false relief for those working within engineering/landscape architecture/urban planning, etc.? Is this simply the newest trend that will soon be dismissed and replaced by another, or are NBS proponents really committed to finding actual solutions, not for a political mandate or two, but for our complex relation with nature?

Endnotes

1. Examples include the hydrophobic and friction-reducing properties of artificial surfaces designed to mimic the topographies of water-repellent leaves as a solution to problems of wear in mechanical systems, linking "nature-based solutions" to industrial design challenges. See J. Benyus, *Biomimicry: Innovation Inspired by Nature* (New York: Harper Collins, [1997], 2002).
2. *Towards an EU Research and Innovation Policy Agenda for Nature-Based Solutions & Re-Naturing Cities. Final Report of the Horizon2020 Expert Group on Nature-Based Solutions and Re-Naturing Cities* (Brussels: European Commission, 2015), 5.
3. *Towards an EU Research and Innovation Policy Agenda*, 6, 27.
4. *Towards an EU Research and Innovation Policy Agenda*, 6,31.
5. *Towards an EU Research and Innovation Policy Agenda*, 6, 33.
6. *Towards an EU Research and Innovation Policy Agenda*, 6, 35.
7. Benyus, *Biomimicry*, 3.
8. C. Nesshöver, et al., "The Science, Policy and Practice of Nature-Based Solutions: An Interdisciplinary Perspective," *Science of the Total Environment* 579 (2017): 1215–27.
9. Nesshöver, et al., "The Science, Policy and Practice of Nature-Based Solutions," 1216.
10. Nesshöver, et al., "The Science, Policy and Practice of Nature-Based Solutions," 1218, table 2.
11. A typical wind turbine has a foundation (made of concrete), a tower (made from steel or concrete), a nacelle (steel and copper), and the blades (from composite materials). Concrete and composites are the most environmentally problematic at end-of-life, since there are currently no established industrial recycling routes for them. Several studies explore the adverse environmental consequences of the disposal practices of turbine blades: either at landfills (takes hundreds of years to degrade; potential release of methane and other volatile organic compounds), incineration (can produce toxic gases, smoke, and soot, harming environment and humans), or mechanical processing (energy intensive and creates health and safety risks). See Ramirez-Tejeda, Turcotte and Pike, "Unsustainable Wind Turbine Blade Disposal Practices in the United States. A Case for Policy Intervention and

Technological Innovation," *New Solutions: A Journal of Environmental and Occupational Health Policy* 26 (Feb. 2017): 581–98. Also, wind turbines are the leading cause of death for bats and birds, and studies show that the hoary bat population could decline by as much as 90% in the next 50 years. See W. F. Frick, et al, "Fatalities at Wind Turbines May Threaten Population Viability of a Migratory Bat," *Biological Conservation* 209 (May 2017): 172–77.

12. R. Lenoble, *Esquisse d'une Histoire de l'Idée de Nature* (Paris: Éditions Albin Michel, 1969).

13. See K. R. Olwig, "The Archetypical City and the Concept of Nature before the Industrial Revolution," in *City and Nature: Changing Relations in Time and Space*, ed. T. Kristense, et al. (Odense: Odense, Denmark: University Press, n.d.), 97.

14. "Nature is that which we observe in perception through the senses. In this sense-perception we are aware of something which is not thought and which is self-contained for thought. This property of being self-contained for thought lies at the base of natural science. It means that nature can be thought of as a closed system whose mutual relations do not require the expression of the fact that they are thought about." A. N. Whitehead, *The Concept of Nature* (Cambridge: Cambridge University Press, [1920] 2015), 2.

15. See R. G. Collingwood, *The Idea of Nature* (Oxford: Oxford University Press, [1945] 1965), 173.

16. BiodivERsA is a network programming and funding research on biodiversity and ecosystem services across European countries and territories, comprising 32 agencies and ministries from 21 European countries. See E. Balian, Eggermont & Le Roux, "Outputs of the Strategic Foresight workshop "Nature-Based Solutions in a BiodivERsA context,'" Brussels, June 11–12, 2014. BiodivERsA report 2014.

17. *Towards an EU Research and Innovation Policy Agenda for Nature-Based Solutions & Re-Naturing Cities—Final Report of the Horizon 2020 Expert Group 'Nature-Based Solutions & Re-Naturing Cities'*. European Commission, Directorate-General for Research and Innovation, (Luxembourg: Publications Office of the European Union, 2015) 24.

18. Nesshöver, et al., "The Science, Policy and Practice of Nature-Based Solutions," 1220.

19. H. Eggermont, et al, "Nature-based Solutions: New Influence for

Environmental Management and Research in Europe," GAIA 24/4 (2015): 245.

20. A. Torre-Marín, M. Snethlage & B. Delbaere, *Nature Works for Regions!* European Centre for Nature Conservation (Tilburg, Netherlands: ENCN, 2012), 10.

21. Torre-Marín, et. al., *Nature Works for Regions!*, 21.

22. Torre-Marín, et. al., *Nature Works for Regions!*, 70.

23. *Towards an EU Research and Innovation policy agenda for Nature-Based Solutions & Re-Naturing Cities - Final Report of the Horizon 2020 Expert Group on 'Nature-Based Solutions and Re-Naturing Cities'* European Union, 2015. Emphasis added.

EIGHT

The Good and Prudent Handling of Things: The Need for Ecological Management

Mark Dibben

THE WORLD WE LIVE IN AND ON is changing rapidly, the result of a thirst for growth, a narrative of growth, and the economism that has dominated our thought particularly over the past three hundred years. Yet it is only a small minority who really care about growth. The problem is that this minority tends to rise to the top precisely because they are expansionist and aggressive and so dominate the rest of us who aren't. The minority then pretend that their own particular view of life—their desire to grow and dominate—is typical of the whole human race and, through the powers of persuasion, the rest of us who are merely trying to get on with our lives tend not to reflect seriously on what growth implies. So growth becomes the accepted mantra of the politics of the West. All mainstream political parties speak of growth as a *sine qua non*. The Western model of economics has an infantile infatuation with growing, and success has come to mean growth. Management has been the architect of that remarkable "success."

This deeply pernicious con trick has led to us living in a period in the Earth's life increasingly understood as the Anthropocene. In the Anthropocene, we have developed the power to change the biosphere in ways only previously available to the geological aspects of Nature, e.g., earthquakes and volcanoes. The difference is that, whereas the chaos they cause has positive consequences, ultimately, for biodiversity, the sort of chaos we—*Homo sapiens*—are presently causing, does not. It's almost all negative. The Anthropocene is a period of mass extinction brought about by *Homo sapiens'* own actions that have wrought fundamental change to the Earth's biosphere. The Earth is only now beginning to adjust to the changes. A pessimistic view is that the Earth is struggling to survive. An optimistic view might be that it is naturally adjusting. If we take this more optimistic view, we might say it is recalibrating. Weather patterns are already changing, and weather events are becoming more severe.

At present, a hundred and, perhaps, occasionally a thousand people are dying in each of these severe weather events. As the recalibration gathers pace and the weather events become yet more severe, however, thousands of people—if not hundreds of thousands—may die at a time; *Homo sapiens* will not escape the recalibration unscathed. As well as the complete extinction of many other species, there will be a partial extinction of *Homo sapiens,* for the Earth will shortly not be capable of supporting the population. This is not simply because of the fact that the population of *Homo sapiens* has tripled in a generation, but because its managerial actions over the course of that generation have significantly degraded the planet. For example, it is obviously not possible for the planet to support animal life into the longer term if, directly as a result of the actions of one of its species, it is losing 1% of its soils every year.[1] One hundred years is a remarkably short time.

There are only two reasons *Homo sapiens* itself will survive and not become extinct. First, we have spread so successfully across the planet that groups of us, purely by default, will be living in those parts of the Earth that remain habitable. Second, as a result of the size of our brain, we seem to have a capacity to adapt that is greater than other species.

Management as Inherent in Nature[2]

This is not to say that we are the only species that engages in management. Most, if not all, creatures engage in managing their environment by making shelter or having special places where they rest and reproduce, finding and storing food, and even creating paths that run to and from the food and shelter. Insects, spiders, birds, fish, reptiles, and mammals all practice management to some degree. Management is inherent in nature. Indeed, it seems to be almost naturally selected for. The alpha pair of a Meerkat group, the dominant male and female in a chimpanzee community, the Silverback in a gorilla troop, to name just three community-dependent social animals, all have to be able to manage their respective entourages—boss them into line occasionally, yes, but also continually work to resolve disputes and thereby keep the group collective functioning effectively as a community, for the benefit of all within the community.

Yet of all the Earth's creatures, it is *Homo sapiens* who is, perhaps most unfortunately, the ultimate management practitioner. We seem to be capable of making the most decisions. We organize, manage, and use the technologies of tools and vocalizations to an extent unseen elsewhere in the natural world. The same is true of the way we also seem to manage our personal behavior, others of our own kind, other species, and the environment so successfully (or not, as the case now seems to be). Managing, and thus management, is by the very force of nature itself the only means we have for coping in and with our lives.

The difference between us and other animals is that, having invented currency to replace food, shelter, and community as the primary value, we have ever-increasingly focused our management skills on the particular purpose of making money, particularly since the Industrial Revolution. This most unnatural commodity has become our all-pervading focus, the measure of quality of life; more so even than the quality of life inherent in the Earth.

The Effects of Scientism and Human Management in the Modern Age

All animal species gather food, most make shelters of some sort, and thus most make their own routes (some very short, others longer than our own) between food and shelter. Yet we have taken these natural acts of management to extremes, so that the making of shelters is about making money, the gathering of food is about making money, the travel is about making money. No other animal manages for the sake of consumption, for the sake of obtaining more than it needs to live. Whereas other animals mange for sufficiency, we manage for excess.

This shift has separated us from the Earth, or so we have thought, in the search for growth as a proxy for (so-called "quality" of) life. To the delight of the pharmaceutical corporations who manufacture antidepressant "happy pills"; happiness has declined while incomes have soared. As David Korten has explained,[3] corporations now rule the world and have done so, in fact, for some time. Management, as *Homo sapiens* has practiced it in recent times, in the modern era, is about using people to improve the wealth of corporations, which offer goods (so positively called!) for human consumption as an end in itself. Worse, this consumption is achieved by the accrual of personal and governmental debt, which is spiraling ever deeper across the so-called "developed" and "developing" worlds. Capitalism is committing suicide.

It follows that we can no longer think about management in the way we did in the modern age. That age, as John Cobb has said so profoundly,[4] is ending. Growth is now in sharp contradiction to sustainability, where sustainability means a genuine coexistence with the rest of nature in a way that is regenerative of nature rather than the depletive relationship that has existed hitherto. The current endpoint of humanity's purpose, the wealth of corporations and the false belief in consumption for happiness, will not matter as the Earth proceeds to recalibrate. What will matter is how we adjust our thinking and how we adjust our acting so that we can be in step with and supportive of that recalibration. We must think about management and its purpose in a new way.

Management needs recalibrating. It needs to become more natural. This requires a mode of thought, a way of understanding, that stands in stark contradistinction from the mode of thought that has dominated the Modern Age.

The Cause and Effect of the End of Neo-Naturalism

Of course, the mode of thought that has dominated the Modern Age is that of science, still underpinned by the presuppositions encouraged by the mainstream understanding of Isaac Newton and René Descartes, namely: (1) that our minds are separate from our bodies, from "matter"; and (2) that the world is made up of passive, inert objects as opposed to active, experiencing subjects. This leads to two fundamental assumptions. First, that scientific explanations are inherently comprehensive, being founded in the study of objects and, second, that the objects of scientific study are understood as being the only real things. Scientism founded a worldview that rightly places *Homo sapiens* in nature, but the reductionist view of nature as passive, material, and mechanistic, dominates the modern worldview. This is in no small part a result of its power as the taken-for-granted (and indeed by and large only acceptably credible) ontology within 'value-free' science research universities. Insofar as their presuppositions are concerned, most scientists exclude subjects of any kind from playing a causal role in the world, even if their own experience of themselves and others demonstrates the opposite is the case. Our lived experience, our common sense no less, recognizes the agency of subjects.

The agency of subjects brings with it an assumption of purpose, which stands in contrast to the scientific focus on function. This focus suggests every part of a system is mechanistic in that its structure and function can be explained entirely by its role in the system, by its place in the achievement of efficient causes. If it has a seemingly purposeful role, it is not because there is a purpose, but rather it is either because of pure chance or of systemic necessity. Subjectivity plays no causal role. This is, by and large, the view that has come to dominate intellectual inquiry insofar as that can be understood to take place within universities.

A second view, mentioned above, used to exist in universities. This view did not suggest we needed to rethink our understanding of *ourselves* (i.e., to focus on even ourselves as isolated objects) as a result of our inclusion in nature. Rather, it suggested we needed to rethink our understanding of *nature* as a result of our inclusion in it. The neo-naturalist approach to comprehending nature lost out, however, due to the rise of the discipline model of research founded on the principle that physics provides the most complete answers. This was despite the fact that because Hume conceptually exposed the mechanistic view's limitations, Kant concluded through his notion of theoretical reason that Cartesian naturalism offered the best and indeed only responsible way to think about the world.[5] This was in contrast to philosophers such as Bergson, James, Pierce, and, most notably, Whitehead, who argued that a more accurate and comprehensive account could be found in understanding processes of changefulness as fundamental to the universe. For Whitehead, in particular, a more comprehensive appreciation of nature could be arrived at by placing the various elements of experience into consistent relation with each other. That is, at the most fundamental level, there is a dynamic connectedness among things. Newton perceived this deeply in his law that "every action has an equal and opposite reaction." However, the implication that to react to the action, that action must first be *experienced*—otherwise there is nothing to react to—has been somehow lost to the beguiling power of Kant's understanding of Descartes. And yet, simply put, if I scratch the table hard enough for a mark to become visible on its surface, it must have experienced my scratching it. Otherwise it would not and could not have changed.

Still, physicists as a whole did not desist in their confidence in the resulting mechanical model and, since other scientists did not seriously question that physics was foundational, the newly-established view of how to engage in legitimate study remained. Serious reflection about alternatives was marginalized for two reasons. First, in becoming a discipline of its own to fit into the new academic model, philosophy excluded such questions from its purview by seriously limiting just precisely what philosophy was deemed to *be*. Second, it was found in the age of scientific discovery that studying human beings as objects using the scientific method revealed significant new insights. The other half of Kant's arguments, concerning what he called practical reason, was to all intents and purposes expunged from the curriculum. Of course, the result is that the dominant refrain is now "there is no alternative." The alternative existed but has been at best simply forgotten or, at any rate, is no longer widely known, and at worst has been perhaps intentionally written out of the academic discourse by the practices and procedures of scientific publication itself.

As universities increasingly organized themselves around the disciplines, they were no longer primarily interested in original thinking about human well-being and the well-being of other forms of life. They were instead increasingly interested in advancing knowledge at the frontiers of disciplinary research. They are now primarily interested in competing *inter alia* for the production of research. The inherently value-free nature of our current research-focused higher education institutions of course means that one so-called "value" supplants all others—the desires of the funder. If the funding body is a government equally bent on delivering global competitiveness, for example, by driving economic growth through innovation, then the higher education institutions are bound to answer its desires *if* (perhaps even *since*) they have no coherent set of values underpinning their research.

Obviously, the pressures are likely even worse where industry is the funding provider. In such an environment, retaining a passive-object, substance ontology is still the most straightforward way of contributing to disciplinary knowledge. Yet this ontology stands in stark contrast to what recent advances in, for example, epigenetics and neuroscience are increasingly demonstrating, namely, that changeful and relational subjective experience is a more universal feature of all life on Earth. Since research is, (in principle, rightly) taught in the classrooms, so the problem passes from generation to generation.

The Abject Failure of Our Management

In the humanities and social sciences, traditional object ontology is seen perhaps most powerfully in the discipline of economics. This should come as no surprise; Philip Mirowski has very clearly pointed out that neoclassical economics adopted Newtonian physics just before it was supplanted by the late nineteenth century relativistic thinking that saw interconnectedness as a fundamental feature of reality,[6] and its essence hasn't changed. One of the fundamental assumptions of our time is that economic growth is the universal panacea. Continuous economic growth is "securely entrenched as the natural objective of collective human effort," placing us on a "Collision Course"[7] with the planet—only one of the effects of which is global warming.

Of course, it is perfectly fine for mainstream economists to come up with ideas about how the economy should theoretically and rationally/objectively work through perpetual growth,[8] and in so doing seemingly ignore the close relation between the thought of Adam Smith and Karl Marx as *philosophers*. For example, one misses a great deal of Smith if one does not read *The Wealth of Nations* through its preceding volume, *The Theory of Moral Sentiments*. That is to say, both Smith and Marx, in seeking to comprehend the realities of human experience, understood that the progressive commodification of useful things with use values detrimentally transforms them into commodities with exchange values; Smith is a good deal closer to Marx than commonly appreciated.[9] It is also perfectly fine for public policy thinkers to come up with ways of turning the theoretical ideas of economics into implementable plans, as long as leaders and managers don't actually go ahead and implement them!

To extend the management consultant and philosopher Nigel Laurie's frequent observation that managed organizations are the medium in which increasing amounts of human activity are pursued, there wouldn't appear to be any likely significant alternative to the managed type of organization on the horizon. Management as a practice is, therefore, likely the only means we have at our disposal for intervening in the world to actually *make a difference*. As but one example, just as soon as an environmental scientist decides to move from describing what she sees to actually intervening for change, she is no longer doing environmental science, she is practicing environmental management.

It is possible to practice management with a different purpose than economic growth. Nonetheless, it is true to say that the predominant type of management in practice today has a Western management focus on delivering the economic imperative of capitalism. It follows that *Homo sapiens'* management thinking and practice of the twentieth and early twenty-first centuries, geared in large part towards delivering economic growth through industrialization, can largely be held to blame for the effects we are now witnessing. *In short, the ecological crisis is the direct result of our species' particular practice of management.*

And so, it is high time we tried to rethink and reimagine management to focus not so much on delivering economic prosperity, but rather on delivering a very different understanding of what prosperity will need to be in the future. A particular type of management has led us into this crisis, and only a different type of management can lead us out of it. We need to work out what that "different type" might be, and how it might be.

Management vitally needs thoroughgoing, serious-minded, commonsense philosophical scrutiny and creative philosophical thought, simply because it is so significant a human activity (even if all its impacts were thought of as wholly benign!). New philosophies of management are urgently required; a sticking plaster will not suffice. As one suggestion, a new mode of management thought might take into consideration a more comprehensive, relational approach, supportive of a more integral way of life and "business." This is a radical rethinking. The ecological crisis now before us is such that nothing less will do.

This radical philosophical scrutiny, founded perhaps in neo-naturalism, is essential. While the corporations and management practices within them are directly causing the environmental crisis, as Christopher Wright and Daniel Nyberg have so powerfully and eloquently explained,[10] there is another primary cause that underpins the thought and action of corporrate leaders and managers, namely, the mode of thought taught in our universities. Results-focused science research in narrow disciplines encourages a human/

nature separation. Once inculcated with this mode of thought, graduates go into business and government and quite understandably apply it.

While corporations are a very big factor in the causes of the crisis we face, the deeper underlying problem is that universities are feeding corporations with people trained in a way of thinking that is not capable of resisting—and is even inherently supportive of—what the corporations are doing. Until we educate people differently, until we teach them to think about management differently so that they enter the world of work with a fundamentally different set of presuppositions, the self-destructive nature of economism cannot be meaningfully addressed. Unfortunately, even management thinking that purports to be founded in process thought is inherently flawed, precisely because it, too, is constrained by the scientism—the stasis axiologies—that are the unknown foundation of the management literature.[11] The result is that even process-informed management theory is shot-through with all the usual fallacies, errors, and misunderstandings.[12]

Requisites for an Ecological Management

Borrowing directly from Aldo Leopold's argument that the boundaries of what we commonly understand as "community" need to be enlarged to collectively include animals, plants, soils, and waters, Dean Freudenberger[13] argues that an ecological civilization recognizes that our human narrative cannot be focused on our use of the Earth for our purposes—anthropocentrism. Instead, our narrative needs to be focused on the realization that we are part of the natural world. To an extent unlike any other species, what we do affects our own future, precisely because it directly affects the future of nature—biocentrism.

The focus cannot be solely on our own well-being in the short term. We must return to a narrative that accepts as plain fact that our well-being in the long term, trans-generationally, depends on the well-being of all species. Our future is linked to theirs, theirs to ours, and, crucially, the narrative must recognize the damage we have done, and that we are therefore obligated to adjust our behavior to help the Earth restore a habitable balance. This is a moral obligation. We must change the narrative from "today, not tomorrow," to "tomorrow, not today." To adapt the marketing slogan of a luxury watch manufacturer: we have never actually owned the Earth; we are merely looking after it for future generations—of our own species and of other species as well.

For this to happen, we must live within the potentials and limitations of renewable resources, not exhaustible ones. Sustainability requires living within the regenerative capacity of the biosphere. We must live today in such a way as to meet our needs, but without jeopardizing the ability of future generations to meet their needs for food, water, soil, health, shelter, community, the arts, and the sciences. After Aldo Leopold, we must learn to recognize that our actions and contributions are correct when they contribute to the beauty, integrity, and harmony of the biotic community—the community of not just *Homo sapiens,* but all species. They are wrong if they have the opposite effect.

This is not to say that we abandon technology and—if it were even possible—abandon cities to return to a nomadic lifestyle. It is rather to say that our technological prowess, and the way we manage and develop it, needs to be geared toward the maintenance and regeneration of the ecosystem's services to us. This is beyond the development of renewable energies such as solar, biological, wind, hydroelectric, and geothermal resources, and it is beyond the reduction of our reliance on depleting resources. It is rather more the development of technology and ways of using that technology—for example, in agriculture—that actively support and enhance nature's *regenerative* capability. In this way, we might move from the 3 Ds to the 3 Rs. That is, we might move from our present *delicate, dependent, and depletive* communities toward *resilient, resourceful, and regenerative* ones.

By *delicate,* I mean our communities are increasingly founded in commuter belts, disconnected from nature and even disconnected from our neighbors. By *dependent,* I mean our communities are increasingly reliant on bought-in goods and services. By *depletive* I mean that being both delicate and dependent, our communities are consuming the Earth's resources in ways that are not genuinely sustainable. *Resilient* communities, by contrast, are well-founded in their connectedness to the land around them and the people in their midst. This makes them inherently appreciative of the natural and social resources of which they are made up and thus capable of surviving and thriving despite economic turmoil. They can do this by focusing on positive contributions to their local social and natural environment, being keenly aware of the connection between themselves and, for example, the farms, the foods, and the soils around them.

Moving away from the 3 Ds to the 3 Rs requires the human species fully (as opposed, perhaps, to tangentially) to appreciate the fact that we are one among many species. Our lives depend upon many others, just as the many others that inhabit our bodies depend on us. All species are interdependent and of intrinsic value in and for themselves. In turn, this requires us to re-focus our education narrative away from the inculcation of an objective, anthropocentric, value-free approach to knowledge and towards an appreciation of the fact that every individual member of every species has a subjective experience; that we are one among many inhabiting the Earth, each with their own right to live, their own purposes, all of which are intrinsically valuable. All education, but perhaps most importantly of all, given its significance as a means for enacting change, management education should be focused on arriving at an appreciation of the ecological complexities of place, both local and global, and how we can turn our ways of being towards supporting that complexity to flourish.

In sum, an ecological civilization requires a narrative that recalibrates our human disposition, our core values, our "use" of resources, our understanding of the nature of civilization, our ethics, our technological purposes, our psychological disposition, our education—and our management—towards the original intention of prudence and goodness. None of these can *any longer* be regarded as mere rhetorical statements. If things remain as they are, bound by economism instead of οἰκονομία (economy), the only way in which corporations would genuinely act in the Earth's interests is if unilaterally binding legislation were enacted, making it such that all corporations had to act in this way.

Without it, any corporation that acts in the Earth's interests places itself at an immediate disadvantage in comparison with its competitors who do not, and will thus likely incur the wrath of their major shareholders for whom they are charged with making sizeable returns on investment.[14] It is highly unlikely such legislation would be forthcoming from within the current narrative. In short, therefore, there must be a new underpinning narrative, genuinely felt and subsumed into our subconsciousness just as powerfully as the modern age economism narrative has been to date. Unlike economism, which is a narrative of our individual success at the expense of the planet, the ecological narrative of earthism is the success of the planet as a whole, from which our success—naturally—derives.[15]

Management has always been about delivering the human narrative, making it a reality for people. It follows that management will continue to be about delivering the human narrative, but that narrative is now intimately bound up in an ecological narrative. So, the underlying purpose of management, as *Homo sapiens* practices it, must return to being natural, in concert with the Earth. Its reason for happening, the focus of its practice, the aim of its leadership, and, as I have been at pains to explain the *mode of its thought* from which its practice springs, must be radically different from what we see today. After all, one opportunity to change our approach, namely, the restarting of economies after the initial Coronavirus crisis, has already been lost. In much the same way as ecological economics rightly places economics within the ecological question and thus gears it to meet the needs of the Earth (c.f. environmental economics, which places the environment as but one of the elements in the mainstream economic model[16]), so the goal of management must now be *not* to deliver economy—the artificial wealth of money—but instead nature's οἰκονομία, i.e., ecology, the natural wealth of the Earth.

My point is we need to look to E. F. Schumacher[17]—an inherently process-oriented thinker—for our economics; we need economics not for a large planet, but for a small one. Management not for corporations, the corporatocracy, but for people. Management for Earthism, not Economism. This is radical—but as far as I can see, it is the only route to a future where the human population survives. On the other hand, perhaps what the rest of nature's οἰκονομία needs most is for the human population not to survive at all.

Endnotes

Author's Note: This essay is founded in the thought of the American theologian, philosopher, and environmentalist John B. Cobb Jr. The author is grateful to John Cobb, Kerryn Higgs, and Colin Tudge for their comments on previous drafts.

1. C. D. Freudenberger, *Global Dust Bowl: Can We Stop the Destruction of the Land Before It's Too Late?* (Minneapolis: Augsburg Fortress, 1990).
2. A shorter version of this section was published in a chapter entitled "Management for Our Common Home," first published in J. B. Cobb, and I. Castuera, eds., *For Our Common Home: Process-Relational Responses to Laudato Si'* (Claremont, CA: Process Century Press, 2015). The author is grateful for the copyright permissions contained therein.

3. D. Korten, *When Corporations Rule the World*, 3rd Edition (San Francisco: Berrett-Koehler Publishers, 2015).

4. J. B. Cobb, "Series Preface: Towards Ecological Civilization," in R. B. Edwards, *An Axiological Process Ethics* (Claremont, CA: Process Century Press, 2014).

5. See A. N. Whitehead, *Process and Reality*, Corrected Edition, ed. D. R. Griffin and D. W. Sherburn (New York: The Free Press, [1929] 1978), 144–56.

6. P. Mirowski, "Physics and the 'Marginalist Revolution,'" *Cambridge Journal of Economics* 8 (1984): 361–79.

7. K. Higgs, *Collision Course: Endless Growth on a Finite Planet* (Cambridge, MA: MIT Press, 2015).

8. This is not to say that all economics does this. E. F. Schumacher's work *Small is Beautiful: A Study of Economics as if People Mattered* (London: Vintage Books, 2011) remains an outstanding example of a radical and influential alternative. It has formed the basis for a number of higher education entities that focus attention on an ecological approach to economics and management, including the Schumacher Centre for New Economics in Massachusetts and Schumacher College in Devon.

9. C. Neesham, and M. Dibben, "Class Conflict and Social Order in Smith and Marx: The Relevance of Social Philosophy to Business Management," *Philosophy of Management* 15/2 (2016): 121–33.

10. C. Wright and D. Nyberg, *Climate Change, Capitalism, and Corporations: Processes of Creative Self-Destruction* (Cambridge: Cambridge University Press, 2015).

11. M. R. Dibben, "Management and Organisation Studies," in *Handbook of Whiteheadian Process Thought,* ed. M. Weber and W. Desmond (Frankfurt/Lancaster: Ontos Verlag, 2008), 91–107.

12. C. R. Mesle and M. R. Dibben, "Whitehead's Process Relational Philosophy," in *Sage Handbook of Process Organization Studies,* ed. A. Langley and H. Tsoukas (London: Sage, 2017); Whitehead, *Process and Reality*.

13. D. Freudenberger, *Global Dust Bowl*; W. Jackson, *Nature as Measure: The Selected Essays of Wes Jackson* (Berkley, CA: Counterpoint Press, 2011); A. Leopold, *A Sand County Almanac* (Oxford: Oxford University Press, 1949).

14. I am grateful to Vijay Sathe of the Drucker School of Management at

Claremont Graduate University for pointing this out in conversation, July 2015.

15. J. B. Cobb, *The Earthist Challenge to Economism* (New York: Palgrave, 1999).

16. H. Daly and J. Farleigh, *Ecological Economics: Principles and Applications*, 2nd Ed. (Washington, DC: Island Press, 2010).

17. E. F. Schumacher, *A Guide for the Perplexed* (London: Vintage Books,1995); *This I Believe—and Other Essays* (Dartington, UK: Green Books, 1997); *A Study of Economics as if People Mattered.*

NINE

Re-embedding the Market:
Institutionalizing Effective Environmentalism

Arran Gare

PHILIP MIROWSKI AND DIETER PLEHWE, in their book *The Road From Mont Pèlerin: The Making of the Neoliberal Thought Collective*[1] and in other works edited or written by them, Quinn Slobodian in *Globalists: The End of Empire and the Birth of Neoliberalism*,[2] and S. M. Amadae in *Rationalizing Capitalist Democracy: The Cold War Origins of Rational Choice Liberalism* and in *Prisoners of Reason*,[3] have revealed the ideological roots and the goals of those behind the massive transformation of economies and societies around the world since the 1970s. Backed by media moguls such as Rupert Murdoch in Anglophone countries and Reinhard Mohn in Germany, financed by billionaires, financial institutions, and transnational corporations, with think-tanks set up around the world, this was a deliberate project to subvert and replace the social democratic consensus that had triumphed in advanced Western countries after the Great Depression and the Second World War. More fundamentally, it was a deliberate effort to undermine democracy and to transform institutions serving democracy into either business corporations, or institutions operating according to the "rational choice" logic of economic actors. The best way to characterize what happened is in terms of Karl Polanyi's characterization of the relation between markets and communities.

While markets have operated within civilizations at least as far back as Ancient Persia and Ancient Greece, what took place in Western Europe, beginning with Britain from the seventeenth century onwards, was something new. It was associated with the creation of fictitious commodities—land, labor and money[4]—culminating in the repeal of the 1795 Speenham Law that had provided economic security for the poor, in 1835. The logic of these fictions, essentially forms of Whitehead's fallacy of misplaced concreteness put into practice, had been fully embraced, dis-embedding markets from communities while imposing market relationships on these communities. Individuals were forced to define their relationships through markets, subordinating them to the logic of markets. The poverty and incredible brutality this engendered, along with dramatic improvements in technology, first in Britain itself, and then other countries, led to struggles to develop institutions to alleviate poverty, protect workers, and control the dynamics of markets, subordinating markets to institutions aiming at democracy, social justice, and the common good of society; that is, to re-embed the market. These institutions included trade unions, socialist and labor parties, the development of representative democracy, the civil service, and institutions of public education.

The social democratic consensus that emerged after World War Two in advanced Western societies can be seen as a triumph of this project that began in the middle of the nineteenth century. The broader social democratic project, in an ambivalent relationship to Communist countries, involved extending these institutions to other countries, freeing what was then known as the Third World from colonialism and neo-colonialism, and supporting efforts such as the Prague Spring in Czechoslovakia in 1968, to liberalize Communist regimes. From this perspective, as Takis Fotopoulos argued, neoliberalism was a struggle to again dis-embed markets from communities and impose the logic of markets on communities, this time, imposing a globalized market dominated by transnational corporations, including global financial institutions.[5] Its success has not only engendered massive concentrations of wealth along with economic insecurity for workers, impoverishment, and economic instability, but has paralyzed efforts to deal with the global ecological crisis.

Before examining what kind of institutions could control markets to serve social justice and the common good, specifically to address local and global ecological destruction, it is necessary to consider more carefully what neoliberalism is and what it entails, and what have been the conditions for its success. Neoliberalism has been directed at democracy, identified by ruling elites as mob rule. To understand what this involves it is necessary to appreciate, as William Norgaard pointed out, that there are three ways to organize complex societies: through bureaucracies, through markets, and through institutions of democracy. These three institutions evolved in this order. It is impossible to totally eliminate any of these for any length of time, although democracy is the most vulnerable. The ideology on which neoliberalism is based originated in Britain with the philosophy of possessive individualism articulated by Thomas Hobbes and John Locke, developed to oppose the ambitions for democracy of the Renaissance-inspired civic humanists.[6] Incorporated into classical and later neoclassical economic theory, this ideology was successful, culminating in the nineteenth-century dominance by Britain and the rise of the global market and European imperialism. Its ideological defense was bolstered by Darwinian evolutionary theory and Social Darwinism, which legitimated the suffering it engendered as creative destruction necessary for progress.[7] The inevitable effect of the logic of the market is to advance technology and concentrate wealth, and this it has done whenever markets have been dis-embedded from communities. Imposing markets requires a great deal of organization, and so is inevitably associated with the growth of bureaucracies.

The challenge to this order came from proponents of various forms of democracy. The quest to overcome poverty and imperialism was indissociable from this quest for democracy, although this was less clear in the case of Germany and the Austro-Hungarian Empire. The modern idea of democracy was articulated by Rousseau, Herder, Fichte, and the liberal Hegelians, including T. H. Green and the British Idealists, and those they influenced, including John Dewey and Alfred North Whitehead. John Stuart Mill was strongly influenced by Herder. Marx was also part of this tradition of thought, influenced by Herder, Fichte, and Hegel, but orthodox Marxists interpreted Marx as a Hobbesian thinker and promoted "plebiscitary" democracy, which was really organization through bureaucracy utilizing markets. However, "humanist" Marxists (those who have actually read Marx's works), Marxist theorists of imperialism, and eco-Marxists are committed to promoting strong democracy. Defending democracy involves rejecting the Hobbesian conception of humans and human reasoning as calculating in the service of acquiring the means to satisfy appetites and avoid aversions, and replacing this with a conception of humans as essentially sociocultural beings able to be cultivated through education so that they can participate in the cultural life of their communities and govern themselves. Hegel and the neo-Hegelians paid particular attention to institutions required to control markets, and the quest for democracy involved a defense of some form of institutionalist economics against classical and neoclassical economics, along with an older form of evolutionary theory going back to Schelling in place of orthodox Darwinian evolutionary theory and Social Darwinism.

It is this tradition of democratic thinking that the neoliberals have targeted, beginning with a circle of Austrian economists cultivated by Ludwig von Mises in Vienna in the 1920s, and then with a conference at the University of Freiburg in 1938. Communism, Nazism, and social democracy were equated with rule by the masses. Walter Lippmann's argument from 1922 that the modern world is too complex for democracy was embraced, along with his argument that ruling elites should "manufacture consent" from the masses through public relations, deluding them about where power really lies.[8] These ideas were central to the Mont Pèlerin society, founded in 1947. Friedrich von Hayek played a major role in this, reviving Lockean possessive individualism against notions of community and ideas of the common good and justice deriving from Athenian democracy, Roman and Renaissance republicanism, and German communitarianism.[9] Particularly as developed by the Chicago School of economics led by Milton Friedman, this led to the ascendency of neoclassical economics, particularly against institutionalist forms of Keynesian economics, developing rational choice theory, and reviving Darwinism and Social Darwinism through sociobiology, and arguing for the deregulation of finance and the globalization of the market. This was not simply a matter of freeing financial institutions and transnational corporations to dominate the world, but through the US military, the International Monetary Fund, and the World Bank, imposing or transforming institutions to enable them to do so. It involved "dethroning politics" and developing institution forms to "encase" the global market from interference from national governments.[10] This was the "Washington Consensus." Their greatest success was not imposing the rule of Pinochet in Chile, the triumph of Thatcher in Britain and Reagan in the USA, but the co-optation of supposedly leftist parties: Deng Hsiao-Ping in China, the Hawke-Keating Labor government in Australia, the Bill Clinton administration in the USA, the Tony Blair government in Britain, and, to a lesser extent, the Gerhard Schröder government in Germany. All of these could be said to have accepted Thatcher's claim that "there is no alternative." The rule of such figures entrenched the rule of the global corporatocracy by subverting the institutions required for the functioning of democracy. These developments have been associated with massive increases in the sizes of bureaucracies, both within transnational corporations, in public institutions, and in the institutions of social control. These developments are all associated with what has been called the "new managerialism," characterized by contractual mechanisms and performance measurements, whereby employment has been rendered precarious, workers have been disempowered, and power concentrated in the hands of corporation managers. The general population have been redefined as consumers rather than workers and citizens.

It is important to emphasize that the disembedding of markets that has taken place over the last forty years has not been a bottom-up, spontaneous reaction to situations, nor has it been a matter of eliminating or reducing the power of non-market institutions to avoid the road to serfdom, as von Hayek implied in his promotion of neoliberalism. The changes that have taken place have been driven by a very small number of people, co-opting others to carry out their agenda. Their real aim has been to protect and augment their interests. While governments have increasingly abandoned the institutions upholding democracy, including providing economic security to the population, they have focused on developing means of social control, including a massive increase in levels of surveillance and, in the USA, the militarization of the police force and the growth of goals. As Wolfgang Streeck observed, "neoliberalism needs a *strong* state to suppress demands from society, and especially from trade unions, for intervention in the free play of market forces ... On the other hand, neoliberalism is incompatible with a democratic state."[11]

Imposing markets along with the new managerialism has been portrayed by neoliberals as necessary to improve efficiency. This entails getting rid of trade barriers and constraints on the movement of capital, deregulating financial institutions to allow countries to specialize in those industries where they have a comparative advantage, eliminating job security, and concentrating power in the hands of managers in order to discipline an overindulged workforce. While succeeding in allowing these people to massively increase their wealth, power, security, and access to previously undreamt of luxuries, neoliberalism has massively slowed down the rate of improvement in economic efficiency compared to the 1945 and 1975 era and, outside the production of computer hardware, peripherals, and telecommunications equipment along with durable manufacturing, the productivity of workers has decelerated, despite advances in technology.[12] The lot of most people in advanced Western countries has deteriorated, as Thomas Piketty[13] has demonstrated. The most significant institutional changes have been associated with the internal organization of transnational corporations and the development of financial institutions on a global scale, both as economic organizations and as agents of financial, political, cultural, and social transformation. This has involved the development of the mind-control industries of advertising and public relations, and the transformation of public institutions, including the institutions of finance, politics, education, and other branches of the civil service. Neoliberalism has also involved insulating these wealthy elites from paying taxes and from the threats associated with growing lawlessness, terrorism, and random violence—the consequences of the social disintegration generated by this concentration of wealth and economic insecurity. Such people are also insulating themselves from the effects of ecological destruction, with wealthy Californians and Chinese buying up land in New Zealand.

While the rise of neoliberalism involved a successful ideological struggle, there have been other reasons for its success. Stephen Hymer, in the 1960s, noted that transnational corporations were growing far faster than domestic corporations and predicted that this would undermine all the achievements of social democracy associated with the nation-state.[14] Hymer anticipated then what David Korten feared would be the outcome of this, where corporations would rule the world.[15] As William Robinson[16] has shown, this has involved transforming the institutions of even the most powerful states into instruments of these corporations for the domination and exploitation of nations. This development was partly associated with what could be regarded as the decadence of social democracy, whereby continued demands by an empowered working class were undermining the profitability of corporations and creating a fiscal crisis of the state, and mass culture was eroding people's capacity to govern themselves. As Pierre Bourdieu argued, the supposed radicalism of many of the New Left was not associated with a coherent vision of how democracy could be extended, but by a resistance to any constraints,[17] demands that could be and, as David Harvey argued, were utilized by neoliberals to co-opt former New Leftists to neoliberalism.[18] In a globalized market, with transnational corporations able to move capital and people freely, and with a decadent Left that went on to embrace deconstructive postmodernism while policing political correctness, it would be impossible to uphold notions of democratic communities even without the efforts of the neoliberals. In many cases, as Takis Fotopoulos[19] has shown, it is for this reason that neoliberal policies have been embraced by formerly left-wing politicians, to discipline the workforce and attract capital within the new global market.

What are Institutions?

To revive democracy and re-embed markets, it is necessary to determine: 1) what institutions are required; 2) what institutional changes are required, and 3) what can actually be developed? It is necessary not only to grapple with the immense power of the global corporatocracy and the corrupt politicians, civil servants, and managers of public institutions, such as universities, that serve the interests of the corporatocracy, but also to grapple with the decadence and effective co-optation by the corporatocracy of the purported opponents of the establishment. It is easy to point to some measures that can be and have been effectively taken, for instance, demanding that the leaders of political parties be directly elected by the rank-and-file members of these parties, as happened with the British Labor Party. However, it is first necessary to consider the more basic issue of defining what an institution is.

Institutions have been defined by institutionalist economists in different ways. Arild Vatn[20] is concerned to uphold and develop the tradition of institutionalist economics that goes back to Thorstein Veblen, who was strongly influenced by C.S. Peirce, William James, and John Dewey, and beyond them, to Charles Darwin and the historical school of economics. According to Peirce, instinct, action, and habit formation precede rational deliberation, which always presupposes habits associated with action. Habits were understood as dispositions to act, although when confronted with failure, people could reflect on and modify their habits. Institutions are complexes of such habits, formed through evolution of societies, but capable of being consciously modified or even deliberately created. Successive institutionalists proposed narrower views about actions and institutions.

The Austrian institutionalists, such as von Mises and von Hayek, argued that institutions, for instance, money, evolved spontaneously and could not be planned, and all change should be left to the spontaneous activity of people rather than being planned. The neo-institutionalists, reconceiving action through game theory, effectively assimilated institutionalist economics to mainstream economics with some modifications, with individuals assumed to be calculating, power hungry egoists, reaffirming the traditional Hobbesian notion of *homo economicus*.

To advance the idea of institution of the classical institutionalist economists, Vatn utilized the work of Peter Berger and Thomas Luckmann, influenced by Marx, Durkheim, George Herbert Mead, and Alfred Schutz. From their perspective, institutions emerge when patterns of activity come to be stabilized, taken to be objective, and then internalized in people's actions. For instance, if a couple end up having meals regularly, and their children come to expect these regular meals, mealtimes become an objective reality. The members of the family then internalize this objective reality in the way they organize their activities. Mealtimes have then become an institution, and patterns of eating have been institutionalized. They involve typified responses to typified expectations and are conceptualized and evaluated in this way. However, in light of Mead's insights, there is more involved than this. Each individual develops the capacity to take the perspective of each of the others on their own activities and on themselves, and then to take the perspective of the whole family on each individual. In this way, they develop a conception of themselves in relation to each other and in relation to the family, while still being capable of spontaneous action, reflecting on these identities and values accorded to their institutions and practices.

Societies, including their communities and organizations, consist of patterns of such institutions interrelated with each other through which individuals chart their lives and forge their identities, thereby maintaining and reproducing these institutions, communities, organizations, and societies and the relations between each of these. Conceived in this way, people form institutions which then form them, including their conventions, attitudes, and normative evaluations. On the foundation of these, they are also able to reflect upon these institutions and associated conventions, attitudes, and normative evaluations and to consciously set about changing them or creating new institutions. While the focus of Berger and Luckmann was on the emergence of institutions from below, they also allowed that institutions could be created from above, by state action for instance. Conceiving of people and institutions in this way challenges the conception of *homo economicus*, that is, that people are calculating egoists with a hierarchy of preferences, and allows that people can evaluate and live in very different ways with different ways of reasoning, according to different institutional contexts. It facilitates examination of what is involved in forming institutions, changing them, and evaluating them not only for the values they uphold and their effectiveness in realizing goals, but for the kinds of people that will be formed by these institutions. This has been the focus of Vatn's work.

One of the major problems that must be addressed when considering institutions is the issue of power. Transforming or creating institutions takes place in a social environment already pervaded by institutions which provide opportunities or limit what people can do, and these opportunities and limits are themselves matters of power relations. The issue of power is not treated in any depth by Vatn, although he acknowledges its importance. Berger and Luckmann did consider power in their in their social theory in noting that the most important form of power in society is the power to define reality. They did not ask the further question of who has the power to define reality, although clearly those who do have this power will also have the power to redefine reality. The social theorist whose ideas are entirely commensurate with those of the classical institutionalist economics of Veblen and Berger, and Luckmann's theory of institutions—but which has provided a thorough analysis of power—is Pierre Bourdieu.

Like Veblen, Bourdieu argued that learning is first and foremost a matter of developing habits, or as he put it, developing a *habitus*. Like Berger and Luckmann, Bourdieu examined the social construction of what we take to be reality, and like Mead, Bourdieu saw one of the most important motives driving people is the struggle for recognition. Later, Bourdieu introduced the notion of field into his social theory, providing an alternative to the notion of system commonly used by sociologists. This concept enabled Bourdieu to deal with macro social dynamics, overcoming the deficiency of the sociologists influenced by Mead, such as the symbolic interactionists, and Berger and Luckmann, in their capacity to deal with these macro-dynamics. In doing so, Bourdieu developed the means to analyze the emergence of fields and the relationship between different fields, including national fields and global fields. The concepts of habitus and field are ideal for advancing institutionalist economics and understanding power relations, and Bourdieu[21] went on to apply these concepts to analyzing the social structures of the economy.

To capture the complexity, diversity, and subtleties of power, Bourdieu referred to capital rather than power. The power to define reality, for instance, is defined by Bourdieu as symbolic capital, and it is associated with being recognized as having the legitimacy to define reality. Much of Bourdieu's work was devoted to understanding the nature of this symbolic capital and the struggles to achieve it. This work was particularly important for explaining the autonomization of fields, differentiating them and their logic from other fields. However, Bourdieu saw other forms of capital as important, for instance, (1) social capital, the network of people who one knows; (2) cultural capital, the appropriate sense of taste and associated practices required to get on; as well as (3) economic and political capital. Capital is defined as what is required to continue participating successfully in the different fields, clearly a concept generalized from Marx's study of the bourgeois mode of production. There is also an exchange rate between the capitals of different fields, and the field of the state as a metafield of power operates largely by controlling this exchange rate.[22] A major component of its operation is symbolic violence: devaluing the status of individuals and groups by devaluing the specific capital of their particular fields.

Vatn also argued that societies must be understood in the context of their environments. This is not the set of items that people are likely to come across. He equated the environment with the biosphere, including not only all the species of life and ecosystems, but the interlinked bio-geochemical processes that keep the whole biosphere functioning.[23] It is necessary to take the environment in this sense into account when formulating policies, and the main problem is to work out what kinds of institutions are required to formulate adequate and effective policies that can augment rather than undermine these processes so that societies improve the health of these ecosystems. Then it is necessary to work out how to transform existing institutions or how to create new institutions that are capable of formulating and implementing these policies.

However, the problem here is that such ecological processes are the ultimate basis of power. As ecologists came to realize, the struggle for survival and the consequent nature of ecosystems is essentially a struggle to access and transform usable forms of energy. This idea has been taken up in anthropology and human ecology, where it engendered a theory of social power based on control of the triggers that release transformations of energy, put forward by Richard Newbold Adams,[24] then further developed by Stephen Bunker (1988)[25] and Alf Hornborg,[26] to analyze the structures of exploitation and ecological destruction in the global economy. Hornborg has also shown the relationship between these structures and the forms of technology that have developed based on such controls over energy transformations. In considering both action and what kind of institutions can be created, it is necessary to face up to the problem that power for the most part tends to accrue to those who control the most effective triggers for the transformation of energy, and these are the people whose environmental impact is likely to be greatest and most destructive.[27]

The Proposals

With this background we can now consider what institutions need to be constructed or transformed to re-embed the market to make it serve the common good of the diverse communities that make up humanity and the global ecosystem. Given the forces and trends at work dominating the world, it will only be possible to change all this if there is a clear, coordinating goal. This goal could be creating an ecologically sustainable civilization; however, while this might be an ultimate end, it does not provide enough guidance for particular situations. What has been involved in the dis-embedding of markets is that it has been a subversion of democracy. This has been seen most clearly by anarchist (i.e., libertarian socialist) thinkers such as Noam Chomsky, Takis Fotopoulos, and Robin Hahnel. In claiming that democracy has been subverted, it is important to appreciate what democracy means. It means people governing themselves, having the power to do so. This requires: (1) a capacity to understand issues on which decisions have to be made, and (2) the economic and political security required to achieve this understanding, so that (3) people are able to assert themselves without fear of retribution, and then (4) put their decisions into action. In the modern world, democracy was associated with the rise of the salariat who had the conditions to be citizens; the destruction of democracy has been associated with the rise of the precariat, who do not. It should be clear that in this sense most of the formerly democratic countries, such as the USA, Britain, and Australia where the public has been almost totally disempowered, can no longer be regarded as democracies.

How can democracy be revived? Quite apart from the problem of seizing back power from the global corporatocracy, and even if we aim to decentralize power as much as possible to localities—unless we embrace anarchist proposals of theorists such as Takis Fotopoulos and Murray Bookchin, democracy can only subordinate markets with the assistance of bureaucracies, that is, through forms of the civil service designed to serve democracy rather than replace it. What is required are professional, open civil services, such as those developed in Sweden under social democracy, in which civil servants were obliged to inform the general public about crucial issues on which decisions had to be made. They were expected to speak out and expose corruption, and they could do this without fear of retribution. Democracy involves legislation and its implementation, including law enforcement, and to re-embed markets it will be necessary to ensure that those with wealth do not subvert the functioning of these institutions through control of the media, funding of election campaigns, and subversion of legal institutions. Upholding such institutions requires a clear idea of what democracy is and what is involved in its corruption. This requires the recovery of educational institutions as public institutions in which the first goal of education has to be enculturing students so that they have the virtues required to be citizens, and in which education upholds the humanities and the sciences committed to the pursuit of truth as a comprehensive understanding of the world. Democracy also requires media facilitating the forms of communication necessary for people to understand the present state of the world. To think clearly about all this, it is necessary to teach students that the world consists of communities of communities, as Daly and Cobb argued in *For the Common Good*, and, following Robert Ulanowicz, that human communities should be understood as within and part of broader biotic communities or ecosystems in which semiosis is appreciated as absolutely central to such communities.[28] Ultimately, to properly comprehend the importance of these ideas, it is necessary to replace scientific materialism with process philosophy.

All this should be evident to anyone who takes time to think about it. It is now necessary to consider work advancing these ideas. Efforts to work out how to achieve democratic control over economic processes are being made, and these are important. Environmentalists have been concerned to show what democracy really means, and to work out what institutions are required to recover democracy. These range from those on the anarchist side of the movement, such as Takis Fotopoulos and Cornelius Castoriadis, to those who could be characterized as social liberals, such as Thomas Prugh, Robert Costanza, and Herman Daly.[29] On basics, they come to similar conclusions. Eleanor Ostrom gained a Nobel Prize for her work, published in *Governing for the Commons: The Evolution of Institutions for Collective Action*,[30] showing the conditions for communities to have the means to ensure that markets serve their communities. Institutions are needed that empower communities to participate in developing and reforming institutions. This requires that multiple levels of institutions able to supply and modify institutions to which people can then make credible commitments, which can be mutually monitored to ensure compliance with their purported goals. Ostrom's work is particularly important when considering setting up new institutions. However, in most cases, what is involved in recovering democracy is modifying existing institutions, often simply freeing them from corruption, or ensuring that emerging institutions develop in a way that advances democracy. The work of Lawrence Lessig in the USA on mobilizing people to overcome the corruption of public institutions, including the legal system, to control funding for politicians, to recover the creative commons through changes in property rights to creative productions to make them more accessible to the public, and to free the internet from domination by power elites,[31] is exemplary in this regard. The more difficult problem is to work out what kinds of institutions should and can prevail in economic activity itself, and how economic institutions should interface with political, legal, and other public institutions. The faith socialists had in socializing the means of production understood as creating a command economy has lost its attraction because of the failures of communist countries. Is there an alternative?

Decommodifying Land, Labor, and Money

To begin with, it is necessary to see what the core problem is. It is, as Polanyi argued, that society is dominated by the pseudo-commodities of land, labor, and money. It is treating these as commodities that is the underlying problem that needs to be overcome. Historically, land was treated as commodity before labor and money, then labor was treated as a commodity, and then money, identified as "capital," mystifying human relations and allowing a predator class who contribute nothing to communities to drain them of their income and wealth.

Money and its permutations are the most obvious problem and the most clearly a manifestation of the fallacy of misplaced concreteness. Money is most problematic in its most abstract form, as finance. It is when finance comes to dominate economies and debt levels increase in the private sector that, as first Veblen and then much later, Hyman Minksy[32] argued, market systems collapse into depressions. It is then that the economy is dominated by rampant speculation, fictitious capital, and Ponzi schemes, with income accruing to predators on the economy rather than producers. So it was predictable that in 2007, when the financial sector in the USA accounted for 40% of net profit and private debt levels rose to levels comparable to what they had been in 1929, that there was a global financial crisis that has not yet been overcome.[33] However, finance is also involved in the globalization of the economy, allowing transnational corporations to make huge profits as rentiers, to drain natural resources unsustainably from the peripheries of the global economy, to avoid taxes, and to undermine workers in the formerly affluent countries.

To understand this, it is necessary to recognize money as an institution, and that markets are inherently unstable because they are prone to destructive wealth concentrations. This is because money has different functions—as a means of exchange, as a measure of value, as a record of credit and debt, and thereby as a store of wealth. This last function is progressively disguised, as the way it is represented changes: from gold and silver, to paper money, to abstract symbols. The result is that the illusion is created that wealth can be accumulated endlessly. This is really the enslavement of debtors, as David Graeber[34] pointed out. Accumulated wealth is not only a source of power that cripples the functioning of the market; it can be used to corrupt other institutions, including political and legal institutions. Overcoming the tendency of finance to dominate and indebtedness to grow, Minsky[35] argued, requires large state institutions associated with heavy investments in long-term projects that can counter the business cycle. Banks should be large, preferably publicly owned, and designed to regulate the economy, not to maximize profits. The goal of government economic policy should be maintaining full employment, not growth of the economy. The financial crisis was a lost opportunity to reorient the entire economies of nations to focus on environmental problems with major investments by states in this, as Nicholas Stern argued.[36]

Other economists have focused on the relationship between countries and the illusions created by so-called "free trade." As human ecologists have observed, through economic globalization and free trade agreements, any economic enterprise that is economically viable is now environmentally unsustainable, and any enterprise which is environmentally sustainable is now economically unsustainable.[37] The doctrine of free trade has been rejected by Cobb and Daly and by Vatn, who argues for state institutions to determine what trade can take place. This should be associated with institutions to control capital flows. Considering that in most places around the world governments are under the control of financial institutions and transnational corporations, others have called for more radical changes. The Italian economists Massimo Amato and Luca Fantacci and the US economist Thomas Greco have argued that the third role of money, as a basis for credit, must end. Amato and Fantacci point to the absence of clearing houses in the international system to reconcile creditors and debtors, despite the need for this having been seen very clearly by John Maynard Keynes when planning the Bretton Woods agreement. What they argue for in in *The End of Finance*[38] is the stripping of money of its function as a commodity, that is, as a store of liquid wealth and the basis of credit. To achieve this, they argue for the implementation of Keynes' proposal for an international Clearing Union in which creditor and debtor countries would reconcile their claims, leaving all involved free of debt. Greco in *The End of Money and the Future of Civilization*,[39] argued that usury be abolished. He has offered a range of alternatives to money to effect exchange relationships and to prevent the use of money as a means of creating credit. Hornborg, as a human ecologist, has defended local currencies, ranging from LETS schemes to city currencies such as the Bristol Pound as a way of delinking local economies from an inherently oppressive and destructive global system based on supposedly free markets.[40] He argues that to enable otherwise ecologically sustainable enterprises to flourish, these currencies should not be exchangeable.

Decommodifying Labor

Labor came to be treated as a commodity after (1) people had been deprived of access to means of production, and (2) factories had been developed as a means to employ such people, and (3) owners of the means of production sold what they produced at a profit over and above what they had invested in labor. The dis-embedding of markets meant ensuring that potential employees had no other way of making a living, so they would have to work in the factories. This relationship changed with the development of unions and involvement of the State under the influence of social liberal, labor, and social democratic parties in ameliorating this condition, maintaining incomes of employees and providing an economic safety net. However, this change was accompanied by the growth of corporations (joint-stock companies), and then transnational corporations. It was unions and the State that created the social democratic order. The emergence of the salariat and the growth of the professions was an effect of this, with people respected for the value of their work and expecting an income based on social justice, rather than the market price for their work. That is, the work they did was to some extent de-commodified. The most successful de-commodification of work has been the development of cooperatives, with the exemplary case being the federation of cooperatives in Mondragón in the Basque Province of Spain. The puzzle is why cooperatives have not been more successful, as John Stuart Mill predicted. It has been shown that following the 2007 financial crisis, cooperatives were more successful than normal businesses.[41]

The development of corporations has been associated with the rise of a managerial class, and to some extent, opposition between managers and the professions. This did not necessarily involve the re-commodification of labor, as shown in Pascale and Athos' study, *The Art of Japanese Management*, focusing on Matsushita Electronics (which includes Panasonic, National, Quasar, and Technics brands). The founder of the company believed that work should be fulfilling, and he defined the market as a means by which people voted for approval for what the corporation produced. Employment was secure, and the company ensured that individuals were able to develop their full potential in a cooperative environment. This development can be partly explained by Japanese culture, which meant that the market was less dis-embedded from the community than in Western countries. Germany also had ameliorated the proletarian condition after World War Two by having representatives of workers on the boards of management of companies, and prohibiting companies taking over each other, a law repealed by the Social Democrats under Schröder. These corporate forms contrast with US companies where, as Joel Bakan has shown in *The Corporation: The Pathological Pursuit of Profit and Power*,[42] a decision by the Supreme

Court requiring companies to always put shareholders ahead of stakeholders locked in this dis-embedding and engendered a brutal form of managerialism that has radically extended instrumentalist attitudes to workers. Taking advantage of the freedom of movement of capital, companies have recreated a completely proletarianized workforce and helped create a global reserve army of unemployed or underemployed. The new managerial class, in alignment with out of control financial institutions, has succeeded in corrupting politicians and becoming the new global ruling class, the corporatocracy. Even Japanese and Scandinavian corporations have been forced to reorganize to succeed in the new globalized economy created by this corporatocracy under the banner of neoliberalism.

The problem is clearly the power of these transnational corporations and the global economic environment they have created. Given their immense power, and the difficulty of developing any viable alternative economic enterprises that could compete with them, given all their advantages, including their capacity to avoid taxes, plunder public assets, and control politicians, the solution might be to co-opt them. One possible path is to transform the very nature of corporations by democratizing them. There are various components to this agenda, including putting both workers and government representatives on boards of management. This was suggested by the institutionalist economist John Kenneth Galbraith in *The New Industrial State*[43] first published in 1967. However, this requires laws that put stakeholders ahead of shareholders. It should be made illegal for companies to take over other companies, or to hive off companies, or allow manager buyouts. This used to be the case in West Germany. Radical Swedish social democrats planned to use worker investment funds to buy out the shares of corporations so that they would own the means of production.[44] The end point would be to emulate the worker-controlled business enterprises that developed in Yugoslavia, or even cooperatives such as Mondragón. While cooperatives have been successful, a great many have failed. It is a major challenge to implement such strategies in an economically globalized world in which politicians have been corrupted, unless there is another major economic crisis.

An alternative strategy that could be pursued immediately is associated with the local delinking that Hornborg has called for, providing a less competitive environment where ecologically sustainable cooperatives can survive and flourish. The libertarian socialists have put forward proposals for cooperative organization of economic activity without markets, or with only simulated markets.[45] However, such organizations can only survive where state governments have already provided infrastructure, policing, and so on, and less radical organizational forms such as those associated with Mondragón could also be pursued. Continued success requires such cooperatives to actively engage in national politics to regain democratic control of the institutions of the state from transnational corporations and the neoliberals, and using this control to insulate nations and broader regions (such as Europe, or Latin America) from the global market through controls of capital flows and trade. Ignoring this, as happened in Argentina after workers had successfully taken control and operated factories after Argentina's economic collapse, led to the election of a government that nullified what they had achieved.

Decommodifying Land

"Land" is the most problematic of the pseudo-commodities, highlighted by the global ecological crisis where civilization itself is threatened. "Land," treated as the least important of the factors of production by economists, stands for the ecosystems of which we are part. It is the most pernicious abstraction and the ultimate in the fallacy of misplaced concreteness. The delusions associated with its commodification are entrenched and disguised by the commodification of labor and then further entrenched by the commodification of money. As Daly and Cobb argued in *For the Common Good*, this has led to a peculiar belief among economists that we can get by without natural resources. As George Gilder was quoted as writing, "The United States must overcome the materialistic fallacy: the illusion that resources and capital are essentially things, which can run out, rather than products of the human will and imagination which in freedom are inexhaustible."[46] The globalization of the economy driven by transnational corporations, neoliberal ideology, and those who have embraced it, has been associated with the development of transnational agribusiness companies, either controlling and transforming traditional forms of agriculture, or replacing them completely with factory farms. There has been a massive increase in use of fossil fuels and mining. It is the supposed efficiency of these agribusiness corporations and mining companies that is claimed by neoliberals to have delivered us not only from famines, but from dependency on natural resources.

Once the fiction of land as a commodity is recognized as such, we must acknowledge, as Vatn argued, that "land" includes all processes involved in the functioning of the biosphere. Vatn, like other ecological economists, conceives humans as part of nature, as having co-evolved with other species that make up existing ecosystems, including the global ecosystem, the biosphere, or Gaia. As active agents in the biosphere, humans modify their environments, creating buildings, transport and communication systems, weapons, and so on. Far from being a product of will and imagination, "land" properly understood, as suggested earlier, is the basis of power in society. This is less evident than it once was because of the forms of energy that are now exploited. As Richard Norgaard[47] argued, the exploitation of fossil fuel has dissociated humanity from the species and ecosystems with which we have co-evolved, and it is the power of those controlling the energy transformations associated with this exploitation of fossil fuels that has enabled them to dis-embed markets and impose their ecological destructive economic forms. When considering what institutions can re-embed the modern, globalized market, this is an aspect of power that must be taken into consideration.

What kinds of institutions could reverse these entrenched illusions actively reinforced by power elites? Freeing people from the illusions created by treating land as a commodity is at least partly dependent on freeing people from the illusions created by treating labor and money as commodities. It is these latter fictions which make the bizarre illusions about land as a commodity, and thereby illusions about our relation to the ecosystems of which we are part, possible. Public ownership of land by itself is not a solution to overcoming these illusions. The Soviet Union was characterized by immense environmental destruction. A pattern of what is wrong is evident. As Sing Chew showed in *The Recurring Dark Ages*[48] the growth of cities, since ancient times, has been associated with destructive exploitation of their peripheries. It has been this that repeatedly has resulted in the collapse of civilizations, with recurring "dark ages." This pattern is repeating itself on a global scale, facilitated by the illusions generated by the commodification of land, labor and money, with the peripheries of the world being the location of the greatest ecological destruction. If this is the case, what is required is struggle by the peripheries, wherever they are, to prevent this exploitation by the core zones of the world economy and those dominating these core zones. In so doing, they will take away from the power elites their means of domination. To achieve, this, limits can be placed on ownership and the extent of markets, ensuring ownership and the benefits of economic activity are local. For instance, absentee land ownership can be made illegal, and there can be limits to how much land is owned, as in Kerala in India. This is particularly important in preventing core zones of the world economy from monopolizing the use of land in peripheries, resulting in the starvation of people in the peripheries, as happened in India after Britain came to dominate it, in Ireland during the potato famine, and in twentieth-century Africa, as Susan George described in *How the Other Half Die*.[49] However, it is also important to limit the core zones' power by limiting their access to natural resources, for instance, by nationalizing mineral resources.

The proposals of Daly and Cobb and Vatn to limit trade, and the proposals of Daly and Cobb to defend small family farms along with local communities, would seem to be the most promising path to the future, although the form of farm cooperatives developed in Denmark should also be promoted. Situated in a broader context, this, I believe, is the essence of the quest for an ecological civilization: a world order of communities of communities, each constrained to function in a way that augments the conditions for the other communities on which it is dependent. This could be characterized as a multi-level federalism, reminiscent of the democratic federalism called for by Peter Kropotkin. It also: (1) concurs with the view of the future of some radical proponents of ecological civilization in China, particularly under the regime of Hu Jintao and Wen Jiabao; (2) concurs with the idea of earth democracy proposed by Vandana Shiva;[50] and (3) overlaps with the idea of inclusive democracy of Fotopoulos.[51] However, more work is required to show what this entails.

Such a world order would be much more complex than implied by anarchists or libertarian socialists, who tend to underestimate the contribution of large-scale organizations in making local communities possible. Unless there is a complete collapse of civilization, the globalizing processes that have created a global order are irreversible. What is required does not involve simply falling back to earlier, simpler socio-economic forms and ways of life. It involves a more complex form of organized decentralization that will have to give a place to differentiated markets of various kinds and large bureaucracies, while fostering genuine democracy at local levels able to control these markets and bureaucracies. We need to create markets and bureaucracies not deluded by the fetish of commodities and the pseudo-commodities of land, labor, and money, and which instead of measuring progress in monetary terms, uphold as the goal of communities the flourishing of life. These will be markets and bureaucracies working to augment rather than to undermine democracy. It is not a matter of local democracy or globalization, but a form of globalization designed to replace the new world order of neoliberalism and transnational corporations by advancing multileveled democracies of communities of communities. The organizations associated with the United Nations are examples of the broader bureaucracies required; the administration of Swiss cantons is a good example of good local government. However, a democratic world order will require citizens whose potential is far more developed than at present. It will require citizens educated to understand and feel viscerally that they are participants in the creative becoming of civilization, humanity, and the global ecosystem. This will involve a development of culture.

Regaining the Autonomy of Cultural Fields

This raises the problem of how to reform or create the institutions that can generate such a high level of culture. It is here that Bourdieu's work on institutions and their formation is particularly important. This is particularly problematic as the institutions associated with the media and education which were central to the development of this culture have been subverted by neoliberals, transforming universities into transnational business corporations, transforming science into little more than means to develop the technology that will enable corporations to make profits, and corrupting science. As Al Gore has argued, hope lies in the development of the Internet. The development of the worldwide web, and the use it has been put to by intellectuals and the general public was unanticipated. However, it has enabled communication and searches for truth, websites such as *Wikileaks* and *Skeptical Science,* and open access journals that have been enormously important for the future of civilization. It opens the possibility of recreating Humboldtian forms of universities in localities all around the world, utilizing what is available online, including lectures from top universities. It is these communities that soon could and should enable local communities to form outside the large cities without being cut off from intellectual life. Ultimately, it should provide the infrastructure for a global culture that inspires and is inspired by the quest for a global ecological civilization.[52] However, what is required above all is a new global grand narrative with a vision of the future that can inspire people to struggle to achieve it, and while being global, can orient people in their particular circumstances. The vision of the future that is most promising is that of an ecological civilization, based on Daly and Cobb's notion of communities of communities, extended to recognize ecosystems of which people are part as also communities, the life of which they should augment with their own lives and ways of living.[53]

Endnotes

1. P. Mirowski and D. Plehwe, eds., *The Road from Mont Pèlerin: The Making of the Neoliberal Thought Collective* (Cambridge: Harvard University Press, 2009).

2. Q. Slobodian, *Globalists: The End of Empire and the Birth of Neoliberalism* (Cambridge: Harvard University Press, 2018).

3. S. M. Amadae, *Rationalizing Capitalist Democracy* (Chicago: University of Chicago Press, 2003); *Prisoners of Reason: Game Theory and Neoliberal Political Economy* (Cambridge University Press, 2016).

4. K. Polanyi *The Great Transformation* (Boston: Beacon, 1957), ch. 6.

5. T. Fotopoulos, *Towards an Inclusive Democracy* (London: Cassell, 1997).

6. C. B. McPherson, *The Political Theory of Possessive Individualism* (Oxford: Oxford University Press, 1962); Quentin Skinner, *Hobbes and Republican Liberty* (Cambridge: Cambridge University Press, 2008).

7. As convincingly argued by R. M. Young in *Darwin's Metaphor: Nature's Place in Victorian Culture* (Cambridge: Cambridge University Press, 1985).

8. W. Lippmann, *Public Opinion* (New York: Harcourt, Brace & Co. 1922).

9. F. A. Hayek, *Law, Legislation and Liberty, Volume 2, The Mirage of Social Justice* (Chicago: University of Chicago Press, 1976.

10. Slobodian, *Globalists*, 20.

11. W. Streeck, *Buying Time: The Delayed Crisis of Democratic Capitalism*, trans. P. Camiller and D. Fernbach (London: Verso, 2014), 56f.

12. R. Gordon, "Does the 'New Economy' Measure Up to the Great

Inventions of the Past?" *Journal of Economic Perspectives* 14.4 (Fall 2000): 49–74.

13. T. Piketty, *Capital in the Twenty-First Century,* trans. Arthur Goldhammer (Cambridge, MA: Belknap Press, 2014).

14. S. H. Hymer, *The Multinational Corporation: A Radical Approach: Papers by Stephen Hymer* (Cambridge: Cambridge University Press, 1979).

15. D. C. Korten, *When Corporations Rule the World*, 2nd ed (Bloomfield, CT: Kumarian Press, 2001).

16. W. I. Robinson, *A Theory of Global Capitalism: Production, Class, and State in a Transnational World* (Baltimore: John Hopkins University Press, 2004).

17. P. Bourdieu, *Acts of Resistance: Against the Tyranny of the Market,* trans. R. Nice (New York: The New Press, 1998), 11ff.

18. D. Harvey, *A Brief History of Neoliberalism* (Oxford: Oxford University Press, 2007).

19. T. Fotopoulos, *The New World Order in Action Volume 1, Globalization, the Brexit Revolution and the 'Left' – Towards a Democratic Community of Sovereign Nations,* 2nd ed. (San Diego: Progressive Press, 2016), 29.

20. A. Vatn, *Institutions and the Environment* (Cheltenham, UK: Edward Elgar, 2005).

21. P. Bourdieu, *The Social Structures of the Economy,* trans. Chris Turner (Cambridge, UK: Polity, 2005).

22. P. Bourdieu and Loïc J. D. Wacquant, *An Invitation to Reflexive Sociology* (Chicago: University of Chicago Press, 1992) 114.

23. Vatn, *Institutions and the Environment*, 231.

24. R. N. Adams, *Energy and Structure: A Theory of Social Power* (Austin: University of Texas Press, 1975).

25. S. G. Bunker, *Underdeveloping the Amazon: Extraction, Unequal Exchange, and the Failure of the Modern State* (Chicago: University of Chicago Press, 1988).

26. A. Hornborg, *The Power of the Machine: Global Inequalities of Economy, Technology, and Environment* (Walnut Creek, CA: Altamira Press, 2001); *Global Ecology and Unequal Exchange: Fetishism in a Zero-Sum World* (Oxford: Routledge, 2013).

27. A. E. Gare, "Is it Possible to Create an Ecologically Sustainable World Order: The Implications of Hierarchy Theory for Human Ecology," *International Journal of Sustainable Development and World Ecology* 7.4 (December 2000): 277–90.
28. A. Gare, "Toward an Ecological Civilization: The Science, Ethics, and Politics of Eco-Poiesis," *Process Studies* 39.1 (2010): 5–38.
29. T. Prugh, R. Costanza, and H. Daly, *The Local Politics of Global Sustainability* (Washington: DC: Island Press, 2000).
30. E. Ostrom, *Governing the Commons: The Evolution of Institutions for Collective Action* (Cambridge: Cambridge University Press, 1990).
31. L. Lessig, *Free Culture* (New York: Penguin, 2004); *Republic, Lost: How Money Corrupts Congress – and a Plan to Stop It* (New York: Hachette Book Group, 2012).
32. H. P. Minsky, *Stabilizing an Unstable Economy* (New York: McGraw Hill, 2008).
33. L. R. Wray, "The Great Crash of 2007 Viewed Through The Perspective of Veblen's *Theory of the Business Enterprise*, Keynes's Monetary Theory of Production and Minsky's Financial Instability Hypothesis," in E. S. Reinert and F. L. Viano, *Thorstein Veblen: Economics for an Age of Crises* (London: Anthem Press, 2012), ch.14.
34. D. Graeber, *Debt: The First 5,000 Years* (Brooklyn, NY: Melville House, 2011).
35. H. P. Minsky, *Stabilizing an Unstable Economy* (New York: McGraw Hill, 2008).
36. N. Stern, *A Blueprint for a Safe Planet: How We Can Save the World and Create Prosperity* (London: Vintage, 2010), 6.
37. K. Mayumi, *The Origins of Ecological Economics* (London: Routledge, 2001), 125.
38. M. Amato and L. Fantacci, *The End of Finance* (Cambridge, UK: Polity Press, 2012) 225.
39. T. H. Greco, Jr, *The End of Money and the Future of Civilization* (Edinburgh: Floris Books, 2010).
40. A. Hornborg, *Nature, Society and Justice in the Anthropocene: Unravelling the Money-Energy-Technology Complex* (Cambridge: Cambridge University Press, 2019).
41. C. S. Bajo and B. Roelants, *Capital and the Debt Trap: Learning from*

Cooperatives in the Global Crisis (London: Palgrave Macmillan, 2011).

42. J. Bakan, *The Corporation: The Pathological Pursuit of Profit and Power* (New York: Free Press, 2004).

43. J. K. Galbraith, *The New Industrial State* (Harmondsworth, UK: Penguin, 1968).

44. D. Sturm, *Solidarity and Suffering: Toward a Politics of Relationality* (New York: SUNY Press, 1998), 145.

45. Fotopoulos, *Towards an Inclusive Democracy*; A. Gare, Review of Takis Fotopoulos, *Towards an Inclusive Democracy*, in *Review of Radical Political Economics* 34.1 (Winter 2002), 97–99; R. Hahnel, *Economic Justice and Democracy: From Competition to Cooperation* (New York: Routledge, 2005).

46. Daly and Cobb, *For the Common Good*, 109.

47. R. B. Norgaard, *Development Betrayed: The End of Progress and aCoevolutionary Revisioning of the Future* (London: Routledge, 1994).

48. S. C. Chew, *The Recurring Dark Ages: Ecological Stress, Climate Changes, and System Transformation* (Lanham, MD: Rowman & Littlefield, 2007).

49. S. George, *How the Other Half Die: The Real Reasons for World Hunger*, 2nd ed. (Harmondsworth, UK: Penguin, 1977).

50. V. Shiva, "Earth Democracy," in *New Socialisms: Futures Beyond Globalization*, ed. R. Albritton, S. Bell, J. R. Bell and R. Westra (London: Routledge, 2004); and *Earth Democracy: Justice, Sustainability, and Peace* (Cambridge, MA: South End Press, 2005).

51. Fotopoulos, *Towards an Inclusive Democracy*.

52. A. Gare, *The Philosophical Foundations for Ecological Civilization: A Manifesto for the Future* (London: Routledge, 2017).

53. Gare, "Toward an Ecological Civilization."

TEN

A Jurisprudence for Human Homeostasis with Nature

Charles Walter

HISTORICALLY, SCIENCE INCLUDES the social sciences and the natural sciences, and the natural sciences include the life sciences and the physical sciences. The scientific method,[1] which Galileo designed for use in the physical sciences, is limited by the fact that there could be many possible similar (ὅμοιος) physical systems with a logical form (μορφή) sufficiently similar that data obtained from the one cannot be used to eliminate the homeomorphisms.[2] For this reason, the scientific method is limited to falsifying hypotheses within confidence limits dictated by experimental error, and it cannot confirm that any hypothesis is correct. This empirical limitation on science itself imposes a criterion of demarcation into inductive logic that is inconsistent with its requirement that all the meaningful statements of empirical science must be capable of being *conclusively verifiable* with respect to their falsity *and* truth.[3] In order to avoid this inconsistency, the scientific method used by many scientists loosens the "conclusively verifiable" requirement to statements of systems capable of being refuted by experience[4] founded on common sense through philosophy, and the philosophy of science, rather than inductive or deductive logic.[5] This commonsense approach is widely used in life sciences where reproducibility is unlikely even between seemingly identical living organisms, and experimental error is therefore likely to be enormous. Popper identified this difference as the "common sense clash" between determinism and indeterminism.[6] This choice dates back at least to Epicurus who wrote to Memeceus, "It would have been better to remain attached to the belief in gods rather than being slaves to the fate of the physicists."[7] Now that physics has begun to recognize that living systems are *nonholonomic*,[8] the end of certainty[9] freed the philosophers from their "tragic choice between an alienating science or an antiscientific philosophy" between which no comprise proved to be satisfactory.[10]

Goal

There is no doubt that, in due course, any life remaining on Earth will become extinct due to global warming as our sun swells into a red giant. However, if human activity is contributing sufficiently to global warming that halting such activity would delay extinction; *premature extinction* can be avoided by halting such activity. So the ongoing global warming debate is about how to falsify the hypothesis "Human activity is contributing sufficiently to global warming that halting it will delay premature extinction." This is clearly a hypothesis involving life and is, therefore, not subject to the conclusive verification required by the scientific method. However, it is capable of being refuted by experience founded on common sense through philosophy and the philosophy of science, rather than inductive or deductive logic.

Four facts stand out:

(a) Global warming is happening.

(b) Human activities that might be a substantial cause have been identified.

(c) During the last hundred years we were "carrying out a large-scale geophysical experiment of a kind that could not have happened in the past nor be reproduced in the future."[11]

(d) The commonsense way to assess the effect of doing something is to stop doing it.

Therefore, the commonsense verification of the human activity hypothesis is to stop the human activities and determine whether abatement is sufficient to justify abandoning them forever. The alternative is to continue to return to the atmosphere the concentrated organic carbon stored in sedimentary rocks over hundreds of millions of years as fossils, during which, if global warming continues, we will never know whether our extinction was premature.

This chapter identifies some additional human activities that might be causing global warming now, followed by some principles for an integral jurisprudence that would provide the legal framework for remedying them.

New Human Biological Characteristics

Anthropologists accept as a biological fact that about 50,000 years ago *Homo sapiens* exhibited numerous new biological characteristics based on newly evolved cultural foundations and cognitive abilities. An important development is language and its use as a nonholonomic restraint on cultural dynamics. Peirce's triadic theory is a philosophical concept postulating the unique nature of language as a space-time process involving symbols, symbol users, and referents and is consistent with the notion that macromolecular coding is a prime candidate for nonholonomic constraints at life's lowest levels of abstraction. Lefebvre's application of triadic theory to introreflexive processes for a physician's psychiatric evaluations of a patient, ethical analysis, and resolving international disputes, and his ingenuous use of iconic calculus and polynomials to represent teleogenic processes such as free will illustrates the use of language as nonholonomic constraints at these higher levels of abstraction.

Here are four additional examples of our "new" biological characteristics:

Extensive help and cooperation beyond close kin is important because it is essential for the unified action necessary for a worldwide, integral jurisprudence. It begins at the intra-community level, when the community response to a member in need is to provide social security and basic needs, and it grows outward to include inter-community resource distribution and worldwide cooperation necessary for global peace and harmony. Failure to use the biological advantages of this process has led to increasing conflict between communities, war, and damage to nature.

Cumulative cultural adaptation facilitates extension of help and cooperation to other communities. In a community-based global environment, it promotes understanding of the needs of other cultures and inter-community trade.

Cooperative breeding promotes intra-community harmony such as the indigenous concept of relative-by-choice ("hunka-parent") used when over-protectiveness of natural parents may hinder an adolescence's passage into adulthood.

Technology, because it requires consumption of new "fixes."

Now, 30,000 years after our ascendance over the Neanderthals with these new biological characteristics, we find ourselves having bypassed life "becoming" (as simple nonholonomic organisms and superorganisms), ending "being" (as incredibly complex nonholonomic tribes and societies), and facing premature extinction.

There is a need to realign ourselves with biology and that "arrow of time" upon which all forms of life ride. To understand and maintain sustainability with nature, we must accept that nature is the mistress and life is her harlequin servant, a *disystem* comprised of self-executing dynamical systems obeying the laws of physics coupled synergistically with "irreversible" systems that restrain physics into the quasi-stable organism biologists call "life." To create an integral jurisprudence for sustainability, we must take care of nature first, then look for life's justice and rewards. We must rely on our intuition and commonsense experience; we must accept that the stakes are too high to fret about "fairness" at nature's expense; that time will tell and not vice-versa.

Homeostasis: Understanding What Life Is

It is apparent that meaningful statements about a biological organism may not be verifiable or even reproducible. This is because individual organisms within a population may vary both from apparently identical members of a population and also individually from time to time. So biologists search for intra- and inter-hierarchal commonality and use variance differently than physicists. Such commonality is used as the basis of conjectures that may be used in proposing fundamental facts and processes of biology. A necessary condition for a workable integral jurisprudence supporting a sustainable relationship between nature and humans is a jurisprudence that is not inconsistent with the fundamental facts of nature and the laws of physics.

A fundamental fact of nature is that all life depends on homeostasis and ends without it. Homeostasis is the maintenance of the stream of matter that biologists call an "organism." All living systems need resources to maintain homeostasis. When homeostasis fails, disease and ultimately death follows. To maintain homeostasis, energy is mobilized as work to reduce physiological fluxes (P) lost through thermodynamically favored fluxes (T). Living systems persist because they tend to satisfy $T + P = 0$. The living Earth population is a communion of human and all other Earth organisms with which we share nature. Since homeostasis exists at every level of biological organisms, from the cellular and eukaryotic to the ecologic and biospheric, we must interact synergistically with other organisms to maintain the dynamic orderliness that is characteristic of life. Therefore, homeostasis exists between humans and nature if we sustain nature synergistically, and our continued existence requires that we use nature in such a manner that the Earth's resources are not depleted or permanently damaged. In other words, a necessary condition for sustainability of the Earth's resources is homeostasis between us and nature. An integral jurisprudence supporting a sustainable relationship between nature and us must require homeostasis of that relationship to avoid its death and human extinction.

Another fundamental fact of nature is that the cell is the basic unit of all forms of life on Earth, and therefore of all organisms. Individual cells developed at the beginning of life on Earth, continued to exist in homeostasis with Earth as the basic unit of life by arising only from preexisting cells, and will no longer exist when homeostasis is no longer sustained by nature's resources.

A closely related fact of nature is that all organisms contain their own descriptions. In single cells, DNA contains a description of its cell, and at all higher hierarchal levels there exists a symbol system, syntactical rules for combining symbols into interpretable statements, and a mechanism for writing, reading, and executing such statements.[12] These writing and reading mechanisms require totally different constraints on the metabolic dynamical processes.[13] Since these physical laws are self-executing, they require no outside enforcement and can ordinarily be represented with differential equations.[14] However, the semantic descriptions require specific rules that provide *nonholonomic* constraints on them. In species with bilateral brains, the existence of such nonholonomic restraints, coupled synergistically with the self-executing dynamical processes, is sufficient for a teleogenic *disystem* comprising "fast" reversible processes obeying the self-executing laws coupled with dissipative processes restraining them. This is sufficient for consciousness, cognition, and teleogenic natural intelligence.[15] Disystems persist at more complex levels of social biology such as dispute resolution,[16] telogenesis,[17] legal reasoning,[18] legal language,[19] and other creative cognitive[20] processes at all higher levels of biology. There is no mystery to life, no need for metaphysics or speculation to explain its *becoming*, *being*, and *extinction*. The natural incorporation of nonholonomic restraint on physics is sufficient to explain all organisms in the universe.

Since a living organism's system is nonholonomic, many of its system parameters are hidden or out of control. As a result, the state of such a system is better described by a domain of points rather than a single state-space point, which suggests the use of fuzzy sets[21] and the theory of possibility for the analysis.[22] The S-Lagrandian dynamics applied to social group evolution indicates linear and despotic dominance hierarchies depending on the differences between individuals in coping with stress with leadership roles assumed by individuals who more readily cope with stress.[23] However, even this ingenuous approach to nonholonomic biological systems requires assumptions that may not apply, especially in highly nonlinear regions.[24]

Sociobiology and Process Philosophies

The American pioneer of sociobiology and preeminent myrmecologist, William Morton Wheeler, brought the concept of homeostasis explicitly into sociobiology in his famous 1911 essay "The Ant Colony as an Organism," wherein he stated, "the insect colony or society may be regarded as ... a living whole bent on preserving its integrity."[25] During the period before Alfred North Whitehead joined the Harvard faculty in 1924, Wheeler was Professor of Economic Entomology in the prestigious Bussey Institute at Harvard elaborating on connections between experimental biology, metaphysics, and philosophy, including geologist James Hutton's notion of "superorganisms" as ecological communities in which every organism existed as a member of an extended community and was dependent upon it.[26] Meanwhile, Whitehead and Bertrand Russell were engaged with the impossible task[27] of describing a set of axioms and inference rules in symbolic logic with which all mathematical proofs could be proven.[28]

In 1929, as biology was experiencing renewed interest in speculation about the connections between experiment, metaphysics, and philosophy, Whitehead produced a handwritten manuscript in conjunction with his 1927-8 Gifford Lectures which he termed "The Philosophy of Organism."

The content of these lectures, which uses emergent sociobiological terminology to describe a philosophical cosmology that basically builds upon and universalizes the speculative biology of the first part of the twentieth century, resulted in Whitehead's magnum opus, *Process and Reality: An Essay in Cosmology*, first published a year later by Macmillan in the United States and Cambridge in England, and as a "corrected edition" fifty years later.[29] After Whitehead joined the Harvard faculty in 1924, he referred to Professor Wheeler as "the only man he had ever known who would have been both worthy and able to sustain a conversation with Aristotle."[30] This convergence between Wheeler's thoughts and Whitehead's late metaphysics has been a neglected chapter in the history of ideas.[31]

Wheeler's magnum opus, *Ants: Their Structure, Development, and Behavior* describes his observed behavior of the world's most widely studied eusocial animal.[32] This magnificent work spans the entirety of biological science, starting with sound experiment, extending through speculative metaphysics, and gestating in the cosmology of living organisms. And throughout the journey, it is pregnant with ideas found in Whitehead's process philosophy of organism. Examples include Wheeler's characterization of an organism as "a continual flux or process rather than a thing or a concept," his recognition of "symbiotic relationships," and his comparisons of biological entities from cellular organisms to human societies.

Differences between Whitehead's process philosophy of organism and Wheeler's philosophical biology existed in areas related to the origin of human feelings, thought processes, metaphysical beliefs, etc. For example, in his Gifford Lectures, Whitehead compared Hume's "'make-believe' character of modern empiricism"—wherein "sensation" arises in the soul from unknown causes—and "reflection" through the eyes as a color." Years later he wrote, "The first principle of epistemology should be that the changeable, shifting aspects of our relations to nature are the primary topics for conscious observation."[33] We can observe how a dog tracks by smell, but don't "know" how a dog "perceives" its world versus of what they are "aware," only that it solved a problem in a more or less reliable manner. On the other hand, Wheeler's distinction between instinctive and plastic behavior[34] illustrates a central question of ontology for philosophers for over two thousand years, what Epicurus had referred to as remaining "attached to the belief in gods rather than being slaves to the fate of the physicists,"[35] and what Popper later referred to as a "common sense clash" between determinism and indeterminism,[36] and Prigogine referred to as Whitehead's "tragic choice between an alienating science or an antiscientific philosophy."[37] To biologist Wheeler the "formal" definition of "instinct" was "a mass of obscurities," "a caricature from the theological dust-bin"[38]; "plasticity" was an organism's "ontological experience (*'historische Reaktionbasis'*) . . . commonly designated as 'intelligence'"[39]; and "the old Thomistic dogmas concerning the nature of the human soul" of no concern.[40]

Now postmodern science provides the means for understanding how this choice is related to the meaning of time, and that the "arrow of time" is not because imperfect human observers are responsible for differences between past and future through approximations they introduce through their description of nature.[41] An important goal for Whitehead was to treat existence as a process.[42] Bergson intuited that "human existence" was a process of continual creation of unpredictable novelty[43]; Prigogine described the spatialization of time itself as incompatible with both the evolving universe and our own human experience.[44] Prigogine believed that the process of "becoming" is the *sine qua non* of the existence of science, of knowledge itself, and that science is the process of a dialogue between humankind and nature.[45] Attempts to understand nature should not be identified with the idea of control, because "what can be controlled is never completely real, and what is real can never be completely controlled."[46] In short, biology itself comprises dynamical processes operating on a time scale dictated by the laws of physics restrained by a synergistically coupled process that is "irreversible" on that time scale. Complex nonholonomic biological processes such as consciousness, empathy, natural intelligence, etc. potentially exist at every level of biological complexity from an isolated single cell to the most complex living thing in the universe.

Sustainability

A jurisprudence upon which the sustainability of the Earth's resources is based requires a clear definition of sustainability; namely, that the Earth's resources are used in such a way that the resources are not depleted or permanently damaged. Five hundred years ago, when the human population was at levels compatible with the Earth's resources, the people of the North American Iroquois Nation understood the need to look out "for the welfare of the whole people, not only the present, but the coming generations, even those whose faces are yet beneath the surface of the ground—the unborn of the future Nation."[47] This philosophy was so widespread in Native American indigenous cultures that it generated the proverb, "We did not inherit the earth from our parents, we are borrowing it from our children." This and other indigenous people knew that nature is the mistress, and life is its harlequin servant.

Serious recognition of our threat to nature begins at the end of the nineteenth century with Svante Arrhenius's hypothesis that sustainability is related to atmospheric carbon dioxide content[48] and his conclusion that the arctic region temperature would rise about 80–90° C if carbonic acid increased to 2.5 to 3 times its 1896 value.[49] Based on the assumption that nearly all the carbon dioxide produced from combustion of fossil fuels extracted from the earth by 1940 remained in the atmosphere,[50] it was suggested that carbon dioxide can influence weather.[51] Fifteen years later, based on the assumption that much of the carbon dioxide produced from combustion of fossil fuels during the Industrial Revolution was absorbed in the ocean, it was suggested that carbon dioxide may pose a significant threat during future decades if industrial combustion continued to rise exponentially.[52] Nevertheless, rather than using established means to create carbon-free fuels, we carried out an untested, dangerous, large-scale geophysical experiment that put us in danger of premature extinction. Fossil fuels—coal, natural gas, and petroleum—were extracted on a massive scale from the Earth's interior, while well-known, inexpensive production of carbon-free fuels was stymied by the financial and political interests of the fossil fuel industry. During the period 1949–2011, our combustion of petroleum, coal, and natural gas in engines, furnaces, appliances, and other devices added over a quarter of a trillion metric tons of carbon dioxide to the Earth's atmosphere.[53] During this period, interests promoting global economic growth, fossil fuel extraction, and its accelerated degradation of biodiversity by carbon dioxide emissions, led to ostensibly free markets that undermined the global need to harmonize prosperity with ecology. Neoliberal interests[54] enlisted the United Nations to create a World Commission on Environment and Development (WCED) to support an unhampered market economy that would not harm the environment. After identifying sustainability problems worldwide, WCED redefined economic development as "sustainable development," and "sustainable development" as "the kind of development that meets the needs of the present without compromising the ability of future generations to meet their own needs" only to find its own definition of sustainable development oxymoronic.[55]

In 2013 a cartoon depicted the frequency of the word *sustainable* as a percentage of all words used in U.S. English texts during the previous fifty years. It then extrapolated that figure into the future and suggested that by the year 2109 the word *sustainable* would itself be unsustainable. That is, all sentences would comprise just the word *sustainable* repeated over and over. Thus, we already live in an age of *sustainababble,* "a cacophonous profusion of uses of the word sustainable to mean anything from environmentally better to cool," where everything we do, buy, and use will go on forever.[56]

Of course, we know it won't, no matter what we do. Eventually, perhaps about a billion years from now, the sun's current phase of development will end; it will swell into a red giant, and the Earth will become too hot for any form of life. But it is unlikely that any species extant today will survive until this natural extinction a billion years hence, because, of the estimated four billion species to have evolved during the last 3.5 billion years, four hundred million are now extinct. Paleontologists believe that during the most recent 540 million years, the Earth has experienced five "mass extinctions," during which at least three-quarters of existing species were lost during relatively short geological intervals. During the hundred million years between "mass extinctions" many species will not survive the continuous natural "background" extinctions or even natural selection.

In an early publication, in which he explores the philosophies and technologies that have brought humankind to the tragic end of nature as a force independent of us, Bill McKibben suggests that these incomprehensible dimensions of geologic time and space obscure the fact that nothing happens quickly.[57] Sixteen years later, he concludes that the key environmental fact in 1989 was the contrast between the pace at which the physical world was changing and the pace at which we reacted to its impact; specifically, in the need for population control ("smaller families"), for reduced consumption, and for stronger, tighter communities.[58]

Is it too late now? How much can we delay premature extinction by using nature in a sustainable manner? Since current estimates are that only 4.7 billion people could live within the Earth's current ecological limits without reducing their consumption, the current world population of 7.6 billion is consuming over 1.5 Earths every day. Based on our projected growth during the next five generations, we will be consuming 2.0 Earths in 2040 and 2.5 Earths by 2118. At best, we have condemned future generations to share the planet's ecological limits with an over-populated Earth due to dissipative technologies and social organizations that harm nature with increasing climate instability for hundreds, perhaps thousands of years. At worst, it may be too late. It is possible that we will become extinct before the end of this century.[59] Indeed, although "the time has arrived to prepare for the consequences of unsustainability, even while we refuse to give up the effort, however quixotic, to shift to true sustainability on some reasonable schedule," it may already be too late."[60] This is a political crime committed by us against nature for which we have no name, no jurisprudence, no justice; if we -try to avoid premature extinction, we must act decisively and create an effective integral jurisprudence to support sustainability.

Jurisprudential Options

A preview of effective governance during a terrifying forced departure from normal resources occurred when shortages were imposed by foreign governments on the entire population of Cuba for political reasons.[61] Fortunately, the hard work of the Cuban people, together with centralized governmental controls, maintained homeostasis with nature.

Unlike the small island of Cuba, in order to avoid premature extinction of the entire human population, an effective jurisprudence supporting a return to sustainability and homeostasis and their maintenance must apply *worldwide* because nature has no boundaries. In order to sustain the Earth's resources, coupled with existing technology and social organization R, a worldwide jurisprudence would have to limit the Earth's entire population P to a number where:

$$R \geq \sum r_i P \quad i = 1, 2, ..., n,$$

Equation 1

r_1 is the fraction of R used by each of n members of population P. Only the currently available resources are known, but R will continue to decrease due to dissipative technologies and social organizations that harm nature, or R could increase due to technological development or social organization that is synergistic with nature. For example, photosynthetic biochemical pathways that have used sunlight to reduce water to molecular hydrogen for over a billion years with zero net production of carbon dioxide could be used to replace natural gas and to fuel coal and petroleum machines. Photosynthetic bacteria from the genus *Rhodopseudomonas* use a simple, three-step process comprising (1) ordinary photosynthesis, (2) heterotrophic fermentation and (3) photosynthetic hydrogen production. There is no net production of CO_2 because the overall reaction is simply $2H_2O \rightarrow 2H_1 + O_2$. The solar energy converted by this photosynthetic process operating at maximum efficiency is approximately $3 \times 10^9 BTU/acre$.[62] Alternatively, green algae from the *Chlamydomonas* genus, such as *C. reinhardi*, yield simultaneous hydrogen and oxygen production in molar ratios close to the theoretical value of 2 to 1, which may result in an even more efficient use of solar energy.

Using molecular hydrogen instead of carbon-containing fuels is important because the only product of hydrogen oxidation is water: $2H_2 + O_2 \rightarrow 2H_2O$. As a consequence, there has been substantial interest in hydrogen-fueled vehicles for at least two hundred years.[63] In 1972, a Gremlin with a cryogenic hydrogen-containing fuel tank was developed at the University of California at Los Angeles and the Los Alamos Scientific Lab in Los Alamos, New Mexico. It carried a 351-cubic inch Ford Boss engine and had no tailpipe emissions except water vapor.[64] U.S. Patent 384426A discloses an open cycle combustion engine using oxygen and hydrogen as fuel in a combination chamber. After being mixed with a surplus gas, it expels only the water of combustion.[65]

Methods for implementing worldwide governmental power to deal with global warming and other threats to industrialization include *centralization, strong* (direct) *democracy,* and various forms in between.

Advocates of centralization prescribe it "as the only means by which our threatened and dangerous civilization will make way for [future generations]."[66] The obvious advantage is that centralization of power (at least temporarily) eliminates friction caused by democratic debate. The obvious problems are that the extent to which power must be centralized depends on self-discipline, and the performance of highly controlled governments is not encouraging for long emergencies.[67] Neither economic development based on consumption in western neo-democratic capitalist republics nor eastern Marxist dictatorships based on constructive postmodernism have delivered sustainability, because governance for real sustainability and successful degrowth depend on their taking responsibility and making tough choices.[68]

Various other forms of jurisprudence have been suggested. One, for example, uses the power of markets and technological innovation to avoid government regulation; another would use the emergence of national and global networks abetted by the internet and advancing communication technology.[69]

In order to survive long emergencies, a worldwide government would have to have strict *rules of law* to ensure *fairness* and *justice* to protect individuals and minorities from tyranny: whether *autocratic tyranny*, in the case of centralized governments, or *democratic tyranny* in the case of strong democracies. In order to escape the autocratic tyranny of an English king, the strong democracy once proposed by Thomas Jefferson and John Dewey granted ultimate power to "we the people" in the U.S. Constitution, while denying them any such power or even much access to it. Advocates claim the problem is not that we're too democratic; it is that we're not democratic enough.[70]

The alternative to a centralization of power with extremely strong rules of law is a strong direct democracy also with extremely strong rules of law. In either case, the rules of law must have the support of a worldwide population of engaged, thoughtful citizens operating in a properly structured setting that facilitates knowledge about societal options.[71]

A jurisprudence supporting a return to homeostasis with nature must be a comprehensive instrument that is democratically approved by the entire Earth population and that governs our use of nature. This would be a single Earth Constitution for a diverse but unified "Earth society" of n people. (*See Equation 1.*) It would be facilitated by a single, iconic Earth language, a single measuring system used by all, etc.

A Proposed Jurisprudence: Constitutional Provisions and Enabling Statutes

Any worldwide jurisprudence designed to facilitate our survival must recognize that nature's remedy for damage caused by exceeding R in Equation 1 is to reduce P. As described previously, only 4.7 billion people can live within the Earth's current ecological limits without reducing their consumption; the current world population of 7.6 billion is consuming over 1.5 Earths every day. Based on our projected growth, we'll be consuming two Earths in 2040 and 2.5 Earths by 2118. Thus, the jurisdiction proposed here *must* incorporate the biological fact that, unless nature halves our population immediately, or we reduce our consumption by half, we comprise a competitive disystem with nature that inevitably leads to our extinction while nature survives. In order for us to survive, we require a synergistic disystem with nature in control and us as its slave. Do we wish for our children and grandchildren to survive? If so, our science and jurisprudence must focus not only on how nature creates competitive disystems that lead to our extinction, but also if there are ways that nature permits synergy to exist, and, if so, how this synergy can be used to benefit both parties in our disystem. Plainly, if we compete with nature, either by force or by choice, we will not survive long. Nature will not hesitate to cause billions of deaths to save itself. Indeed, history shows that it cannot do otherwise.

A contribution to the 2017 Whitehead conference in the Section on "Whitehead, Mathematics, and Logic" describes some of the ways nature provides otherwise competitive disystems that can evolve naturally into synergistic disystems. For example, when there is a sequence of metabolic events:

$$X_1 \rightarrow X_2 \rightarrow \ldots \rightarrow X_i \rightarrow \ldots \rightarrow X_n$$

Equation 2

The final step to X_n may be required to control the entire process. If the sequence involves viral mutations that terminate with a highly infectious, lethal X_i, the result may be a pandemic that biologists expect to be much worse that the Severe Acute Respiratory Syndrome (SARS) epidemic sixteen years ago. However, if additional natural mutations lead to a much more highly infectious but nonlethal X_n, the result could be like inoculation of smallpox by cowpox.

This chapter proposes an ecocentric worldwide jurisdiction based on the principles enacted by the citizens of Ecuador in September 2008 in their constitutional *Derechos de la naturaleza* (Rights of Nature), and by the citizens of Bolivia in their *Bolivia (Plurinational State of) Constitution of 2009* and its enabling statute *Framework Law on Mother Earth and Integral Development of Living Well* (*La Ley Marco de la Madre Tierra y Integral Desarrello para Vivir Bien*) enacted on October 15, 2012. The primary difference between the approaches used in Ecuador and Bolivia is that Ecuador established its jurisprudence rather neatly within its new constitution, whereas Bolivia wisely also created an *enabling statute* for the provisions in its new constitution. The anthropomorphic use of *Pacha Mama* in Ecuador is equivalent to *Pachamama* and *Madre Tierra* in Bolivia for *la naturaleza* and the use of *Mother Earth* for *Nature* in English.

Article 71 of the Ecuadorian Constitution boldly asserts (1) that "La naturaleza or Pacha Mama has the right to integral respect for Her existence and for the maintenance and regeneration of Her life cycles, structure, function, and evolutionary processes" and (2) gives standing to "all persons, communities, peoples and nations...to enforce the rights of Nature." The Ecuadorian State is required to "give incentives to natural persons and legal entities and to communities, to protect nature and to promote respect for all of the elements comprising an ecosystem."

Article 72 asserts that "nature has the right to be restored" and requires that "the State shall establish the most effective mechanisms to achieve the restoration and shall adopt adequate measures to eliminate or mitigate harmful environmental consequences."

Article 73 requires the Ecuadorian State to apply "preventative and restrictive measures on activities that might lead to extinction of species, the destruction of ecosystems or the permanent alteration of natural cycles."

Article 12 establishes a "human right to water" and asserts that water is an unalienable "national strategic asset for use by the public,... and essential for life."

Article 13 establishes that "persons and community groups have the right to safe and permanent access to healthy, sufficient and nutritional food" and that "the Ecuadorian State shall promote food sovereignty."

Article 14 establishes the right "to live in a healthy and ecologically balanced environment that guarantees sustainability." The Ecuadorian Constitution declares environmental conservation, the protection of ecosystems, biodiversity, the integrity of Ecuador's genetic assets, the prevention of environmental damage, and the recovery of degraded natural spaces matters of public interest.

Article 15 requires the Ecuadorian State to promote the use of environmentally clean technologies and nonpolluting sources of energy; it specifically prohibits energy sovereignty from being achieved to the detriment of food sovereignty or effect the right to water established in Article 12, and it amounts to a constitutional prohibition on the development, ownership, marketing, and use of agrochemicals, biological and nuclear weapons, pollutants, and genetically modified organisms that are harmful to human health or jeopardize the integrity of ecosystems.

Article 57 guarantees indigenous people and communities twenty-one listed collective rights including their intellectual property from all forms of appropriation.

Title I, Chapter I of the Bolivian statute establishes the purpose, scope, application, and goals of the statute in Articles 1–3. Chapter II defines the terms used in the statute and establishes seventeen principles (including the precautionary principle) that must be applied in enforcing the statute in Articles 4 and 5.

Title II deals directly with *values of living well in an alternative to capitalism* (*Valores del vivir bien como horizonte alternativo al capitalismo*) in Chapter 1, and in connection with integral development in Chapter II, and rights, obligations, and duties in Chapter III, and generally with the scope of the objective of living well in connection with integral development in Chapter IV.

Title III deals with the bases and orientation of integral development in harmony with Mother Earth.

Title IV sets forth protections and guarantees of nature's right for living well. Title V deals with the politics, tools, and institutionalization of harmony with Mother Earth.

Generally speaking, the Bolivian statute is specifically based on an integral jurisprudence wherein it is the obligation of the state and the people to use the *precautionary principle* to prevent human activities from causing extinctions and alterations of the "cycles and processes that ensure life." This means that if an action or policy has any suspected risk of causing harm, in the absence of a scientific consensus that the action or policy is not harmful, the burden of proof that it is not harmful is on those proposing the action. Title II, Chapter III, Article 10 requires the state to develop policies to protect nature from exploitation by demanding international recognition of environmental debt to nature through "financing and transfer of clean technologies that are effective and compatible with the rights of Mother Earth." In addition, Article 11 establishes an obligation for people to uphold and respect the rights of nature, to promote synergy with it, and to report violations of its rights.

The enactment of these constitutions by direct democratic vote in Ecuador and Bolivia (but not in common law jurisdictions in the western hemisphere) is a result of deep-rooted indigenous and *compesino* movements which survived the genocide of Hispanic invaders in South America, whereas the possibility for such survival in the north was exterminated by the full-scale genocide committed by northern European invaders in the United States and Canada.

Despite these democratically elected ecocentric constitutions, and despite the Bolivian enabling statute, their implementation has been severely inhibited by imperialistic global economics fueled by greed and growth. Despite attempts at worldwide governance in the League of Nations and the United Nations, there is no respite from the metastasizing effect of over-population resulting from capitalism practiced by imperial neo-democratic republics (e.g., the United States and its allies), the more centralized oligarchies (e.g., Russia and its allies), the even more centralized neo-Marxist dictatorships claiming newly-coined monikers such as "constructive" postmodernism (e.g., China and its allies), as these veto- and nuclear-armed nations capture their inequitable share of Earth resources from the growing population of indigenous people throughout the world, many of whom have maintained their homeostasis with nature. These failures to respect the laws passed by the indigenous people of Ecuador and Bolivia have stymied attempts to reestablish worldwide homeostasis with nature. Therefore, this chapter sets forth ten additional Earth Constitution provisions and enabling statutes to maintain homeostasis between *Homo sapiens* and nature.

1. A provision establishing nature's identity as the primary source of R in Equation 1, along with enabling statutes that create both criminal and civil liability for any action by any person or entity that harms nature or diminishes R, regardless of intent, with the burden of proof on the person or entity who allegedly caused the harm. The standard for the burden of proof is to reject the hypothesis "the action caused the harm" with a confidence of at least 99 percent. Additional provisions to establish the standing of nature as a legal entity with a legal right not to be harmed.

2. In addition to the Bolivian provisions and enabling statutes establishing the strong precautionary principle as a required test that must be made and passed before any action that might harm nature, provisions and enabling statutes to establish the strong precautionary principle as a required test that must be made and passed before any action that might diminish R is taken. For purposes of these provisions, the precautionary principle applies whenever knowledge is limited. Also, enabling statutes to

enact both criminal and civil liability on any person or entity who engages in any such activity that was not successfully tested by the strong precautionary principle, regardless of whether or not the action is harmful, and to create the burden of proof on those who argue that a proposed activity will not cause harm as scientifically rejecting the hypothesis "the act will cause harm" with a confidence of at least 99 percent.

3. A specific provision denying legal standing or "personhood" to corporations and other business entities in addition to the provisions establishing the standing of each person as a legal entity.

4. A specific provision requiring all expenses incurred during all elections to be authorized and paid for by the Earth government and that no such expenses shall be paid for or reimbursed by any other entity or individual in addition to the other provisions requiring various actions by the world government.

5. A specific provision establishing a common iconic language for worldwide communication intended to supplement the diversity of local languages.

6. Provisions and enabling statutes establishing the rights of each person to equal shares of R in Equation 1 as set forth by:

$$r_i = r_{i+1} \qquad i = 1, 2, ..., n-1$$

Equation 3

and enabling statutes establishing criminal and civil liability for any action that harms any person by diminishing his or her r, regardless of intent, with the burden of proof on the person who caused the harm to reject the hypothesis "the act caused harm" with a confidence in excess of 50 percent.

7. Provisions and enabling statutes establishing strict and fair governance of P in Equation 1 until it is reduced to levels supportable by R, with criminal liability for bearing a living child without authorization by the Earth government.

8. A provision prohibiting the extraction of fossil fuel from the Earth and enabling statutes making it a felony to extract fossil fuels from the Earth; also criminal liability for failing to replace current high, overconsumptive technologies with available sustainable technologies approved by the Earth government.

9. Specific provisions replacing consumptive social and economic

systems based on growth or competition with systems more closely based on our genetically evolved cultural foundations and cognitive abilities.

10. Provisions for establishing and using the metrics of sustainability and homeostasis to meet the needs of future generations, and for rapid amendment of the worldwide constitution when needed for homeostasis or sustainability.

Effect of Covid-19 Pandemics on Creating Global Jurisprudence

The enactment of the global "rule of law" required to achieve sustainability and reestablish homeostasis with nature is a binary decision for the world population to make or not make. During the presentation of this paper at the 2017 Whitehead conference, a common response was that humans would never give up national independence and be subject to global rule of law enforced by the laws of nature. Several years ago, the late Pete Seeger is reputed to have said, "If we are still here a hundred years from now, we'll be sharing." To conclude, I adopt Seeger's hope as a warning to share or cease to be.

Nature's source of energy for life on earth is solar energy. When it is absorbed by photosynthetic vegetable life that fixes carbon dioxide and reduces it into carbohydrate and molecular oxygen, the carbohydrate serves as a stable, transduced source of solar energy for animal life that converts it back to carbon dioxide. Nature's balance between vegetation and animal life is controlled by the laws of biology. Excess reduced carbon is ordinarily stored deep in the earth and excess carbon dioxide is stored in frozen tundra and the oceans. Today, the storage space is overflowing and contributing to a warming of the Earth.

A substantial amount of carbohydrate hydrogen may be reduced further into molecular hydrogen by photosynthetic microorganisms and from thence oxidized naturally into water. It is this molecular hydrogen that is available to mankind as a natural transduced source of solar energy available as a carbon-free fuel upon combustion to water. The only chemical difference between using molecular hydrogen and hydrogen carbons as fuels is that the product of hydrogen combustion cannot contain carbon dioxide. Thus, molecular hydrogen is a natural, transduced form of solar energy produced by photosynthetic microorganisms. It replaces hydrocarbons as a combustible fuel that does not produce carbon dioxide. If our society had replaced hydrocarbons with molecular hydrogen as a combustible fuel, no carbon dioxide would have been added to our atmosphere from its combustion in vehicles, for heat, or any other purpose.

Instead, nature has been notifying us of our carbon dioxide abuse for at least 125 years. How long do we have to stop the abuse before nature begins to defend itself from our "sustainababble"? Beginning with Arrhenius's warning that worldwide temperatures would rise about 8°–9° C if carbonic acid increased to 2.5 to 3 times its 1896 value, and ending with Seegers' time for sharing, the time to act was three or four generations ago. We ignored the threat when we failed to adopt molecular hydrogen as our natural, carbon-free form of transduced solar energy. We failed to act fifty years ago when neoliberal interests promoted global economic growth and fossil fuel extraction (with its accelerated degradation of biodiversity) ostensibly for free markets, but which actually undermined the global need to harmonize prosperity. Now we continue to permit these same neoliberal interests to use electricity instead of molecular hydrogen as their sustainababble transduced form of solar energy for electric cars that require batteries and are destined to further damage nature and thereby prematurely exterminate several billions of our species.

Fortunately, we know from the laws of biology that the action-delay time to reestablish homeostasis with nature during mutating viral pandemics is two or three years. During the first year of the COVID-19 pandemic, two million humans died. Is this a message from nature reminding us that it is the mistress and life is her harlequin servant? Whatever the case, it compels the world's population to establish a global rule of law to achieve sustainability and share before it is too late. Electric cars may buy us a few years until we have to protect nature from exposure to spent battery fluids. But time is clearly of the essence.

Endnotes

1. G. Galileo, *Discoursie e Dimonstrazioni Matematiche: intorno a due nuove scienze* (1638).
2. Not to be confused with "homomorphisms," the word that should be used in topology for identical forms.
3. M. Schlick, "Die Kausalität in der gegenwärtigen Physik," *Naturwissenschaften* 19 (1931): 150.
4. K. Popper, *The Open Universe: An Argument for Indeterminism* (New York: Routledge University Press, 1982), 18.
5. H. Gauch, *Scientific Method in Practice* (Cambridge: Cambridge University Press, 2003).
6. Gauch, *Scientific Method*, xix.
7. J. Barnes, *The Presocratic Philosophers* (New York: Routledge University Press, 1979).
8. H. Pattee, "Laws and Constraints, Symbols and Languages," in *Toward a Theoretical Biology*, ed. C. H. Waddington (Edinburgh: Edinburgh University Press: 1972), 248–56.
9. I. Prigogine, *The End of Certainty* (New York: Free Press, 1997).
10. Prigogine, *The End of Certainty*, 10.
11. R. Revelle and H. Suess, "Carbon Dioxide Exchange Between Atmosphere and Ocean and the Question of an Increase of Atmospheric CO_2 during the Past Decades," *Tellus* 9.1 (1957): 18–27.
12. Pattee, "Laws and Constraints, Symbols and Languages," 248–56. See also H. Pattee, "Dynamic and Linguistic Modes of Complex Systems," *International Journal of General Systems* 3 (1977): 259–66, 260.
13. Pattee, "Laws and Constraints, Symbols and Languages," 263.
14. C. Walter, "The Validity of Using a Quasi-Steady State Approximation for the Reversible Michaelis-Menten Mechanism of Enzyme Action," *Journal of Theoretical Biology* 44 (1974): 219–40; C. Walter, in *Biochemical Regulatory Mechanisms in Eukaryotic Cells*, ed. E. Kun and S. Grisolia (New York: John Wiley, 1970), 355–489; C. Walter, R. Parker, M. Ycas, "A Model for Binary Logic in Biochemical Systems," *Journal of Theoretical Biology* 15.2 (1967): 208–17; and C. Walter, "A Model for Sustained Rhythmic Binary Logic in Biochemical Systems," in *Quantitative Biology of Metabolism*, ed. A. Locker, (Cham, Germany:

Springer-Verlag Press, 1968), 38–44.

15. C. Walter, "Natural Models of Intelligence" in *Computer Power and Legal Reasoning*, ed. C. Walter (New York: West Publishers, 1985).

16. C. Walter, "The Disystem: a Fundamental Process of Nature," *Cybernetica* xxxiv no. 1 (1991): 5–21; C. Walter, "Effect of Legal Structure on International Stability" in *IFAC Proceedings* (1983).

17. C. Walter, "Teleogenic Behavior Based on Granular Control," in *Automated Analysis of Legal Texts: Logic, Informatics, Law*, ed. A. Martino and F Socci Natali (Elsevier Science Pub., 1986).

18. C. Walter, "Natural Models of Intelligence."

19. C. Walter, *Computer Power and Legal Language* (New York: Quarum Books, 1988).

20. Pattee, "Dynamic and Linguistic Modes of Complex Systems," 259–66.

21. C. Walter, "Teleogenic Behavior Based on Granular Control"; C. Walter, "Elements of Legal Language" in *Computer Power and Legal Language*, 13–19.

22. U. Sandler and L. Tsitolovsky, "The S-Lagrangian and a Theory of Homeostasis in Living Systems," *Physica A* 471 (2017): 540–53.

23. U. Sandler, "S-Lagrangian Dynamics of Many-Bodied Systems and Behavior of Social Groups: Dominance and Hierarchy Formation" *Physica A* 486 (2017): 218–41.

24. U. Sandler, "S-Lagrangian Dynamics, 225.

25. W. Wheeler, "The Ant Colony as an Organism," *J. Morphology* 22.1 (1911): 307–25

26. R. Nash, *The Rights of Nature: A History of Environmental Ethics* (Madison: University of Wisconsin Press, 1989), 59.

27. K. Gödel, "Über formal unentscheidbare Sätze der Principia Mathematica und verwanter Systeme," *Monatshefte für Matematik und Physik* 38.1 (1931): 173–98.

28. A. N. Whitehead and B. Russell, *Principia Mathematica* (Cambridge: Cambridge University Press, 1925, 1927 & 1927), 1, 2, & 3.

29. A. N. Whitehead, *Process and Reality*, Corrected Edition, ed. D. R. Griffin and D. W. Sherburne (New York: Free Press, 1978).

30. G. Parker, "Biographical Memoirs of William Morton Wheeler," *National Academy of Sciences: Biographical Memoirs* 19 (1938): 220.

31. D. Sölch, "Wheeler and Whitehead: Process Biology and Process Philosophy in the Early Twentieth Century," *J. Historical Ideas* 77.3 (2016): 489–507.
32. W. Wheeler, *Ants: Their Structure, Development, and Behavior* (New York: Columbia University Press, 1910).
33. A. N. Whitehead, *Modes of Thought* (New York: Free Press, 1968), 337.
34. Wheeler, *Ants*, 518–45.
35. Barnes, *The Presocratic Philosophers*.
36. Popper, *The Open Universe*, xix.
37. Popper, *The Open Universe*, 10.
38. Popper, *The Open Universe*, 520.
39. Popper, *The Open Universe*, 531.
40. Popper, *The Open Universe*, 351.
41. Prigogine, *The End of Certainty*, 1–7.
42. Whitehead, *Process and Reality*.
43. See H. Bergson, *l'evolution créatrice* (1927).
44. I. Prigogine, personal communication (1972); see also *The End of Certainty*, 58–59.
45. Prigogine, personal communication.
46. V. Nabokov, *Look at the Harlequins!* (New York: McGraw-Hill, 1974).
47. G. Dekanawidah, *The Great Binding Law of the Iroquois Nations* (c. 1390–1525).
48. S. Arrhenius, "On the Influence of Carbonic Acid in the Air upon the Temperature of the Ground," *Philosophical Magazine and Journal of Science* 41.5 (1896); T. Chamberlin, "An Attempt to Frame a Working Hypothesis of the Cause of Glacial Periods on an Atmospheric Basis," *Journal of Geology* 7 (1899); S. Arrhenius, *Lehrbuch der kosmischchen Physik* 2 vols. (Leipiz: Hirzel, 1903).
49. Arrhenius, *Lehrbuch der kosmischen*.
50. See G. Callendar, "The Artificial Production of Carbon Dioxide and Its Influence on Temperature," *Quarterly Journal of the Royal Meteorological Society* 64 (1938); "Variations of the Amount of Carbon Dioxide in Different Air Currents," *Quarterly Journal of the Royal Meteorological Society* 66 (1940).

51. Callendar, "The Artificial Production of Carbon Dioxide."
52. R. Revelle and H. Suess, "Carbon Dioxide Exchange Between Atmosphere and Ocean and the Question of an Increase of Atmospheric CO2 during the Past Decades," *Tellus* 9.1 (1957): 18–27.
53. U.S. Energy Information Administration (EIA) estimates for carbon dioxide emissions from energy consumption from coal, natural gas, and petroleum products.
54. Free-enterprise classical liberals such as U.S. President Ronald Reagan and British Prime Minister Margaret Thatcher.
55. Limitations imposed by the state of technology and social organization on the environment's ability to meet the needs of both present and future populations may be inadequate for intergenerational equity.
56. R. Engelman, *State of the World 2013: Is Sustainability Still Possible?* ed. E. Assadourian (Washington, DC: Island Press, 2013), 3–4.
57. B. McKibben, *The End of Nature* (New York: Random House, 1989).
58. McKibben, *The End of Nature* (2005 edition).
59. B. Barry, *Why Social Justice Matters* (Cambridge, UK: Polity Press, 2005).
60. Engelman, *State of the World 2013*, 12.
61. P. Murphy and F. Morgan in *State of the World 2013*, 12.
62. C. Walter, "Unpublished Lecture Notes," University of Houston Department of Chemical Engineering (1975).
63. Francois Isaac de Rivaz is credited with designing the first hydrogen-fueled internal combustion engine in 1807.
64. C. Walter, personal experience breathing emissions at the Los Alamos Lab (1975).
65. P. Dieges, US Patent No. 3844262 (A) "Vaporization of Exhaust Products in Hydrogen-Oxygen Engine" (1974).
66. See R. Heilbroner's article in *Challenge*, May-June 1975: 27.
67. D. Orr, "Governance in the Long Emergency," in *State of the World 2013: Is Sustainability Still Possible?*, ed. Worldwatch Institute (Washington, DC: Island Press, 2013), 280–82.
68. S. Lorek, S. and D. Fuchs, "Strong Sustainable Consumption Governance—Precondition for a Degrowth Path?" *Journal of Cleaner Production* xxx (2011): 1–8.

69. Orr, in *State of the World 2013*, 281–83.
70. H. Myerson, "Did the Founding Fathers Screw Up?" *American Prospect* (2011), 16.
71. Orr, in *State of the World 2013*, 291.

PART THREE
Organic Religion

ELEVEN

Divine Wilder/ness:
Nature, Panentheism, and Eco-Theological Ethics

Andrew M. Davis

And in journeying into the wilderness areas—feeling the pulsations of life unmanipulated by humans—we journey into the very God whose body is that wilderness. As our senses join soil, air, water and wilderness, they join God. -Jay B. McDaniel[1]

THESE ARE WILD AND PRECARIOUS TIMES to find oneself alive. With the threat of environmental catastrophe looming large, we have heard from all variety of disciplines as to what kind of response is needed to curb—and possibly survive—the potentially dire ecological effects of human civilization. While it is often the case that theology is devalued in secular culture—treated as though its contributions have long been exhausted—we cannot (and should not) ignore the religious and theological undercurrents involved in the ecological crisis.[2] These undercurrents have been both for good and for ill. Some theology has no doubt exhausted itself into irrelevancy and even aggravated our ecological situation further with passive and escapist undertones. Nevertheless, it should not be denied that *theology matters*—and matters greatly for our ecological precarity. To object to this amounts to essentially denying that "ideas" have any practical consequence in and for our world. The environmental crisis, to be sure, has many complex and mutually related contours: philosophical, scientific, political, and economic. But the *theological contours* are essential, in that they harbor creative resources that rouse not only *deep reverence* for the sacredness of nature, but also *ethical action* on its behalf. Gordon Kaufman nicely captures the central thrust of theology in this regard: "Theology is not merely a rehearsal and translation of tradition; it is (and always has been) a creative activity of the human imagination seeking to provide more adequate orientation for human life."[3] In this respect, an *ecological shift* in the concept of God and God's relation to, and interaction with, the world can have deeply salvific consequences for our environmental situation. David Buchdahl rightly states that "A change in the conception of God is a cultural event of some magnitude, especially because the character of a culture is heavily influenced by the notion of God that predominates within it."[4]

In dialogue with key ecological insights of philosophers, theologians, and other voices of significance, my goal in this chapter is to articulate the value of "panentheism" as an eco-theological response harboring great ethical relevance. As a theological position, panentheism is understood broadly as the view that the divine reality is *inclusive of* and also *immanent within* the world. As such, it does much to reenchant our vision of and participation in nature as a *divine wilderness*. In contrast to the ecological detriments of popular theology, panentheism is an alternative position of *divine wilder/ness* which calls for a re-imagination of divine attributes and activity and also, thereby, the necessity of our own ethical action in and for the world.

In the spirit of Buchdahl's words above, I look first look to what I call the central *theological pillars of ecological passivity* as they are exhibited in much cultural theology today.[5] I focus principally upon the negative ecological consequences of *monarchical omnipotence* and *divine externality*. I then offer a vision of panentheism as an *ecological God* unhindered by these passive implications. I explore the positive ecological value intrinsic to panentheism's vision of *divine proximity* as *inclusion, immanence,* and *evolution*. From these convictions, I then develop a creative eco-theological vison of divine attributes, activity, and the human ethical imperative. These include *eco-sacramental suffering*; *divine persuasion and the omnipotentiality of love*; *divine call and creaturely response*; and the divine-human collaborative ethic I call *ethical theosis*. I conclude with a brief overview and call to action.

Theological Pillars of Ecological Passivity

There is no doubt that for many religious people, certain perceptions of the world and their responsibilities toward it are filtered through their dominant vision of God. This is true on both personal and collective levels. Indeed, realization that "theory" inevitably affects "practice" in this way immediately raises "theology" to a place of significance. Many have spoken to the spiritual or religious roots underlying our current environmental situation. Al Gore, for example, insisted that the more he searched "for the roots of the global environmental crisis," the more he became convinced that it is "an outer manifestation of an inner crisis that is, for lack of a better word, spiritual." We have, he states, "misunderstood who we are, how we related to our place within creation, why our very existence assigns us a duty of moral alertness to the consequences of what we do."[6] Speaking to the role of Christian anthropocentrism in perpetuating ecological peril, historian Lynn White Jr., similarly comments that "since the roots [of the ecological crisis] are so largely religious, the remedy must also be essentially religious . . . we must rethink and refeel our nature and destiny."[7] In no other way are these comments more significant than when applied to the doctrine of God. If part of the religious consciousness is to imitate and be in harmony with the supreme reality of the universe, then how God is conceived goes a long way in affecting the internal workings of the world.

Monarchical Omnipotence: "God is in Control"

Of all of the attributes traditionally assigned to "God," there is perhaps one that risks breeding ecological passivity more than any other: divine omnipotence. For many, it is largely taken for granted that "God" refers to the omnipotent ruler of the universe by whose fiat all things are willed and controlled. Such a vision of omnipotent sovereignty has been a hallmark justification of climate complacency. There are several striking examples we can give in this regard.

In 2012, Republican Senator James Inhofe published a book under the revealing title, *The Greatest Hoax: How the Global Warming Conspiracy Threatens Your Future.* Aimed against those he refers to as climate "alarmists," he confidently maintained that "God is still up there, and He promised to maintain the seasons."[8] Elsewhere, Inhofe has spoken of the arrogance of human beings who think that they "would be able to change what He is doing in the climate."[9] These comments demonstrate a vision of God whose omnipotent control cancels out the need for human action with respect to the climate. Inhofe's logic in this regard equates essentially to saying "we cannot change what God wills for the climate, so we shouldn't even try." What is even more concerning, however, is that in 2015, Inhofe became chairman of the Senate's Committee on Environmental and Public Works.[10]

In a similar way, well known conservative radio personality Rush Limbaugh appealed to the "intellect" saying "If you believe in God, then intellectually you cannot believe in manmade global warming." We are not so "omnipotent," he states, that we "could destroy the climate."[11] Human beings do not have the power, but God does. Here again is a justification of human inaction based purely upon theological assumptions of omnipotence. These examples coincide well in evangelical leader David Crow's theological ultimatum that "man is not in control. God is! Everything in the sky, the sea and on earth is subject to His control."[12] The global environmental crisis, in other words, is not in human hands, but in God's.

A strong commitment to divine omnipotence is also behind the denial of evolution as the natural process by which the world came to be. According to a recent Gallop poll, 40 percent of Americans believe that the world was supernaturally created within the past 10,000 years.[13] Omnipotence remains front and center. After all, why would an omnipotent God require 13.7 billion years to create the world, its ecology, and its creatures? To deny evolution is also to deny any continuity between human beings and nature, which leads to a bifurcation of the two. Is it not an insult to humanity to say that they share common ancestors with "lesser" creatures like primates? The human realm, in other words, is thought to be a "special creation" apart from, and superior to, all other creatures. What is more, if the world can come about *ex nihilo* through the omnipotent snap of the divine fingers, then the ultimate worth of the world to God can certainly be put into question. Even if it were the case that the world was destroyed in environmental decay, could not God simply (and quickly) create another world as God had done "in the beginning?" These few examples show that extreme understandings of divine omnipotence and control can dangerously correlate with ecological passivity. Unfortunately, it doesn't stop there.

On a governmental level, it should be said that theological protections of monarchical omnipotence have fed right back into the establishment of political positions whose own acclaimed "omnipotence" so often overrides all claims to "greatness." Something of this mentality could be seen in the Trump administration, which generally viewed climate concerns as suspect. It could be seen in what for many was the distressing announcement that the United States had officially withdrawn from the Paris Climate Accord. This epoch-making global agreement was established by 195 countries in 2015 to reduce greenhouse emissions and to curb rising global temperatures. "Our withdrawal from the agreement," Trump stated, "represents a reassertion of American workers' sovereignty."[14] And yet, for many believers, the "sovereignty" of American workers itself is justified by the omnipotent sovereignty of the God who "blesses" America. Some have gone so far as to insist that it was God who elected Donald Trump through the divine will—and may well do so again. Should this be the case, one is not advised to oppose him or his policies! This was made frighteningly clear in a statement by evangelical activist Mary Colbert. Pointing to the illusory nature of our democratic political process, she insists that we in fact "do not choose" our leaders, we rather "recognize" the ones God has chosen through the divine will. Such recognition of the chosen one of God, in Donald Trump in particular, will bring blessing; but woe to those, she insists, who "come against the chosen one of God." You will reap "curses" throughout generations, "curses like you have never seen."[15]

One remains astonished at such perspectives. In truth, such statements exhibit nothing more than the fright of theological barbarism. As a counter voice, few have spoken against such barbarism more powerfully than Alfred North Whitehead. "The glorification of power" he states, "has broken more hearts than it has healed."[16] This has certainly been the case among governments and nation-states, the deification of whose power has crushed more nations than it has healed. "This worship of glory arising from power," Whitehead continues, "is not only dangerous: it arises from a barbaric conception of God." What is more, Whitehead supposes "that even the world itself could not contain the bones of those slaughtered because of men intoxicated by its attractions."[17] Given the prevalence of theological barbarism and the gravity of our ecological situation, it is understandable that many have agreed with Charles Hartshorne: omnipotence is a "theological mistake."[18]

Divine Externality: "Not of This World"

What is God's "locus" with respect to the universe? Recalling Inhofe's conviction above: God is still "up there." That God is often conceived as "up there" and "out there," separate from and external to the universe, is widely assumed in popular cultural theology. In this vision, God has created a world "outside" of God's self. To many, it is clearly not the case that God is "here"; after all, isn't this why "He" had to "send" His "Son" from somewhere else? And isn't this why Jesus said he would "go and prepare a place for us" presumably *other than* this earthly vale of tears, bacteria, and Covid-19?

The practical ecological danger in these notions suggests a focus not on this world, but on some "other" world, beyond and better than this one. Indeed, one of the most popular Christian brands today—often seen on bumper stickers and clothing—is the acronym "NOTW," standing for "Not of This World." Popular books and television series surrounding notions of an apocalyptic "rapture" and a sinful world "left behind," have also bred complacency and raised deep questions as to why one should really care for the environment at all.

Conceiving the divine realm or the goals of religion as essentially external to the world of nature risks drawing one's attention away from the world completely. If Larry L. Rasmussen is correct, the implications of modeling our own lives upon divine exteriority could be serious: "If you put God outside and set him vis-à-vis his creation, and if you have the idea that you are created in his image, you will logically and naturally see yourself as outside and against the things around you." When it comes to the natural world, he states, "the environment will seem to be yours to exploit."[19] In this way, Sallie McFague's distinction between treating the natural world as a "hotel" verses a "home" readily applies.

> If we belong here, if the earth is our home, then it follows that we will want to take care of it. The Western hotel sensibility views the earth as if it were a set up for our convenience, with endless supplies of hot and cold running water, gourmet room-service meals, and luxurious fresh towels that, when we have used them up, can be tossed in the middle of the room as we drive on down the highway for more of the same. But we are coming to realize that the earth is not a hotel, and we had better start treating it as a home.[20]

Certainly, the "domination" and "escapist" mentality of certain expressions of Christian faith have treated the world in an overly anthropocentric way, as if it is ours to exploit and then escape. Deep tensions persist between this conviction and that of responsible "stewardship" in the biblical narrative. Take, for example, conservative pundit Erick Erickson's recent Tweet, "I worship Jesus, not Mother Earth. He calls us all to be good stewards of the planet, but doesn't mean I have to care about global warming."[21] The notion of human stewardship is scarcely reinforced if God is conceived as "elsewhere" to a world that will ultimately be "left behind" in apocalyptic culmination. No one, after all, has ever treated a hotel as if it were a home. One brilliant response fired back at Erickson: "I worship Jesus, not the poor. He calls us all to feed the hungry, but that doesn't mean I have to care about starving people."[22]

Coupled with omnipotence, divine externality also has a tendency to assume that divine action would be supernaturally enacted *from the outside*. In popular understanding, if God is seen to "act," it is often imagined to consist in external breaks or suspensions of the natural processes of nature. That God *can* supernaturally interrupt natural process in this way reinforces divine control of nature and thus human passivity on its behalf. Indeed, if things get bad enough, God can intervene to save us. In addition to being otherworldly, this salvation is also focused almost exclusively upon human beings. God's sympathies are purely anthropocentric. What is important is personal "human salvation," not salvation of the "hotel" in which we and a myriad other creatures are temporarily housed.

Not only are divine sympathies anthropocentric, God is also conceived in overly anthropomorphic ways in the dominant cultural view. One need only recall Michelangelo's painting of the creation of Adam on the ceiling of the Sistine Chapel in Rome to be reminded of the prevalence of this popular theological imagination. This imagination has a tendency to view "God" as a person-like being separate from and outside of the world—even if supernaturally active within it. On such a view, the goals of religion are again not oriented toward the world as such, but rather toward a divine being and a heavenly kingdom "beyond." As long as "religion" and "theology" are seen to consist in such views, it is no surprise that today's "cultured despisers," as seen, for example, in the "new atheist" movement, are calling for their repudiation.

One is reminded of Friedrich Schleiermacher's dialogues with those despisers of religion for whom "no room is left over for the eternal and holy being" that, for them, is conceived as lying "beyond the world."[23] It is precisely the vision of a fierce anthropomorphic deity and the presumed "otherworldly" nature of religion that such despisers find so reprehensible: "Fear of an eternal being and reliance on another world seem to you to be the hinges of all religion and that is, on principle, contrary to you," Schleiermacher states.[24] Schleiermacher, of course, agrees that those who make a strong distinction between this world and another world beyond "delude themselves," but he also insists that they show the "greatest contempt" for "true religion."[25]

It is here, however, where the challenges of today's despisers and the creative reformulations of theologians can come together. It is not uncommon to witness hostile dismissals of theology and religion as such, those which—as in the case of "new atheism"—even call for its eradication. It must be admitted that such enthusiasm is extremely shortsighted. After all, it is unlikely that "theology" or "religion" will ever fade from the interior human landscape (*homo religiosus*). This wish is both irresponsible and unrealistic. If theology as such has *no* chance of eradication, the only other option is *better theology*. Given the consequences of religious and theological ideas for our world, and our shared drive to overcome barbaric theology, the "newness" of today's atheism should rather consist in *them becoming theologians*.

The practical shadow side of robust notions of divine omnipotence and divine externality for our ecological situation seem clear. If, indeed, "God is in control," and humankind is ultimately "not of this world," it becomes virtually impossible to stimulate ecological action on theological grounds. This needs to be the shared goal not only for those who adhere to the claims of theology, but also for those who do not. A new theological stimulus is needed: a theological vision that is *wilder* than dominant cultural sensibilities. Indeed, to reenchant nature as a divine wilderness, we require a theological shift toward *divine wilder/ness*.

An Ecological God: Panentheism as Divine Wilder/ness

To address our environmental crisis, a creative eco-theological response is required, one with an internal structure that necessarily counters the troubling issues upheld by the pillars of ecological passivity. These pillars, as we have seen, largely surround notions of divine omnipotent control and divine externality. As a theological position, "panentheism" (Gr. "all-in-God") is the view that the divine reality is *inclusive of* and also *immanent within* the natural world.[26] It is a position that holds much potential for reenchanting our vision of nature as a *divine wilderness*. In contrast to the ecological detriments of popular theology, panentheism offers an alternative position of *divine wilder/ness* which calls for re-imagination of divine attributes and divine activity and also the necessity of our own ethical action in the world. As I develop it here, it harbors not only the resources that spur deep reverence for the sacredness of nature, but also the ethical imperatives to take action on its behalf.

Divine Proximity: Inclusion, Immanence and Evolution

Whereas popular theological sensibilities tend to emphasize God's radically transcendent separation from the world, general understandings of pantheism tend to emphasize God's radically immanent identification with the world. While the former risks breeding passivity by virtue of divine separation, the latter risks breeding passivity by virtue of divine identity. Because God has been exhausted into and as the world itself, John A. T. Robinson insists that pantheism suffers from an "indifferentism...which has to maintain that evil is in some way illusory or unreal."[27] In a similar way, Jürgen Moltmann states that pantheism must "ignore the negative element in the world."[28] More clearly still, David Ray Griffin is adamant that "the worst implication of pantheism" is that "whatever happens is divine, and therefore right, no matter how horrible."[29] Understood in this way, it is hard to see how pantheism offers an adequate eco-theological basis from which to form an environmental ethic.[30]

Panentheism, however, is able to mediate between these two extremes by virtue of its fundamental affirmation of *divine inclusion,* on the one hand, and *divine immanence,* on the other. As the etymology of the word suggests, "pan-en-theism" grounds the transcendent autonomy of the divine, in that all things are *included* and therefore *within* the divine. As such, God will always be "more" than the sum total of things as the very *soul of the universe*. In this way, panentheism agrees with most forms of theism in that God is distinct and transcendent; however, panentheism insists that divine transcendence is that of *all-inclusiveness* rather than separation or exclusion. As Elizabeth Johnson has stated, divine transcendence in panentheism "is a wholeness that includes all parts, embracing the world rather than excluding it."[31]

This very conviction, that the reality of God as such *includes* the world of nature and its activities *within* its own life, holds immense ecological implications. Indeed, of all the places one could start in a doctrine of God, panentheism begins with this basic conviction: that the world, far from being external to or separate from God—is actually its *indwelling participant*. Trees, soil, water, animals—all find their ontological embeddedness within God. And divine inclusion, it should be stressed, should not be imagined as some kind of aloof containment, but rather *intimate interpenetration*, such that the world remains in God and God remains in the world as its deepest animating source. For panentheism, God remains the intimate precondition for a living reality. In Whitehead's words, "The world lives by its incarnation of God in itself."[32] Consider the simple diagram below (Fig. 11.1) which communicates the uniqueness of panentheism from common renderings of both theism and pantheism. The broken line of the universe represents the mutual immanence of both God and the universe. The locus of the universe is in God, but God also interpenetrates the universe as its dynamic and interactive ground.[33]

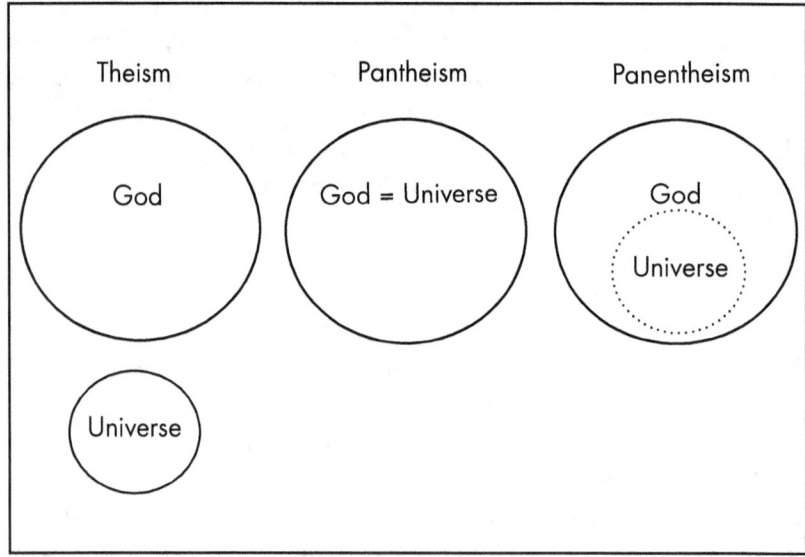

Figure 11.1

John Cobb and Charles Birch have developed an eco-theological vision in which God can appropriately be called "Life," not only because "the immanence of God in the world is the life-giving principle but also because the life-giving principle is itself alive." They insist that "a lifeless principle could not ground or explain the urge to aliveness that permeates the universe." As a life bestowing reality, grounding all things in an interconnected matrix of being and becoming, God is "the supreme and perfect exemplification of the ecological model of life."[34] This position immediately calls into question any form of theology or religion nurturing goals of evacuation from this world or visions that locate God "somewhere" else rather than right here and now as the inclusive and immanent Life of the universe itself.

What is more, for panentheists the world of "creation," far from being a one-and-done event of the past, is rather viewed as a continuous process (*creatio continua*) that is grounded in the primordial vision of God and channeled through the freedom and creativity of creatures. Human beings are not created separate from or outside of nature, but remain continuous with the evolutionary process as one of its most unique exemplifications. They cannot be abstracted or considered without recourse to their status *in and as nature*. This thought alone can help shift our orientation towards the natural world. Because human beings must exemplify wider principles of the natural world, nature cannot be considered without recourse to inner categories of experience, value, and purposeful intent. In this way, nature more readily deserves respect, consideration, and compassion—for out of it we were born and on it we continually depend.

Rather than denying (on theological grounds) the reality of evolution, panentheists see evolution as infused with deep theological significance. As the very divine means by which "creation" is (even now) coming into being, an evolutionary world demands that God cannot be exterior or separate, but must be involved, immanent, and intricately allied with the ecological thrust of the world process. It was Aubrey Moor who spoke powerfully of the theological significance of Darwin's discovery, saying, "Darwinism appeared, and, under the disguise of a foe, did the work of a friend. It has conferred upon philosophy and religion an inestimable benefit, by showing us that we must choose between two alternatives. Either God is everywhere present in nature, or He is nowhere."[35] Whitehead, too, underscored this central conviction, insisting that "God is *in* the world or nowhere, creating in us and around us. This creative principle is everywhere," he states, "in animate and so-called inanimate matter, in the ether, water, earth, human hearts... this creation is a continuing process."[36] Countering common theologies that imagine a world devoid of God, for panentheists, "the diaphany of the divine," as Teilhard de Chardin famously wrote, is "at the heart of a glowing universe." The divine radiates from the "depths of blazing matter."[37]

In such a world where God is present as the innermost organic interior, one's religious orientation must drastically change. It will not include an "other worldly" drive, but rather what Whitehead has called "world loyalty,"[38] and Teilhard a "cult of the earth."[39] Such loyalty is linked directly to the notion that all creatures participate in the circumambient reality of God. "Our sense of the importance of our actions in relation to other creatures is reinforced by the idea that God is immanent in all beings," Griffin states, "so that each species is a unique mode of divine presence."[40] One cannot, therefore, look at the natural world as something to be exploited and disregarded; rather one ought to consider Teilhard's words as to the resulting shift in religious consciousness that can take place when the wilderness of nature is re-conceived as the wilder/ness of a universal divine milieu.

> God reveals himself everywhere, beneath our groping efforts, as a *universal milieu,* only because he is the *ultimate point* upon which all realities converge.... It follows that all created things, every one of them, cannot be looked at, in their nature and actions, without the same reality being found in their innermost being—like sunlight in the fragments of a broken mirror—one beneath its multiplicity, unattainable beneath its proximity, and spiritual beneath its materiality.[41]

For both Teilhard and Whitehead, divine inclusion and immanence means that God is *internal* to creatures and creatures are *internal* to God. Not only must this central panentheistic conviction change our ethical concern on behalf of all sentient creatures, it must also radically alter our perspective on nature as a whole. Nature becomes reenchanted as a divine wilderness—the divine body—in which all things participate and through which they are sustained. The various panentheistic metaphors which communicate this mutually immanent, all-encompassing eco-vision are continual reminders that the divine wilder/ness we inhabit is not a temporary hotel, but our sacred home, infinitely deep with the divinity.

In addition to viewing nature as the "the body of God," Sallie McFague has spoken of "the entire cosmos" as the "habitat of God."[42] In a similar way, Glen A. Mazis speaks of the natural world as the divine "surround," insisting that we dwell in an "ecospiritual reality, a divinity of the earth." "The surround, of which we are a part," he states, "is the source of spiritual inspiration and the object of reverence, the gift-giver to all living and nonliving beings and the necessary focus of our care."[43] Idealist philosopher James Lindsay once called God the "Great Universal" and recently, Theodore Walker and Chandra Wickramasinghe have insisted upon panentheism as "panoramic theology," where God is the all-inclusive whole of reality itself.[44]

All of this encompassing language helps reenchant nature and our experience of the world. For panentheism, the value of the natural world is fundamentally grounded in its intimate relation to God; and "this relationship" as John Cobb states, "is such that faith in God expresses itself as the affirmation of the world and involvement in it."[45] Speaking from his own Christian context, Cobb's deep seated conviction is that, "when the affirmation of the world is cut off from faith in God, it ultimately undercuts itself, and that a devotion to the divine which turns its back upon the world is a rejection of the God known in Jesus Christ."[46] How different this conviction is from the passive voices heard above! Cobb is right: any notion that we are, with God, "not of this world" must be fundamentally rejected as anti-religious and anti-Christian. Panentheism effectively turns this perspective upside-down. More and more individuals are agreeing with Jay McDaniel that "it is from a panentheistic perspective ... that Christians have most to learn in developing images of divine love for nature."[47]

It should be said, however, that while a shift in our understanding of divine proximity is a huge step forward for our ecological situation, an alternative vision of divine attributes and activity is also needed. This alternative vision must flow from affirmations of inclusion and immanence and work to deepen our ethical imperatives with respect to nature. To this end, something *wilder* than omnipotent control, supernatural interruptions, and anthropocentrism is required.

Eco-Sacramental Suffering

For panentheists, the claim of divine "passibility"—God's affective suffering—is understood to necessarily follow from divine inclusion of, and immanence in, the natural world. It would be odd, after all, if the divine reality that both encompasses and is interior to the world was devoid of feeling what the world itself feels. Nevertheless, that the world does not really add anything to God has been a hallmark claim not only of "classical philosophical theism," but also popular cultural theology, which often portrays God as a kind of unsympathetic ruler who watches the kingdom of earth from a distance. Far from simply observing our ecological situation passively or unsympathetically, for panentheism, God is rather an *active participant*, experiencing and suffering with the environment and the various creatures (including human beings) that belong to it. This is what divine immanence demands. Just as human beings suffer with their bodies, so God suffers with the divine body of creation. This eco-theological conviction is no small matter when considering a theological stimulus to action, for God, too, is counted among the victims of our ecological disregard. It is the divine body that suffers our ecological indifference and exploitation. To disregard the suffering of the environment is to *disregard the suffering of God*. Paul Fiddes's words apply nicely to divine suffering and our ecological precarity in this way.

> If God suffers then God too ... is to be numbered among the victims and not among the torturers, murderers and oppressors ... God protests with the protesters because God too suffers. There is mutuality between the two experiences: if God suffers then God too protests and a God who protests against suffering cannot be the cause of it, or God would be protesting against God.[48]

Fiddes's words are striking when applied to our ecological situation, for contrary to the passive opinions expressed above, God is not causing or willing our ecological crisis, but rather *suffering its detriments*. It is human beings who have been the "torturers, murderers and oppressors" of nature. God, too, protests with the environment and its creatures who continually suffer our ruinous ways of life. And because "God suffers their sufferings," Griffin is right to state that "God presumably wants the suffering of the creatures to be minimized and their flourishing maximized." If indeed that is the divine desire, can we afford to not also have it as our own? "It is right, then, to give special attention to preventing suffering and enabling flourishing," Griffin states, "especially with regard to those creatures who can suffer the most, and whose potentials can be most severely thwarted."[49]

The eco-theological ethic embedded in divine suffering is such that to alleviate the suffering of the environment is to alleviate the suffering of God—whose very body *is that environment*. We can state it in an even stronger fashion: God is incapable of being relieved from suffering *unless human beings act* against the injustices perpetuated against the natural world. Far be it from religious believers to be passive in the face of divine suffering. Rather, divine suffering counters any notion of ecological passivity on theological grounds. It is a call for action extending from divine protest.

What is more, for panentheism, ecological suffering can be viewed as the sacramental presence of the suffering God. To see the suffering of other creatures is to also see the suffering of the God immanent in them. This calls for a fundamental shift in the way we view the suffering of the natural world and its inhabitants. Jay McDaniel states, for example, "as we humans watch a starving pelican chick, we are watching God. For God is actually there, in the chick, suffering with it. Even as worldly creatures are immanent to God, God is immanent within them."[50] The destruction of wildlife, the pollution of rivers and oceans, and the genuine disregard for ecology among many religious believers, simply cannot hold when it is *God who is suffering, too*. It may be, however, that one of the prime reasons people are often suspicious of the notion of divine suffering is because they may think that suffering is *all that a suffering God does*. Certainly, if God is utterly debilitated in suffering, the value of a panentheistic vision seems dubious. The question remains whether God does something more than just suffer with the world.

Divine Persuasion and the Omnipotentiality of Love

The question of how God acts in the world and with what kind of power must be central to any eco-theological endeavor. As we saw above, popular cultural theology leads one to say that divine action requires external and "supernatural" interventions. Furthermore, God's power is often imagined to be unhindered omnipotence that fundamentally controls environmental conditions. The statements above by Inhofe, Limbaugh, Crow, and Colbert all testified to this. The presupposition of divine inclusion and immanence in panentheism, however, offers an alternative framework from which to rethink divine activity, divine power, and our own ethical action.

With a vision of the world *within* God, talk of God's external "intervention" loses all meaning. God's working with the world is not external to the world but rather finds its efficacy among the internal ecological workings of the world itself. According to Griffin, "divine influence is understood as part and parcel of the world's normal causal relations and never an interruption thereof."[51] As opposed to supernatural interruptions, therefore, panentheism can be framed as a "theistic naturalism," whereby the *internalization of divine action* belongs to the very nature of God's relationship with the world. Divine power for panentheism is then necessarily *relational and persuasive* in nature. This is not to say that God is impotent, but rather that authentic divine power is that of a *persuasive and poetic love which calls one to act*. Contrary to the idea of one exterior agent acting upon another, this is an evocative and inward power lovingly entangled within the world's own power and continually calling it into salvific possibilities beyond the detriments of the past. Whitehead expresses this vision compellingly.

> God's role is not the combat of productive force with productive force, of destructive force with destructive force; it lies in the patient operation of the overpowering rationality of his conceptual harmonization. He does not create the world, he saves it: or, more accurately, he is the poet of the world, with tender patience leading it by his vision of truth, beauty, and goodness.[52]

Should our world suffer ecocide, divine power is *not* the kind of power that can quickly snap another world into existence. Nor is it a power that can coercively counter an ecological situation that is rampantly out of control. It is rather the power of persuasive and loving possibility that has coaxed the world from chaos to cosmos for some 13.7 billion years. Far from being a creative means that monarchial omnipotence could have avoided, evolution remains *the only way for God to bring about a world at all*. Working with the wilderness of nature as it is, divine power is redemptive and vulnerable, enveloping the world with the loving presence of what *can be*. In the face of our ecological crisis, this is a power which offers back to the world potentials of redemption that transcend the destructive ecological patterns of the past. It is a faithful power of possibility which allows for the transformation of our ecological precarity into the triumphs of mobilization, collaboration, and compassionate action.

This redemptive power of the possible we might call God's *omnipotentiality*. We can agree with Ivone Gebara in this light when she states that "to speak of pan-en-theism is to consider the potentialities of the universe, the potentialities of life, and the potentialities of human life as always open-ended."[53] Indeed, the divine life grounds the possibilities of what still can be, even in the face of environmental destruction. As such, it is imperative that omnipotentiality be conceived as a power which, as Catherine Keller states, "does not do *for* or *to* us but 'makes possible' our own action." "We are responsible, able to respond," Keller states, "because [divine] potentialities vastly exceeding our own predictable capacities flow through us."[54] With this understanding of divine power, then, nothing can change without human response.

Divine Call, Creaturely Response

Central to the divine wilder/ness of panentheism is its underlying eco-theological ethic. We have already seen that this ethic grows out of affirmations of inclusion, immanence, and divine suffering. This ethic is also a direct outgrowth of commitments to a naturalistic vision of divine activity and the persuasive calling of divine omnipotentiality. God, we repeat, *cannot* supernaturally intervene or control all things.[55] Although immanent to God, the world retains its own creative freedom, a freedom which God necessarily works in and through to achieve the goodness of what can be. The naturalism of this "in and through" emerges as an *invitation to act*, a call to actualize in the world what God can *only do through creatures*. Indeed, "invitational" verses "unilateral" accounts of divine agency have deep implications for our ecological situation. While the former breeds *ethical activity*, the latter breeds *ethical passivity*. Divine invitation can be understood as a "call forward," one which John Cobb has identified as an objective "aspect of experience." God, he insists, is the "One Who Calls."[56] Marjorie Suchocki elaborates, saying "God calls; creation responds. God then responds to the creation's response, and building upon it, calls yet again. Through call and response, the creation comes into being as world. It is incremental, gradual, with creation participating in its own becoming."[57]

Such a call-and-response relationship between God and creatures reinforces the old theological adage that "God has no hands but our hands." For panentheism, therefore, there is a deep sense in which God is *dependent upon creatures to achieve the aims of creation*. Put differently, our ethical action is indispensable to the actualization of divine aims in the world. In this way, Etty Hillesum speaks insightfully of human beings as the "only ones who can 'enable God to be God' through acts of radical, hospitably, love and justice."[58] Taking this statement seriously means that the efficacious reality of God in the world is contingent upon human attentiveness and action. Similarly, Richard Kearney has spoken of "the God who may be," saying that "God can be God only if we enable this to happen."[59] John Caputo's distinction between God's "insistence" and God's "existence" also applies here. While God *insists*, it is up to human beings whether God will *exist* or not: "The name of God is the name of an insistent call or solicitation that is visited upon the world, and whether God comes to exist depends upon whether we resist or assist this insistence."[60]

These are compelling statements at the heart of a panentheistic eco-theological ethic. That God *only* works "in and through" the world is a conviction that reinforces the gravity of human action to address the environmental crisis. Ethical passivity has no place in such a theology. To speak of a God who is "up there" as Inhofe stated above, creates a vision of the world which can be "left behind." The "Kingdom of Heaven" is somewhere else, somewhere "out there." Yet this is far removed from the Galilean prayer which calls this kingdom to earth. It is through human beings *enacting the divine call* that a new ecological livelihood is possible. For Kearney, the "God-who-may-be offers us the possibility of realizing a promised kingdom by opening ourselves to the transforming power" of divine ideals. "Each human being carries within him/herself the capacity to be transfigured in this way and to transfigure God in turn—by making divine possibility ever more incarnate and alive."[61] For Whitehead, the divine ideals for the world *are* the kingdom of heaven, and "the kingdom of heaven is with us today" as a persistent call for its actualization.[62]

Ethical Theosis

Through this vision, we can state the panentheistic ethic in an even stronger way. It is not simply a matter of God being passively immanent to human beings as they work in the world; rather, when human beings answer the divine call they *become God* as God acts to transform our ecological situation. This incarnational unification of divine and human action is what I call *ethical theosis*: the alignment of one's own ethical activities such that they share a unified identity with those of the divine. This takes imagination. Far from being *only* an eschatological notion, theosis can be a realized vision here and now when divine promptings for the world are actualized by human agents in each moment. This is a vision grounded in the mutual relationship between God and humanity as collaborators in the world. Speaking to the "divinization of our activities," Teilhard's incarnate panentheistic vision exemplifies an ethical theosis where divine action and human action coincide in the world.

> Through the unceasing operation of the incarnation, the divine so thoroughly permeates all our created energies that, in order to meet it and lay hold of it, we could not find a more fitting setting than that of our action ... in action I adhere to the creative power of God; I coincide with it; I become not only its instrument but its living extension.[63]

Teilhard's vision is such that God "awaits us every instant in our action, in the work of the moment."[64] Whitehead, too, insists that "every event on its finer side introduces God into the world."[65] For Abraham Joshua Heschel, "God is waiting to be disclosed, to be admitted into our lives." "Our task," he states, "is to open our souls to Him, to let Him again enter our deeds."[66] All of these statements are a profound reorienting call to the moment at hand. Quoting Isaiah 43:12, ("Ye are my witnesses, saith the Lord"), Heschel elaborates: "when you are my witnesses I am God, and when you are not my witnesses I am not God."[67] It is human action which "witnesses" the actual *existence* of God's healing vision in the world. When applied to our ecological situation, the message for religious believers is clear: our environmental crisis is an opportunity to fulfil our fundamental religious vocation: to *become God to the world*. Paul Knitter's words are a concise and clear statement of the panentheistic vision of ethical theosis.

> God is always "God with"; and humans are always "humans-with." When these two realities are really with each other—God with humanity, and humanity with God—that is when they are really their fullest, truest selves. The unity between what I call God and myself is one in which God genuinely acts as God insofar as

I act in a truly human fashion. If God is indeed acting through us, that means that God cannot be "in" unless God is "through." So, it is not just the case of God acting in me, but me *being God as God acts in the world*.[68]

Realizing that God is dependent upon human action in efforts to restore our ecological situation can be both profound and petrifying, for the weight of this responsibility is always a *call to act*. It is far too often the case that we would prefer someone else to act instead of ourselves. Our ecological condition requires massive mobilization, collaboration, and creativity from religious believers. Many continue to feel paralyzed and pessimistic toward the possibility of countering our environmental state. Passivity, however, is not an option when faced with the divine ecological cry of our time. It was Emmanuel Levinas who insisted that "To know God is to know what must be done."[69] Indeed, our theology should be such that one cannot affirm the reality of God and remain inactive.

Conclusion: Divine Wilderness, Divine Wilder/ness

The role of theology for our ecological condition is paramount. Because theory inevitably affects practice, a cultural change in the conception of God can have a huge impact upon our environmental situation. A large part of our crisis is theologically and religiously derived and can only be countered with a novel theological response. New theological notions need to be developed and disseminated throughout our culture, with creative contours that fundamentally transform our vision of nature and our actions toward it. As Kaufman has written: "Theology is not merely a rehearsal and translation of tradition; it is (and always has been) a creative activity of the human imagination seeking to provide more adequate orientation for human life."[70] Contrary to the theological pillars of ecological passivity, the inclusive and immanent vision of panentheism not only reenchants nature as a *divine wilderness*, but also reorients human purpose as participation and "world loyalty." In comparison to the all-controlling and "other worldly" detriments of the dominant cultural theology, this vision is one of *divine wilder/ness* in its re-imagination of divine attributes and activity, and also its inherent eco-theological ethic. Eco-sacramental suffering, persuasion, and the divine redemptive power of omnipotentiality, all reinforce human ethical activity on behalf of the environment. Divine-human interaction is and always remains one of call and response unification—that of ethical theosis. A divine cry is heard from the environment. It is this cry that awaits the deification of our deeds and the apotheosis of our actions. As our actions "join soil, air, water and wilderness, they join God."[71]

Endnotes

1. J. McDaniel, *Of God and Pelicans* (Louisville: Westminster John Knox Press, 1989), 91.

2. Whitehead's comment is relevant in this regard: "It is customary to under-value theology in a secular history of philosophical thought. This is a mistake, since for a period of about thirteen hundred years the ablest thinkers were mostly theologians." A. N. Whitehead, *Adventures of Ideas*, (New York: The Free Press, 1967), 129. Applied to our ecological situation, this statement remains important, as theologians today remain some of the most creative and valuable voices for change.

3. G. D. Kaufman, *Theology for A Nuclear Age* (Manchester: Manchester University Press, 1985), 20.

4. Quoted in W. G. McLoughlin, *Revivals, Awakenings, and Reform* (Chicago: University of Chicago Press, 1978), 215.

5. In this chapter, by "cultural theology" or "popular cultural theology," I mean the pervasive assumptions about "God" that reign over much of American society. These labels refer more to a dominant lay image of what it means to be "God," rather than to what sophisticated philosophical traditions—classical, modern, postmodern or otherwise—have insisted.

6. Quoted in L. L. Rasmussen, "Cosmology and Ethics," in *Worldviews and Ecology: Religion, Philosophy and the Environment*, ed. M. E. Tucker and J. A. Grim (Maryknoll, NY: Orbis Books 1994), 174.

7. Quoted in G. Sessions, "Deep Ecology as a Worldview," in *Worldviews and Ecology*, ed. Tucker and Grim, 207.

8. J. Inhofe, *The Greatest Hoax: How the Global Warming Conspiracy Threatened Your Future* (Washington, DC: WND Book, 2012), 70–71; quoted in D. R. Griffin, *God Exists but Gawd Does Not: From Evil to New Atheism to Fine-Tuning* (Anoka, MN: Process Century Press, 2016), 308.

9. Quoted in B. Tashman, "James Inhofe Says the Bible Refutes Climate Change," *Right Wing Watch*, August 3, 2012; in Griffin, *God Exists but Gawd Does Not*, 308.

10. Griffin, *God Exists but Gawd Does Not*, 308

11. In D. Edwards, "Limbaugh: Christians 'Cannot Believe in Manmade Global Warming,'" *Raw Story*, August 14, 2013; quoted in Griffin, *God Exists but Gawd Does Not*, 308, 309.

12. D. Crowe, "Katrina: God's Judgment on America," Beliefnet, September 2005; quoted in Griffin, *God Exists but Gawd Does Not*, 309.

13. See: https://news.gallup.com/poll/261680/americans-believe-creationism.aspx.

14. C. Domonoske and C. Dwyer, "Trump Announces U.S. Withdrawal from Paris Climate Accord," *NPR News*, June 1, 2017.

15. S. Palma, "Christian Activist: "God will curse the children and grandchildren of those who opposed Trump, *DeadState*, April 4, 2017. See video at http://deadstate.org/christian-activist-god-will-curse-the-children-and-grandchildren-of-people-who-opposed-trump/.

16. A. N. Whitehead, *Religion in the Making* (New York: Cambridge University Press, 2011), 45.

17. Whitehead, *Religion in the Making*, 44–45

18. C. Hartshorne, *Omnipotence and Other Theological Mistakes* (Albany: State University of New York, 1984).

19. L. Rasmussen, "Cosmology and Ethics" in Tucker and Grim, *Worldviews and Ecology*, 173.

20. S. McFague, *The Body of God: An Ecological Theology* (Minneapolis: Fortress Press, 1993), 57.

21. E. Mazza, "Christian Conservative: Jesus Wouldn't Want Me to Care About Global Warming," *Huffpost*, June, 1 2017.

22. Mazza, "Christian Conservative."

23. F. Schleiermacher, *On Religion: Speeches to its Cultured Despisers,* ed. and trans. R. Crouter (Cambridge: Cambridge University Press, 1996), 3.

24. Schleiermacher, *On Religion*, 11.

25. Schleiermacher, *On Religion*, 16.

26. Although etymologically panentheism locates the world *in* God, many panentheists also read the term in reverse: "theos-en-pan." This indicates the mutual immanence of the position. In other words, panentheists usually insist that the world cannot be *in* God without God also being *in* the world. Thus Philip Clayton is correct to say that "the etymology is a bit misleading... since in most cases the 'in' actually has at least *two* meanings: all things are in God, and God is in all things" ("Panentheism: East and West," *Sophia* 49 [2010]: 184). Panentheism has a rich intellectual history and creative contemporary expressions continue to emerge. See J. W. Cooper, *Panentheism: The Other God of the Philosophers* (Grand Rapids: Baker Academic, 2006); P. Clayton and A. Peacocke, *In Whom We Live and Move and Have Our Being: Panentheistic Reflections on God's Presence in a Scientific World* (Grand Rapids: Eerdmans, 2004); A. M. Davis and P. Clayton, eds., *How I Found God in Everyone and Everywhere: An Anthology of Spiritual Memoirs* (Rhinebeck: Monkfish, 2018); G. Brüntrup, B. P. Göcke, L. Jaskolla, eds., *Panentheism and Panpsychism: Philosophy of Religion meets Philosophy of Mind* (Brill: Mentis: 2020).

27. J. A. T. Robinson, *Exploration Into God* (Stanford: Stanford University Press, 1967), 118.

28. J. Moltmann, *Crucified God* (New York: SCM Press, 1974), 277.

29. D. R. Griffin, *Reenchantment Without Supernaturalism: A Process Philosophy of Religion* (Ithaca, NY: Cornell University Press, 2001), 142.

30. This is not to say that pantheism is a position devoid of reverence and devotion to nature. As a vision that considers the universe as a whole as sacred, Griffin states that pantheists "regard the world with the same reverence that Christians, Jews and Muslims have for God. On this basis, pantheists may be motivated to protect nature, but there is no moral injunction to do so, because pantheism holds that literally everything is equally divine." For Griffin, an "is-ought" problem plagues the position: "Pantheism, therefore, provides no basis for distinguishing between 'is' and 'ought'—between what is the case and what ought to be the case. There is, accordingly, no basis for saying that we should protect nature for future generations: The universe is sacred no matter what happens" *(Protecting Our Common, Sacred Home: Pope Francis and Process Thought* [Anoka, MN: Process Century Press, 2016], 58).

31. E. A. Johnson, *She who is: The Mystery of God in Feminist Theological Discourse* (New York: Crossroad, 1992), 231.

32. Whitehead, *Religion in the Making*, 49.
33. This diagram is my own. It first appeared in Davis and Clayton, *How I Found God in Everyone and Everywhere*. See my "Conclusion: Returning to God *After* God."
34. C. Birch and J. B. Cobb Jr., *The Liberation of Life: From the Cell to the Community* (Cambridge: Cambridge University Press, 1981), 195.
35. Quoted in Arthur Peacocke, "The Challenge and Stimulus of the Epic of Evolution to Theology," in *Many Worlds: The New Universe, Extraterrestrial Life and the Theological Implications,* ed. Steven J. Dick (Philadelphia and London: Templeton Foundation, 2000), 109.
36. As reported by L. Price, *Dialogues of Alfred North Whitehead* (Jaffrey, NH: David R. Godine, 2001), 366.
37. *Pierre Teilhard De Chardin: Writings Selected With an Introduction by Ursula King,* Modern Spiritual Masters Series (New York: Orbis Books, 2004), 32.
38. Whitehead, *Religion in the Making*, 49.
39. *Pierre Teilhard De Chardin,* 52.
40. D. R. Griffin, "Whitehead's Deeply Ecological Worldview" in *Worldviews and Ecology,* ed. Tucker and Grim 201.
41. *Teilhard De Chardin,* 72.
42. McFague, *The Body of God,* 183.
43. G. A. Mazis, "Ecospirituality and the Blurred Boundaries of Humans, Animals, and Machines" in *Eco-Spirit: Religions and Philosophies for the Earth,* ed. L. Kearns and K. Keller (New York: Fordham University Press, 2007), 155,
44. See J. Lindsay, *A Philosophical System of Theistic Idealism* (Los Angeles: Hardpress Publishing, 2012) and T. Walker and C. Wickramasinghe, *The Big Bang and God: An Astro-Theology* (London: Palgrave Macmillan, 2015).
45. J. B. Cobb, *God and the World* (Philadelphia: Westminster Press, 1965), 10.
46. Cobb, *God and the World,* 9.
47. McDaniel, *Of God and Pelicans,* 26.
48. P. S. Fiddes, *Participating in God: A Pastoral Doctrine of the Trinity* (Louisville: WJK Press, 2000), 161–62.

49. Griffin, "Whitehead's Deeply Ecological Worldview," 204.
50. McDaniel, *Of God and Pelicans*, 30.
51. D. R. Griffin. *Panentheism and Scientific Naturalism: Rethinking Evil, Morality, Religious Experience, Religious Pluralism, and the Academic Study of Religion* (Claremont, CA: Process Century Press, 2014), 156.
52. Whitehead, *Process and Reality*, 346.
53. Quoted in C. Keller, "The Body of Panentheism," in *Panentheism Across the World's Traditions,* ed. P. Clayton and L. Biernacki (New York: Oxford University Press, 2014), 79.
54. Keller, "The Body of Panentheism," 80.
55. Due to the recent work of Thomas J. Oord, such a view is now being more widely embraced on a popular level. See T. J. Oord, *God Can't: How to Believe in God and Love after Tragedy, Abuse, and Other Evils* (SacraSage Press, 2019); *Questions and Answers for God Can't* (Grasmere, ID: SacraSage Press, 2020); *The Uncontrolling Love of God: An Open and Relational Account of Providence* (Downers Grove, IL: Intervarsity Press, 2015).
56. Cobb, *God and the* World, 45.
57. M. Suchocki, *Divinity and Diversity: A Christian Affirmation of Religious Pluralism* (Nashville: Abingdon Press, 2003), 28–29.
58. Quoted in R. Kearney, *Reimagining the Sacred: Richard Kearney Debates God,* ed. James Kearney and Jens Zimmerman (New York: Columbia University Press, 2016), 258.
59. R. Kearney, *The God Who May Be: A Hermeneutics of Religion* (Bloomington, IN: Indiana University Press, 2001), 2.
60. J. D. Caputo, *The Insistence of God: A Theology of Perhaps* (Bloomington, IN: Indiana University Press, 2001), 14.
61. Kearney, *The God Who May Be*, 2.
62. Whitehead, *Process and Reality* (New York: Free Press, 1978), 351.
63. *Teilhard De Chardin*, 75.
64. *Teilhard De Chardin*, 75.
65. Whitehead, *Religion in the Making*, 140.
66. A. J. Heschel, *Man is Not Alone: A Philosophy of Religion* (New York: Noonday Press, 1951), 154.

67. Heschel, *Man is Not Alone*, 243–44.
68. P. F. Knitter, *Without Buddha I Could Not be a Christian* (Oxford: Oneworld, 2009), 23. Emphasis mine.
69. Quoted in R. A. Cohen, "Emmanuel Levinas: Judaism and the Primacy of the Ethical" in *The Cambridge Companion to Modern Jewish Philosophy*, ed. M. L. Morgan and P. E. Gordan (Cambridge: Cambridge University Press, 2007), 246.
70. Kaufman, *Theology for a Nuclear Age*, 20.
71. McDaniel, *Of Gods and Pelicans*, 91.

TWELVE

Images of Lions:
Psalm 104 as a Metaphor
for a Processual View of Creation

Robert Gnuse

The geological column with its testimony to a diverse range of fossils and the great age of the Earth was accepted by eighteenth and nineteenth century churchmen. They viewed it as the way in which God created the world and believed that essentially Genesis 1 was describing that process in its own language. They viewed the fossil record as a testimony to God's logical unfolding of life in the world order. Most suggested that God engaged in a continual process of "special creation" to generate all the species. Their view of world order was expressed best in the early nineteenth century beliefs of Paley who envisioned the world as arranged in clockwork fashion by God.

Charles Darwin devastated this world view by suggesting that the evolutionary advance was not fueled and directed by the infinite wisdom of God, but rather was a blind process driven by the principle of survival—the survival of the fittest. Furthermore, species were mutable; one could evolve into another species. Paley's clockwork view of things was crushed, along with notions of "special creation." In short, Darwin removed the God hypothesis from the evolutionary paradigm. This initially effected a negative reaction from churchmen, who took great umbrage at the removal of God from the natural process and at the articulation of a model which saw violence as the chief mode of evolutionary advance.[1] However, some theologians and social ethicists adjusted in the late nineteenth century by advocating a theological "social Darwinianism" which became an intellectual hallmark paradigm of the Gilded Age.[2]

In the 1920s in the American South, the paradigm of "scientific creationism" first began to arise among Seventh Day Adventists. It was a wholesale rejection of evolution, and it naively assumed that the entire evolutionary theory began with Darwin and deserved total repudiation. Scientific creationists, like the nineteenth century theistic evolutionists, recoiled against a model that portrayed nature as "red in tooth and claw," with an evolutionary advance driven by apparent blind chance. They were repelled by Darwin's vision of the violence and cruelty in creation as a constituent of the fabric of nature, and preferred to see a natural order that originally was benign in nature, and would return to the pristine state of harmony (and vegetarianism) in the animal world with the second coming of Jesus.[3] One can even observe that romantic vision of the future eschatological animal world in the theological and artistic traditions of the early nineteenth century.

I live in the heartland of Roman Catholic "scientific creationism" in southern Louisiana. Two of my three children were taught "scientific creationism" in New Orleans Roman Catholic high schools. As chairperson of the Religious Studies Department at Loyola University in New Orleans (2003–2009), most of the angry phone calls I received from surrounding-area Roman Catholics complaining about our "liberal" religion department usually included references to the fact that we accepted and taught evolution in our religion classes. They also complained about the teaching of world religions. Their reservation about evolution, of course, is that it replaced God with a mindless, brutal process of competition for survival. My first response was that this godless theory of evolution is godless only when it is taught by godless instructors, and one could say this about virtually any field of instruction (i.e., "godless economics," e.g., Rand Paul and "Vienna economics").

My response to their concerns about the violence of nature in the Darwinian worldview is that perhaps they should have looked more closely at some of the biblical passages that accept and even embrace the violence and the predatory nature of the natural order, and can even treat it in somewhat laudatory fashion as part of the presence of God in creation. For this chapter, I look in particular to Psalm 104, which is significantly dedicated to the theological praise of God's created order. In noteworthy fashion, the biblical author says in vv. 21–22,

> The young lions roar for their prey, seeking their food from God.
> When the sun rises, they withdraw and lie down in their dens.

This is a dramatic image; the affirmation of a lion hunting its prey. Even more dramatically, the author declares this to be in some sense a divinely willed activity. As Rogerson and McKay noted, this text acknowledges the "dark side of the natural world—'nature red in tooth and claw.'"[4] I recall a National Geographic television show that I watched a number of years ago in which a lion was eating a young gazelle, while the gazelle was still obviously alive. I thought that I certainly did not want my children to watch this show. I would have difficulty affirming that this activity was divinely willed by God and indeed worthy of several lines of praise in a great hymn. Perhaps I am a brainwashed nineteenth-century romantic, but this is what our biblical author did. Our biblical author also accepted and praised the cycles of life and death in the natural order. In verse 29b, we are told of the entire animal realm, "when you take away their breath, they die and return to their dust." In the next line, verse 30a, the author affirms how life comes out of death and the next generation of animals are born, "When you send forth your spirit, they are created; and you renew the face of the ground." This verse not only envisions the transience of life, but the significance of how each new generation replaces the older generation, so that out of death comes new life symbolically.[5] The vision of nature as a violent world of eat and be eaten appears to be clearly affirmed and praised by the psalmist. In the words of Artur Weiser,

> Because the psalmist envisions the world in the light of God's affirmation of it, he does not stop at the tragic aspect of dying, but discerns in the coming into being and passing away of living things the conquest of death by means of the continual process of re-creation by the ever-active, ever-living God.[6]

The choice of lions in the Psalm is a most apt allusion. Lions are usually characterized as being those creatures on the top of the food chain. In order for them to survive, especially if there are a decent number of lions in the pride, a lot of meat is required. The animals they consume, of course, are herbivores, for the most part, which require plant life to survive.

This means that you need a verdant environment in the savannah where the lions live. Other animals are also necessary for the overall ecological system in which the lions live. Indeed, the lion is king of the beasts, the lion is the top of the food chain, and a fully developed ecological system is required for the continued existence of a healthy and strong pride of lions. An individual lion must consume 140 kilograms of food daily and a lion pride requires between 50 and 100 lions to maintain genetic diversity. The ecosystem for such a pride must contain a great degree of fauna and flora. The lion is a "keystone species" as Shugart states.[7] The lion is a most appropriate symbol for the totality of the ecological order in the environments where they are to be found. Commentators suggest that the biblical author indeed uses the lion as a symbol for all wild animals.[8] Though the biblical author was probably not aware of this, we can nonetheless read the psalm and see the lion as the symbol for the totality of the ecological order and the balanced natural infrastructure of life. In the Ancient Near East, lions were symbols for royal power, and in artistic representations, kings often portrayed themselves as hunting lions, in quest perhaps for mystical union with them.[9]

In the book of Job we find passages that describe lions in their predatory mode of existence. The texts are comparable to the imagery in Psalm 104, but I prefer to focus upon the language in Psalm 104 because the entire psalm is a hymn to the natural order, and lions are thus seen as part of that great natural order. But the texts in Job are at least worthy of mention. In Job 38:39–40 we read, "Can you hunt the prey for the lion, or satisfy the appetite of the young lions, when they crouch in their dens, or lie in wait in their covert?" This passage likewise speaks of the predatory nature of the lion in the natural world order. It also bespeaks human finitude by our inability to provide for lions in the way in which they survive in the competitive natural order.

In Job 4:10–11 we hear the tragic story about the death of lions, "The roar of the lion, the voice of the fierce lion, and the teeth of the young lions are broken. The strong lion perishes for lack of prey, and the whelps of the lioness are scattered." Norman Habel believes that this last passage is a metaphor for the wicked.[10] Even if it is a metaphor for human society, the imagery reflects the real tragedy of the natural order wherein starvation and death are the tragic consequences in a world where so often only the fittest survive.

Psalm 104 is a long and beautiful hymn of the natural order. The lion reference is only part of it, and greater attention is given to the story of how God masters or defeats the waters of chaos. It is a hymn that truly speaks about the dynamic order of life in the world, and the whole hymn bespeaks the wonder of the life processes. The psalm stresses dependence of all in the created order upon God through "regular, ordered, and manifold channels."[11] As Artur Weiser noted, "The relation of this nature-hymn to the story of creation in the first chapters of Genesis is like that of a colored picture to the clear lines of a woodcut."[12] Critical scholars have suggested that it was a psalm inspired by the fourteenth century BCE Egyptian hymn produced by the pharaoh Ikhnaton, the Hymn to the Sun. James Henry Breasted was the first to make this suggestion in the early twentieth century. Subsequent authors have noted the affinity of the biblical psalm with the Egyptian hymn.[13] Most contemporary scholars suspect that our biblical author was not directly familiar with that Egyptian hymn, but more likely was familiar with intermediary hymns which came to Israel from Phoenicia.[14] But that is all wonderful speculation. We simply do not have enough texts to make a solid case for any grand decision on this matter.

What are the implications of this text for process thought, and in particular process thought which has directed its attention to the ecological order? The psalmist clearly affirms the grittier aspects of the created order, the story of predatorial killing and eating. Had our nineteenth century theological forebearers, who were squeamish with Darwin's "survival of the fittest," looked more closely at this text, perhaps they could more easily have affirmed that God is present in the cycle of life and death in the great food chain. Some of them did, but in general it seems that most Christians did not. Recognizing the presence of the divine in the great "circle of life" (to steal a term from *The Lion King*, most appropriately), is to see God as most vividly involved in the process of our world. We can speak with Bernhard Lang, who said of this passage in Psalm 104 that the crying of the young lions is a prayer to God for food.[15] Furthermore, to thus affirm the cycle of life and death is also to affirm the underlying forces behind the evolutionary process. This is an explicit way of accepting the evolutionary process and declaring that God is present in that process. It is, in effect, to say that God is present in the carnivorous lions, in the predator dinosaurs, in the very simple one-celled creature that eats another one-celled creature. God is present in the process; God is present in evolution, for God is present in the hunt. In the ancient world, often a goddess was portrayed as "Lord of the Animals," and in turn, the biblical authors portrayed Yahweh as "Lord of the Animals" in response. Passages in Psalm 104:21–22 and Job 38:39 are part of that Old Testament affirmation.[16] We must recapture that imagery in our theological portrayals of God. We must see God as "Lord of the Animals," "Lord of the Created Order," "Lord of the Evolutionary Process," and a God who is in the natural process. One botanist observed that when the first unicellular organism turned and consumed another single-cell organism, the development of life was truly underway. Process theologians looking at the text of the lions in Psalm 104 can without hesitation say that God was present in that first unicellular devouring organism. God is, indeed, "Lord of the Evolutionary Process."

For Christians to accept that God is present in the evolutionary process, even in the violent aspects of the natural order, may enable them to view God as active in the process in other ways, too. It can make them comfortable with viewing religion itself as an important and integral part of the evolutionary process. Religion can be seen as part of the human evolutionary advance as it enables people to adapt and survive in the world. Most significantly, religion draws people together into a group or community larger than the nuclear family, and this group provides greater protection for the individuals who constitute the group, for it binds them together in a cooperative process for survival in the hostile world environment.[17] The evolution of religion actually replaces the kinship structures of family, which is bound together by a deep genetic commitment, but religion gives people the sense that they belong to a larger family. Groups of humans who were "religious" had a better possibility of survival in the history of human evolution.[18] Combined with this is the speculative insight that religion and contemplation of the divine becomes possible when our minds evolve the ability to ponder what the minds of other people might be thinking of us, thus producing social skills in human interactions, and further leading us to suspect that there is a Greater Mind somewhere that is observing our behavior in addition to those around us.[19] For process theologians, such evolutionary advance is believed to occur with the presence of the divine involved in the process. To accept that the divine may have undergirded the evolution of religion in the natural process of universal evolution, and not through some spectacular external revelation, as we have been wont to say for so many years, can be made possible when we acknowledge the presence of the divine in the nitty-gritty, earthy, and even bloody and competitive process of evolution. God bless the lions; God bless the carnivores.

Endnotes

1. A. Peacocke, "Biological Evolution and Christian Theology—Yesterday and Today," in *Darwinism and Divinity*, ed. J. Durant (Oxford: Basil Blackwell, 1985), 101–30.

2. R. Hofstadter, "The Coming of Darwinism," in *Evolution and Religion: The Conflict between Science and Theology in Modern America*, ed. G. Kennedy (Lexington, MA: Heath and Company, 1957), 3–14; J. Moore, "Herbert Spencer's Henchmen: The Evolution of Protestant Liberals in Late Nineteenth Century America," in Durant, *Darwinism and Divinity*, 76–100.

3. R. Numbers, *The Creationists: The Evolution of Scientific Creationism* (Berkeley, CA: University of California Press, 1992), 54–139; D. Pleins, *When the Great Abyss Opened: Classic and Contemporary Readings of Noah's Flood* (New York: Oxford University Press, 2003), 43–66.

4. J. W. Rogerson and J. W. McKay, *Psalms 101–150* (Cambridge: Cambridge University Press, 1977), 27.

5. Rogerson and McKay, *Psalms 101–150*, 27.

6. A. Weiser, *The Psalms*, trans. Herbert Hartwell (Philadelphia: Westminster, 1962), 670.

7. H. Shugart, *Foundations of the Earth: Global Ecological Change and the Book of Job* (New York: Columbia University Press, 2014), 226–29.

8. A. Anderson, *The Book of Psalms*, Vol. 2: *Psalms 73-150* (Grand Rapids, MI: Eerdmans, 1972), 723.

9. B. Doak, *Consider Leviathan: Narratives of Nature and the Self in Job* (Minneapolis: Fortress, 2014), 204–06.

10. N. Habel, *Finding Wisdom in Nature: An Eco-Wisdom Reading of the Book of Job*, The Earth Bible Commentary Series 4 (Sheffield, UK: Sheffield Phoenix Press, 2014), 43.

11. Rogerson and McKay, *Psalms 101–150*, 27.

12. Weiser, *The Psalms*, 666.

13. Weiser, *The Psalms*, 666.

14. M. Dahood, *Psalms III: 101-150* (Garden City, NY: Doubleday, 1970), 33.
15. B. Lang, *The Hebrew God: Portrait of an Ancient Deity* (New Haven: Yale University Press, 2002), 85.
16. Lang, *The Hebrew God*, 84.
17. D. S. Wilson, *Darwin's Cathedral: Evolution, Religion, and the Nature of Society* (Chicago: University of Chicago Press, 2002).
18. F. MacIntyre, "Was Religion a Kinship Surrogate?" *Journal of the American Academy of Religion* 72 (2004): 653–94.
19. J. Bering, *The Belief Instinct* (New York: Norton, 2011).

THIRTEEN

Toward an Ecologically Awakened Islamic Humanism

Farhan A. Shah

MY ENDEAVORS AS A MUSLIM PHILOSOPHER to re-form or redefine the Islamic calling in relation to the pressing existential issues of our time emerges from a profound love and care for the innumerable unborn generations, which, although they lie outside the limits of immediate vision, ought to be considered as the most important portion of living communities. Trial and error are always part of positive historical evolutions. And as our collective experiences demonstrate, it is the future, and its potential members, that should guide the present attitudes and policies. Put differently, our immediate interests should be subordinated and, if need be, sacrificed for the sake of posterity; of that unborn infinity which gradually discloses itself from generation to generation. As moral agents, we cannot afford to remain indifferent to this biological truth.

In April 2017, my colleagues and I, in Claremont, CA, realized the above during a one-day conference on Muhammad Iqbal and Alfred North Whitehead. The express purpose of this conference was to explore the process-oriented potential of Islam that emerges from the qur'anically inspired writings of Iqbal and, further, to adumbrate the main points of an Islam of creativity, guiding us toward an "integral ecology," that lives for respect and care for human and nonhuman communities of life. Iqbal was a Muslim philosopher and the spiritual father of Pakistan who, as it happens, was also an informal student of Whitehead, concurring with Whitehead that the very energy of the universe, found in human life and in nature, is creative. For Iqbal, as for Whitehead, God works with, not against, this creativity.

In many contexts I speak of process Islam as a form of Islamic Humanism. I realize, however, that the phrase can be misleading and off-putting, if the word "humanism" suggests a Promethean perspective asserting that "man is the measure of all things." I realize as well that for many process thinkers, with their ecological orientation, the phrase can also suggest a reductive anthropocentric approach that neglects the intrinsic value of the more-than-human world.

I do not intend the word to have these connotations. In Islam the Qur'an itself speaks of the whole of creation on the analogy of a tree of life, or a single organism, emerging from and returning to its divine source. An Islamic Humanism will see the value of human life and human rights as situated within, not apart from, this larger whole, itself becoming through time, with each creature having *intrinsic value*. Therefore, a humanism understood as *anthropocentric* in this sense is alien to the Islamic outlook.

The chapter is intended to clarify, even though partially, this point, bringing my perspective shaped by a holistic approach to the qur'anic scripture and Muhammad Iqbal's process-oriented philosophy into conversation with the larger project of *constructive postmodernism*, which is to encourage and cultivate ecological worldviews that stress the interrelationality of the whole of life and that invites us, in the midst of unsustainable courses, toward the development of just and sustainable communities throughout the world—the Islamic world much included. My sense is that Islam, as interpreted by Iqbal, can make a powerful contribution to this deeply humane—and, yes, ecologically awaked humanistic—hope.

Salient Features of Eco-Humanism

The main features of eco-humanism, inspired by the qur'anic scripture and Muhammad Iqbal's philosophy, can be summed up as following: (1) The ontological dignity and freedom of humanity; (2), human rights as universal and the corresponding duties; and (3) the interrelationality and radical interdependence of all creation. We will briefly look into points one and two, and then deal with the last point in somewhat more detail.

Human dignity and freedom

Human dignity transcends the barriers of ethnocentrism and encompasses humanity *en masse*, regardless of gender, sexual orientation, functionality, ethnicity, age, etc. The Qur'an asserts in a sonorous way: "Verily, We have created all humans worthy of dignity and honour" (17:70). The prophet of Islam, in his farewell address (632 CE), categorically asserted that "there is no superiority of a black over a white or a white over a black. All of you humans belong to the same single stock."[1] Furthermore, the dignity and value of the human person finds its ultimate expression in her/him being "someone" and not "something." Stated differently, the human entity is an "end in itself," thus omitting collective identities such as family membership or citizenship from the scheme of things.

Furthermore, the qur'anic notion of human dignity is associated with mainly three characteristics: (1) that every human being is born with an innate personhood, entitling all humans to equal respect; i.e., human dignity connotes catholicity; it is an ascription to every member of *homo sapiens*; (2) dignity also connotes inalienability, i.e., dignity is noncontingent; and (3) unconditionality; it is an essence necessitating no performance, i.e., it is a God-given ontological property rooted in the human being itself. As such, it is not contingent upon such variables as social prowess, mental or somatic abilities, or genetic endowment. Further, this rooted dignity does not admit of grades. Human dignity cannot be gradually achieved. It is a binary function that allows no middle ground. This position is opposed to the Hobbesian concept of dignity as the price set on an individual agent by the commonwealth, a position that admits of gradation of dignity and that uses a utility function; i.e., the intersubjective judgements of the market.[2] On the contrary, the touchstone of general societal position—determining one's relative status—rests chiefly on modes of human activity. As the Qur'an asserts: "And for all there are ranks according to what they do" (46:19). That is, since the element of interior causality is rooted in every member of the human species, self-determining agents, in their activities, direct their being toward values, and as such determine themselves. Put differently, human beings create themselves. And, as actions are organically linked to creative becoming, by consciously choosing between the various possibilities open to one, a person becomes morally good or morally impoverished.

Therefore, a distinction ought to be made between a God-given ontological innate dignity on the one hand, and how individuals, as a subjective "I," operate with their power of self-determination—which is also organically connected to one's sense of responsibility for actions—and thus determines their own identities and moral values.

Human rights

Human dignity and freedom are intimately related to civil liberties and human rights. Human rights are judicial principles employed against states in order to protect human beings from structural injustice. The prime function of inalienable rights is the enhancement of the common good and also to furnish healthy environments in which human beings can work out their individual potentialities by pursuing an open future.

Indeed, human rights are essential in order to develop sustainable communities. However, there is a general tendency to regard human rights as if they were passed on from some limitless row of pleasurable items. Rather, we need to recognize that human rights are first and foremost *possibilities*, not *actualities*. In other words, human rights can only be "realized" by the fulfilment of duties to "realize" these rights. No obligations, no human rights possibilities turned into actualities. For example, if refugees have a natural *right* to sustenance and protection, then non-refugees have the *responsibility* to supply them with food and shelter. In order to realize the right to free speech, citizens have a duty not to curb the right to free expression. Rights separated from responsibilities will only stay as potentialities or cherished but abstract ideals. We ought to have an *interrelational* approach to the implementation and understanding of human rights.

Just as human dignity and freedom encompasses the human species as a whole, so are basic human rights all embracing, transcending the binary model of a we/they divide. The us-versus-them distinction undermines the more inclusive way which emphasizes the larger whole to which "we" and "they" belong, that is, the human species as an organic whole. In the Qur'an, we read the following verses emphasizing humanity's organic unity: "Humanity is but one single community" (10:19, 2:213).

Anthropocentrism

The last point is related to anthropocentrism. There have been, and still are, anthropocentric tendencies in most civilizations. Briefly stated, the notion of anthropocentrism—derived from the *homo mensura* sentence—was formulated by the pre-Socratic Greek philosopher Pythagoras, who asserted that man is the measure of all things. Furthermore, the dualism developed by Descartes juxtaposes the human mind to all things, even to the human body. This mode of dualism also reckons animals devoid of any subjectivity, thus they can be turned over to science for objective study. The image that is affirmed on the basis of the *homo mensura* dictum and Cartesian dualism quickly develops into human arrogance and reductionist attitudes towards planetary life as dead matter to be used for human profit only. From a Muslim process perspective, humanism does not stand for human entities as the sole denizens of planet Earth, or that human dignity is the only fact to be reckoned with, at the cost of the larger spectrum of nonhuman species and their capacity for enjoyment. This perspective easily mutates into an unfortunate view that is bereft of respect and responsibility for other living organisms and nature in its totality.

With this backdrop in mind, can Islam help us to redirect our energies and visions to the effort to save what can be saved and build on the wreckage something of lasting value?

The Islamic Notion of Stewardship

As a mode of actual living, Islam rejects the mechanistic view of the universe, which pulverizes everything into facts and figures, information and numbers, without recognizing the life-experiences and subjectivity of living entities. In the Islamic tradition, we can identify a position that challenges the longstanding mode of anthropocentrism and mechanistic dualism, a form of "deep ecology." According to the Qur'an, the Earth and everything in it belongs not to humans but to God. In Islam, humans are referred to as *caliphs*, which literally means "guardians." Our roles as guardians on Earth implies the sacred errand to protect the Earth, its material and nonmaterial resources. Humans are free to use these recourses in their own interest, not in unrighteous ways, but rather in a way creative of cultivation of the Earth and its biological diversity. Thus, in Islam there is no space for "human dominion" over planet Earth. The concept of God's unity (*Tawheed*) implies, among other things, world-unity. And since human beings are free agents, their freedom implies responsibilities toward their surroundings.

One of the central pillars of a qur'anically inspired deep ecology is that (1) every living entity has an *intrinsic value* of its own, and hence cannot be considered exclusively in instrumental terms; and (2) that no human being has any right to cut down the richness and plurality of planetary creation, except in the interest to meet *vital human needs*. The term "vital needs" implies that human beings can only satisfy fundamental needs essential for their life on planet Earth. Lastly, the nonhuman world ought to be recognized as communities of subjects (*ummam*), just as the human species. The classical Arabic term *ummam* is a plural form of the term *Ummah*, a term Muslims use in order to refer to other believing communities.

The metaphors of the Qur'an to personalize nonhuman communities indicate an interrelational paradigm. As communities interact with each other and have complex networks, we are encouraged by the qur'anic worldview to recognize that the animal world and nature are not ripped apart, but rather organically linked with the human world. This deep symbol of interconnectedness, which flows through the idea of God's unity, points toward the great wisdom of *radical interdependence*, i.e., we are members of one another and equal before one God. Human communities do not exist as self-enclosed entities but as interactive entities. We are what and who we are through our relationships with others. The welfare of the world contributes to our welfare, and its illness and decay impoverish us as well.

Muhammad Iqbal's Organic Approach

Muhammad Iqbal has made several remarks conducive to the development of an Islamic process-oriented ecology. In one of his pregnant remarks, he states: "All is holy ground. As the Prophet so beautifully puts it: The whole of this earth is a mosque."[3] If the whole of the Earth is a "mosque," this could then lead to the conclusion that all of the denizens of Earth, human as well as nonhuman, are sacred and interconnected (reflecting the presence of Divine energy and God's unity). In other words, all life deserves our outmost respect by widening our horizons, thus including nonhuman actualities such as animal organisms and nature in our decision-making and policies in order to secure environments that promote the overall wellbeing of our dwelling place. Further, the naturalism of the Qur'an is only a recognition of the fact that humanity is connected with nature, and this relation must be used not in the interest of unrighteous desire for domination, but in the nobler interest of preserving and enhancing the organic wholeness of life. There is also a hadith (traditions based on reports of the sayings of the Prophet of Islam) which reads: "Allah is kind only to those who are kind to His creations."[4] Explained differently, our opportunity and fulfilment is to love and serve God by serving God's creation by expanding our zone of existential responsibility, transcending reductionist anthropocentrism and a dualistic framework.

The above is a version of humanism that not only is human-centered, but a version that expands the circle of our sensibilities concerning other nonhuman creatures and the biosphere as well. In other words, this humanism goes *beyond* anthropocentrism and embraces a more organic view of all forces of life. It is humanistic as well as biocentric in that each living being is a subject of its own life and not just an object for others, with intrinsic value. Intrinsic value, like creativity, is *universal*.

John Cobb and Whiteheadian Thought

In this context, a passage of John Cobb deserves our attention. For Cobb, to believe

> that a human life is 'of more value than many sparrows' (Matthew 10:31) does not warrant the conclusion that sparrows are worth nothing at all. Indeed, it presupposes the opposite. The heavenly Father cares even for sparrows; how much more for human beings! This certainly means that people too should be concerned more about a human being than a sparrow. Much more! But it does not warrant the teaching that sparrows exist only as a means to human ends... God is pictured as loving the creatures and caring for them, not only human beings, but the sparrows as well.[5]

Cobb's views can be infused into the Iqbalian vision of "all is holy ground," productive of paving the way for a humanism characterized by respect for humanity's innate dignity combined with "world-loyalty," as Whitehead calls it:[6] a world-loyalty in which our self-interest is joined with our commitment to be creative partners with God in the quest for the welfare and enjoyment for all of creation.

To recapitulate, the foundational keys of an Islamic eco-humanism are as follows: (1) every member of the human species is endowed with an intrinsic, hence, inviolable, dignity and freedom; (2) human rights are universal/all-embracing; (3) humanism, far from being purely human-centered, needs to be blended with respect and profound concern for the ecosphere and nonhuman species, i.e., in addition to humans having intrinsic value, so do other living beings (biocentric).

Organic Islamic Humanism

We can identify this version of humanism as "Organic Islamic Humanism," which is an attitude spacious enough to include all creatures, just as God includes every being in the Divine life, i.e., panentheism ("all-in-God"). Humans are thus significant creatures and God's companions in creating a world that is just, sustainable, and joyful: a world of nurturing communities where no life is left behind, and the other animals and the Earth are treated with respect and care.

This, however, entails a risk. As God's power is *persuasive* rather than *all-controlling*, God offers us only novel possibilities to transcend our facticity, to see all things differently, to imagine what has never yet been dreamed. God works to open others to respond to new visions and to actualise them in concrete ways. God urges, lures, and persuades. Human beings decide, perpetually marching toward futures filled both with possibilities of greater enjoyment and authenticity and destruction. As beings with a unique capacity for conscious freedom, it implies the possibility of also rejecting divine aims. That is, heightened freedom in relation to the temporal order necessarily means increased freedom in relation to God. Muhammad Iqbal captures this profoundly existential risk and burden of responsibility, thus: "To permit the emergence of a finite ego who has the power to choose, after considering the relative values of several courses of action open to him, is really to take a great risk; for the freedom to choose good involves also the freedom to choose what is the opposite of good. *That God has taken the risk shows His immense faith in man. It is for man now to justify this faith.*"[7]

Endnotes

1. A. Shabbir, *Islam as I Understand* (Lauderhill, FL: OurBeacon Books: 2010), 35.
2. T. Hobbes, *Leviathan*, ed. Richard Tuck (Cambridge: Cambridge University Press: 1991).
3. M. Iqbal, *The Reconstruction of Religious Thought in Islam* (Palo Alto, CA: Stanford University Press: 2012), 123.
4. A. Shabbir, *A Selection of Ahadith* (Lauderhill, FL: OurBeacon Press: 2001), 15.
5. J. B. Cobb in B. Epperly, *Process Theology: A Guide for the Perplexed*

(New York: T&T Clark International: 2011), 114.
6. A. N. Whitehead, *Religion in the Making* (Cambridge: Cambridge University Press, 1996), 49.
7. Iqbal, *The Reconstruction of Religious Thought in Islam*, 68.

FOURTEEN

A Shortcut on the Jain Path of Liberation
Aparigraha **as** *Ahimsā in Process Philosophy*

Wm. Andrew Schwartz

According to Marketdata Enterprises, Americans spend more than $60 billion (yes, billion with a "b") trying to lose weight each year.[1] To put this in perspective, if the US weight loss industry was a country, its national GDP (Gross Domestic Product) would be among the top 70 richest countries in the world. But why do we spend so much money on something that is a simple matter of "calories in, calories-out?"[2] A caloric deficit of approximately 3500 is equivalent to 1 lb. of weight loss.[3] This isn't a secret; it's math and science. Life is fundamentally the transmission of energy.[4] Calories are a way of measuring energy. When we eat, our bodies use the food for energy, measured in calories. If we consume fewer calories than our body needs for energy, we find the energy elsewhere—burning existing fat and muscle stores for the requisite energy. Therefore, eating nutrient-rich foods that are lower in calories, coupled with exercises that burn calories, is a basic formula for successful weight loss. So why do Americans spend $60 billion a year trying to shed pounds if it's so simple? Because we're looking for an easier path—a special diet, a rare supplement, or a new regiment—that will guarantee faster results with less work. We spend $60 billion each year looking for weight loss shortcuts.

As big as the weight loss industry is, it pales in comparison to faith-based revenue. A recent study from Georgetown University discovered that the US faith sector is worth $1.2 trillion,[5] which is roughly the equivalent of the national GDP for countries like Mexico, Spain, and Australia.[6] Now, if religion was understood as a business, salvation/liberation would be its bestselling product. So, what if there was a shortcut to liberation? What if I told you I've uncovered the ultimate secret—that with faster results and less work, you could achieve salvation? Why adhere to those old models of liberation that take multiple lifetimes before you see results, if you can shed karmas faster and easier than ever before? In what follows, I will attempt to convince you that process philosophy provides a shortcut on the Jain path of liberation.

The Jain Path of Liberation

Jainism is an ancient Indian religious tradition that is thought to have inspired Gautama Buddha and Mahatma Gandhi. Perhaps best known for images of monks and nuns wearing filters over their mouths (*muhapatti*) in order to avoid harming microorganisms in the air, Jain ascetics have a reputation for taking their vows very seriously—even to the point of voluntarily fasting to death (*sallekhanā*).[7]

Liberation, in Jainism, is a matter of shedding karmas. According to Jain belief, humans and other creatures are, in their true selves, pure souls (*jivas*). Unlike other religious traditions in India, for whom karma is a universal principle of causation, in Jainism karma is actually a physical, dust-like, substance that attaches itself to the soul. When this happens, karmic matter weighs down the soul, imprisoning it within a body.[8]

Jain thinkers have developed a quite sophisticated theory of karma, postulating various types of karmic particles, each with unique impacts on the *jiva* and accumulated through different activities (mental, verbal, and physical). As Paul Dundas explains, "the basic structure of karma in Jainism is comparatively straightforward. Karma is divided into eight categories, found as early as the 'Expositions of Explanations' [a.k.a. the Bhagavatī Sūtra], which are in turn divided into two categories of four: the 'harming' (*ghātiyā*) karmas and the 'nonharming' (*aghātiyā*) karmas."[9] Some karmas have a knowledge obscuring effect (*jñānāvaraṇīya* karmas), which prevent the *jiva* from having omniscience—an innate quality of the unfettered *jiva*. Other karmas determine the length of one's life (*āyas* karmas). And due to the physical nature of these karma particles, varied karmas impart different colors upon the soul, which is determined by the quality of the mental activities motivating one's actions. All in all, Jainism has much to say about the nature of karma.

The path to liberation (*mokṣa*) is ultimately a simple matter of "karmas in, karmas out." Achieving a karmic deficit is accomplished by shedding existing karmas and preventing the accumulation of new karmas. When successful, the *jiva* is released from karmic bondage, eventually allowing the pure soul to ascend to *siddhashila* (the abode of liberated beings). Heinrich Zimmer puts it this way, "Cleansed from karmic matter, and thereby detached from bondage, this perfect one ascends in complete isolation to the summit of the universe. Yet, though isolated, he is all-pervading and endowed with omniscience; for since its essence has been relieved of qualifying individualizing features, it is absolutely unlimited."[10]

So how does one go about shedding karmas? Just as Jainism has an elaborate system of categorizing karmas, there is also an elaborate account for how karmic matter is attracted to, attached to, and released from the *jiva*. The core of this path to liberation is ascetic purification. As Jeffery Long explains,

> The idea behind the Jain path of ascetic purification is that, by ending the influx of karma to the soul through cultivating equanimity and expelling the already present karma through ascetic practice, the soul eventually becomes karma free. Its full potentials of infinite knowledge and bliss then manifest. One thus attains kevala jñāna—omniscience, or absolute knowledge. One is then a Jina, or conqueror. The only remaining karma adhering to the soul will be of a kind that does not obstruct the soul's inherent characteristics.[11]

The Jain path of purification is outlined by five "great vows" (*mahāvratas*) designed for the purpose of eliminating karmas.[12] Two of the most prominent of these great vows are *ahimsā* (nonviolence) and *aparigraha* (non-possession). For Jain monastics, *aparigraha* (अपरिग्रह) entails owning no personal property whatsoever (freeing oneself from karmic inducing desires through non-attachment), while *ahimsā* (अहिंसा) is more about how we interact with others (attempting to do no harm). Both *aparigraha* and *ahimsā* are considered core features of the Jain path to liberation.[13]

Unlike many religions, Jainism has been uniquely uniform throughout the centuries. In fact, there are only two significant sects within Jainism: *Svetambara* (White Clad) and *Digambara* (Sky Clad). The main difference between these two sects is a disagreement about the central tenant of *aparigraha* (non-possession). The Digambara monks are called "Sky Clad" because they are fully nude. Since wearing clothes typically involves owning apparel, clothing is considered a violation of the tenant of non-possession. That means wearing clothes is a stumbling block on the path to liberation for Digambara monks. Svetambaras, on the other hand, take a different interpretation regarding possession and allow their monks and nuns to dress in plain white garbs. What's significant here is that disagreement about how to interpret the vow of *aparigraha* is one of the main reasons for the only significant division within the Jain tradition. As Long notes, "The correct interpretation of *aparigraha* for ascetics is of course the main issue that differentiates Svetambara and Digambara monks. Both groups agree that an ascetic should only possess the bare minimum requirements for practicing the Jain ascetic path, such as the whisk for protecting small creatures from harm. But the Svetambaras include clothing among these requisite items, whereas the Digambaras do not."[14] The way of *aparigraha*, which is essential to the path of liberation, includes both an *attitude* of non-possessiveness as well as a *physical detachment* from material objects.

Also essential to the Jain path of liberation is the vow of nonviolence. *Ahimsā* is perhaps the most well-known (and is certainly the most widely discussed) feature of Jain belief and practice. Among other things, the principle of *ahimsā* informs Jain dietary restrictions. Not surprisingly, doing no harm includes not killing. Hence, Jains adhere to a strict vegetarian lifestyle, since killing animals to consume them is considered a form of violence. Perhaps less obvious is the Jain commitment to avoid eating root vegetables such as potatoes, garlic, onions, etc. since harvesting such plants disrupts the soil and the organisms living in the soil. Additionally, in so far as harvesting root vegetables entails up-rooting them, this is considered unnecessary violence against plant life.[15] I say "unnecessary violence," because there is an acknowledgment in Jainism that some degree of violence (harm) to other beings is an inevitable part of life. Similarly, process philosopher Alfred North Whitehead explains that, "all societies require interplay with their environment; and in the case of living societies this interplay takes the form of robbery ... life is robbery. It is at this point that with life morals become acute. The robbery requires justification."[16] For Jains, the inevitability of violence is not a free pass to harm indiscriminately—the robbery requires justification. As such, Jainism offers a gradation of the moral quality of varied actions. For example, it's much better (lower harm) to consume a mango that has fallen off the tree rather than to cut down the tree to harvest the mango. Similarly, it is better to eat lettuce, whose leaves can be picked without pulling up the roots (which means the plant can continue to live and produce), than to eat a carrot which needs to be uprooted. This gradation of value is categorized into six different mental states (*leśyās*) which correlate to six colors imparted onto the soul as a result of karmic matter accumulated from actions rooted in these six mindsets. The least admirable is the black *leśyā*, a perspective that is devoid of compassion and mercy. This mindset is often portrayed as the one chopping down the tree to harvest the fruit. The most admirable is the white *leśyā*, which embodies *ahiṃsā* and the Jain path to liberation. This mindset is typically depicted as the one collecting fruit that has ripened naturally and fallen from the tree.[17]

In Jainism, *ahiṃsā* is not simply about nonviolence to fellow humans, or even mammals, but all living entities. It's not simply about actions but also intentions (states of mind). The Jain metaphysical formulation (which includes identifying air bodies, water bodies, plant bodies, etc.) is critical to their ethic (including *ahiṃsā* and *aparigraha*), and the path of liberation.[18] It is to this interconnection between metaphysics, ethics, and liberation, we now turn.

A World of Objects: Substance-Based Metaphysics

What sort of "things" are there, and how are these "things" related? According to John Cobb, this is the central question of traditional philosophy.[19] The dominant narrative throughout the Western world has been that reality is ultimately made up of independent and enduring substances. Since the time of Plato, substances have been widely considered the most fundamental building blocks of reality, because they are independent (relying on nothing external for their existence), and eternal (enduring unchanged through time). In philosophy, the term "substance" corresponds to the Greek word for "being" (*ousia*). Substance-based ontologies prioritize being as the most fundamental kind of entity. As C. Robert Mesle explains,

> In the West, Plato firmly established the primacy of Being when he argued that this world of change is merely a shadowy copy of a realm of eternally unchanging forms. Following the Platonist (not

the Bible), Western Christian theologians asserted that God was the ultimate unchanging reality. Finally, in the Enlightenment, René Descartes and others argued for Being over Becoming by insisting (contrary to many of their own observations) that the world is composed of physical and mental 'substances,' especially including human souls, that (1) exist independently and (2) endure unchanged through change.[20]

According to substance-based metaphysics, the world consists of objects/things (instances of being). In the case of René Descartes—the "father of modern philosophy"—there are two types of "things" that make up reality, physical things (extended matter) and mental things (human minds/souls). Cartesian dualism is not simply an anthropological dualism (between human minds and human bodies) but also a metaphysical dualism that set humanity apart from the rest of the physical world, since only humans were thought to possess minds. This dualism works in tandem with Descartes's anthropocentrism, emerging from his famous *"cogito, ergo sum"* (I think, therefore am I) which places the "Self" at the center—a core characteristic of the modern worldview. The human subject became the sole source of value, as all other physical entities were reduced to the status of machines, possessing only instrumental value. Put simply, from substance-based metaphysics, we get the primacy of being, and with the help of Descartes, a dualistic and mechanistic worldview that renders the more-than-human inert and devoid of any intrinsic value, subjectivity, or purpose.[21]

Descartes's fingerprints can be found all over contemporary society. With colonialism, imperialism, and globalization, the core framework of the European Enlightenment was never contained within Europe. Perhaps the most significant area of influence has been upon the scientific worldview. In late modernity, when human beings were shown to be products of evolution and fully part of nature, the door was opened for rethinking nature as having some of the properties Descartes attributed only to humanity (e.g., subjectivity, purpose, and intrinsic value). But rather than elevating the more-than-human world to the status of subjects, scientists chose to study humans in the way they had previously studied the nonhuman world—as machines. A new narrative emerged, asserting that only one kind of "thing" comprised reality: physical substances. Descartes's dualism was replaced by reductive physicalism (a.k.a. materialism).[22] This reductive narrative spawned the pursuit of pure knowledge. What followed was the rise of "value-free" education and the creation of academic disciplines arranged according to purity (e.g., mathematics and physics being purer than psychology and sociology). In more recent years, the notion of pure, value-free, scientific research has come under scrutiny,[23] but the roots of this oft unacknowledged worldview run deep.

The modern worldview sees the world as a collection of objects. Objects are distinct from subjects. Subjects alone have agency and value. As John Cobb explains,

> it would be meaningless to speak of a value apart from a subject. It is subjects that are intrinsically valuable. Only a subject can be something in and for itself. An object, qua object, exists for something else. It can have only instrumental value, and that value must be instrumental to the value of some subject. The question, then, is where subjectivity is to be found.[24]

From the Cartesian perspective, subjectivity is found in humans alone. The rest of the world consists of objects that exist for human subjects.

In Jainism, the purifying practice of *aparigraha* is not a vow of poverty. It's not about renouncing modern comforts. Nonpossession is only superficially about physical possession. At its core, *aparigraha* is an attitude of nonpossession, and as an attitude it is infused with a worldview. Just as traveling long distances at night increases the risk of *hiṃsā* (harm), so too does a metaphysic that depicts the world as constituted by objects increase risk of *parigraha* (possession). A substance-based metaphysic introduces unnecessary stumbling blocks on the Jain path to liberation. Might an alternative metaphysic serve to remove these stumbling blocks and expedite the path toward liberation?

A World of Subjects: Process Metaphysics

What sort of things are there, and how are these things related? Process philosophers in the tradition of Alfred North Whitehead give primacy to event, not being—to experience, not substance. In process thought, the world is not constituted by independent enduring substances, but interdependent moments of experience called "actual occasions." As John Cobb explains,

> Whitehead's judgment was that the actual entities that make up the world are all "actual occasions." This means that they are

happenings, occurrences, or events, rather than substantial entities that endure unchanged through time—an occasion of human experience is not to be understood as a person experiencing. *There is no person beneath or behind the experiencing.* The act of taking the past into account and constituting itself with a view to the future *is* the actual occasion. The person is constituted as a long series of such occasions growing out of one another and out of the body.[25]

Experience, not substance, is fundamental. As Whitehead himself states, the "final real things of which the world is made up" are "drops of experience, complex and interdependent."[26] To ground ontology in experience has a significant impact on subject-object thinking. Experience entails subjectivity. The experiencing subject is the center of values felt. As Philip Rose argues, "Because of the relational nature of his metaphysical scheme one can say, in effect, that for Whitehead 'to be' is *to be the source of values given and the centre of values felt*."[27] Two important things result from this perspective. One, as experience is fundamental to the nature of things, subjectivity is also fundamental, since all experiencing entities are subjects. To be a subject is to be a center of experience—a center of felt values. Second, subjectivity is extended to all actual occasions, not just human ones. All existing entities are experiencing entities. And all experiencing entities are subjects. This view has been promulgated by process philosophers under the heading of "panexperientialism."[28] As C. Robert Mesle encourages,

> Imagine that experience/feeling/emotion goes *all* the way down to subatomic particles. Imagine that electrons, protons, neutrons, and other subatomic "particles" are drops of spatial-temporal experience. They experience their physical relationships with the world around them as vectored emotions—feelings that drive them this way and that. Think of energy as the transmission of physical feelings.[29]

Now, this isn't an attempt to do away with the notion of objects. In process thought, each subject is also an object. When we are the center of values felt we are subjects, and when we are the source of values given for others we serve as objects. There is a fundamental difference, however, between the process conception of objects and the substance approach. In substance-based ontologies, objects are a category of being. Some things are objects and others are subjects. In an event-ontology, object and subject are not categories of being but classifications of relations. To serve as the source of values given is to provide objective datum for the experience of another subject (to relate to that subject as an object). As John Cobb notes, "Without subjects there can be no objects, since to be an object is to be such for some subject. Whitehead said that 'apart from the experience of subjects there is nothing, nothing, nothing, bare nothingness.'"[30] In process philosophy, the world is constituted by an interdependent process of becoming, whereby each entity can only be understood in terms of its relations—relating both as subject and object. This subject-object oscillation is captured by David Ray Griffin who writes,

> all enduring individuals are serially ordered societies of momentary "occasions of experience." This doctrine, according to which enduring individuals, such as molecules and minds, are analyzable into momentary events, is fundamental to process philosophy's reconciliation of final and efficient causation and, therefore, of freedom and determinism. The salient point is that each enduring individual, such as a living cell or a human mind, oscillates between two modes of existence: the *subjective* mode, in which it exerts final causation or self-determination, and the *objective* mode, in which it exerts efficient causation upon subsequent events.[31]

We must not dwell in our own subjectivity. We must remember that the objects of our experience are also themselves subjects of experience. Afterall, "the universe is a communion of subjects rather than a collection of objects.... Existence itself is derived from and sustained by this intimacy of each being with every other being of the universe."[32] Only objects can be possessed. When we recognize that the world is not a collection of objects to own, but a community of subjects to be known, nonpossession becomes a whole lot simpler.

Aparigraha **as** Ahiṃsā: A Shortcut to Liberation

Now, this perspective is not foreign to the teachings of Jainism. This is not a case of Whiteheadian philosophy swooping in with all the answers to save the backward Jainas. Indeed, the subjectivity of all living beings is central to the metaphysics of Jainism.[33] Nevertheless, the influence of mechanistic thinking in the scientific worldview continues to pull our attention away from those truths spoken in the Jain tradition. What process philosophy uniquely offers Jainism is an alternative—not to reductive physicalism, but to substance ontologies. And substance thinking, tied to being, yields possessive attitudes through objectification. "An object, qua object, exists for something else."[34] If the world is seen as a collection of objects, then the world around us exists for us. These objects are our objects. The world belongs to humanity. From this framework, nonpossession (*aparigraha*) is nearly impossibly. Hence, a substance-based metaphysic that depicts the world of being as constituted of objects introduces unnecessary stumbling blocks on the Jain path to liberation.

But that's not all. Possession requires objectification. If the world is in fact comprised of subjects, possession entails treating living subjects as objects that exist for me. When we claim possession over other living beings (objectifying them), in this act we do harm to them. *Parigraha* is also *hiṃsā*. Possession is violence. Therefore, it stands to reason that karmic accumulation multiplies when we have an attitude of possession toward a world of subjects. Alternatively, practicing *aparigraha* as *ahiṃsā*, grounded in a process metaphysic, should multiply our karmic shedding for a more expedient and efficient path toward liberation.

Additionally, process metaphysics—as a metaphysics of compassion—naturally lends itself toward a more nonviolent approach to others. To know a subject is a relational endeavor that Alfred North Whitehead describes as "sympathy." Whitehead's theory of prehension is fundamentally a matter of "feeling the feeling *in* another and feeling conformally *with* another" (compassion).[35] In a world constituted by drops of experience, "to be" is simultaneously to be the center of values felt (subjective mode) and the source of values given (objective mode), such that all experiences are value experiences. To experience value is to feel. Hence, in process philosophy, the fundamental nature of reality is compassion—a web of interdependent relations of mutual indwelling and feeling the feeling in one another. The realization that the world, as a community of subjects, is constituted by relations (interdependent indwelling) lends itself toward the compassionate knowing of others. Such compassion can greatly enhance one's efforts to "do no harm," as it minimizes otherness and maximizes togetherness.

So, you want to shed some karma? You know that nonpossession is one of the core strategies for dropping that karmic weight, but you can't stop seeing the world around you as one massive buffet of temptation.

Everywhere you look there are objects to be owned rather than subjects to be known. You know that nonviolence is another core strategy for shedding karmas, but you can't stop objectify a world of experiencing subjects. You're trapped in a harmful mindset of possession and violence. What's a Jain to do? Be a process philosopher! A process metaphysic makes it easier to practice both *aprarigraha* and *ahimsā*—two of the most significant vows on the Jain path to liberation—by seeing *aprarigrawha* as *ahimsā*.

Endnotes

1. G. William, "The Heavy Price of Losing Weight: Shedding Pounds Can Be Expensive, But The Costs Don't Have To Be As Bloated As You Might Think," in *U.S. News* (January 2, 2013).

2. It's worth noting that I'm not advocating for GDP as an adequate measure of a nation's success; nor am I advocating for weight loss regimens that simply seek to cut calories. In both cases, I think wellbeing and health are better measures than market activity and caloric deficits. Please consult your physician when considering significant weight loss strategies to improve your health, and please consider ignoring the advice of neoliberal economists when seeking to build wellbeing economies.

3. See this short piece published by the Harvard Medical School, available at https://www.health.harvard.edu/staying-healthy/simple-math-equals-easy-weight-loss (accessed September 13, 2020). However, recent studies are challenging this standard view. Our bodies are complex, dynamic, living systems, so this "simple" formula is really an oversimplification of how weight loss occurs. That said, going into detail about human physiology would be a distraction from the core purpose of this paper and the general guideline holds true—consuming fewer calories than you burn (a caloric deficit) leads to weight loss.

4. I am unaware of anyone having referred to the philosophy of Alfred North Whitehead as a "philosophy of calories," but his philosophy of organism does consider the transmission of energy to be fundamental to the nature of things. In process thought, the transmission of energy is a scientific description of what Whitehead calls "prehension" (specifically, the transmission of physical feelings).

5. L. Brown, "Georgetown Study: Religion Worth $1.2 Trillion in U.S. Economy, More Than Google and Apple Combined," in *CNS News*

(September 16, 2016).

6. See data from the World Bank, https://data.worldbank.org/indicator NY.GDP.MKTP.CD (accessed September 13, 2020).

7. For a good discussion of these practice see Christopher K. Chapple, "A Jain Ethic for the End of Life," in *Death and Dying: An Exercise in Comparative Philosophy of Religion*, ed. T. D. Knepper, L. Bregman, and M. Gottschalk (Switzerland: Springer, 2019), 99–114.

8. For a brief introduction to the Jain theory of karma, see P. Dundas, *The Jains* (New York: Routledge, 1992), 97–104.

9. Dundas, *The Jains* 99.

10. H. Zimmer, *The Philosophies of India,* Princeton Classics Edition (Princeton, NJ: Princeton University Press, 2020), 305.

11. J. D. Long, *Indian Philosophy: An Introduction*, (New York: I. B. Tauris, forthcoming), 78.

12. For a more thorough discussion of this, see P. S. Jaini, *The Jaina Path of Purification* (Delhi: Motilal Banarsidass Publishers, 1998).

13. While Jain monastics take the "great vows," all other Jains (regular folks) take modified "small vows" (*anuvratas*), which are the same five principles, but not as strict. For example, while *aparigraha* for monks means owning no personal property whatsoever, *aparigraha* for the household means avoiding greed or obsessive preoccupation with belongings. In both cases, nonpossession is about maintaining an attitude of nonattachment to worldly possessions.

14. J. D. Long, *Jainism: An Introduction* (New York: I. B. Tauris, 2009), 109–110

15. In Jainism, the category of being is subdivided into three parts. The lowest are the *nigoda* (one-sensed submicroscopic organisms). Above that are earth bodies, air bodies, water bodies, and fire bodies (also one-sensed). The highest category includes plants and animals, which is further subdivided into hierarchies based on the number of senses possessed. Comparably, Whitehead's philosophy also includes a gradation of value that is tied to the capacity for greater or lesser intensity of feeling. For a discussion of *ahimsā* and the Jain view on categories of being see, C. Key Chapple, *Nonviolence to Animals, Earth, and Self in Asian Traditions* (New York: SUNY Press, 1993), 10–12.

16. A. N. Whitehead, *Process and Reality,* Corrected Edition, ed. D R. Griffin and D. W. Sherburne (New York: The Free Press, 1978), 105.

17. While I won't go into detail here, I am aware of the potential problems with coloring value (black is worst, white is best, etc.) That said, the other colors used in Jain *leśyā* theory are blue, grey, red, and yellow. And according to Jain cosmology, these colors are not arbitrary reflections of social perspectives on race and ethnicity in India, but literal coloring of the soul through karmic particles.

18. *Ahimsā* also has implications, especially for monks, on issues of travel and mobility. How one moves through this living world is an ethical matter. Hence, both Svetambara and Digambara monks make use of small broom-like whisks to gently sweep their walking path to avoid stepping on small creatures. The faster one travels, the more difficult it is to take care of the living creatures on your route. The farther one travels, the greater the risk of harming lifeforms as you journey. Hence, cars and planes are often avoided by Jain monks. Also, travelling at night is far riskier than traveling during the day, since there is a greater chance of stepping on critters you don't see.

19. J. B. Cobb, Jr., *A Christian Natural Theology: Based on the Thought of Alfred North Whitehead* (Philadelphia: Westminster Press, 1965), 23.

20. C. R. Mesle, *Process-Relational Philosophy: An Introduction to Alfred North Whitehead* (West Conshohocken, PA: Templeton Foundation Press, 2008), 8.

21. For a thorough account of Descartes's framing of the modern worldview, see J. I. Kureethadam, *The Philosophical Roots of the Ecological Crisis: Descartes and the Modern Worldview* (Newcastle upon Tyne, UK: Cambridge Scholars Publishing, 2017).

22. Of course, not all thinkers advocated for Cartesian dualism, or the later reductive physicalism. And while Alfred North Whitehead was not alone in his rejection of these dominant narratives, they are indeed dominant. Still today you will find very few scientists speaking of minds or souls. Instead, you'll get discussion of brains and bodies, with the assumption that everything can eventually be explained from the purely physical realm of objects.

23. As Maria Mies beautifully points out, "They can only propagate the slogan 'Knowledge is power' with impunity—and people believe in this phrase—because scientists since Bacon, Descartes and Max Weber have constantly concealed the impure relationship between knowledge and violence or force (in the form of state and military power, for example) by defining science as the sphere of a pure search for truth.

Thus, they lifted it out of the sphere of politics, that is, the sphere of force and power. The separation of politics (power) and science which we feminists attack is based on a lie. It does not exist and it has never existed, that value-free, disinterested pure science, devoted only to the infinite search for truth, which is legally protected as scientific freedom in our constitutions. Even those scientists who only want to satisfy their presumably irresistible urge for pure knowledge and research cannot do so unless such basic research is funded. And it is not difficult to identify militaristic, political, and economic interests behind this funding of fundamental research" (M. Mies, "Feminist Research: Science, Violence, and Responsibility," in *Ecofeminism*, ed. V. Shiva and M. Mies [New York, NY: Zed Books, 1993], 46).

24. J. B. Cobb, Jr., "Whitehead's Theory of Value," available at https://www.religion-online.org/article/whiteheads-theory-of-value/, accessed September 19, 2020.

25. J. B. Cobb, Jr., *Whitehead Word Book: A Glossary with Alphabetical Index to Technical Terms in Process and Reality* (Claremont, CA: P&F Press, 2008), 16, 19, emphasis added.

26. Whitehead, *Process and Reality*, 27.

27. P. Rose, *On Whitehead* (Belmont, CA: Wadsworth Publishing Co, 2001), 3, emphasis added.

28. Panexperientialism was coined by David Ray Griffin in contrast to panpsychism. Griffin believes that experience is more fundamental than consciousness. Only the most complex creatures enjoy conscious experiences. Simple but animate creatures and inanimate objects do not experience consciousness. The capacity for consciousness emerged in evolutionary history smoothly from less complex species with mentality but not consciousness (i.e., "smooth emergence"). Complex creatures capable of conscious experience represent a miniscule percentage of entities known to exist, and conscious experience represents a miniscule percentage of the experiences of conscious beings.

29. Mesle, *Process-Relational Philosophy*, 35–36.

30. J. B. Cobb Jr., *Back to Darwin: A Richer Account of Evolution* (Grand Rapids, MI: Wm. B. Eerdmans Publishing Co., 2008), 254.

31. D. R. Griffin, *Reenchantment Without Supernaturalism: A Process Philosophy of Religion* (Ithaca, NY: Cornell University Press, 2001), 6.

32. B. Swimme and T. Berry, *The Universe Story* (San Francisco:

HarperOne, 1994), 243.

33. For an example of this, see V. R. Gandhi, "Religion and Philosophy of the Jainas," edited by N. J. Shah (Ahmedabad: Jain International, 1993).
34. Cobb, "Whitehead's Theory of Value."
35. Whitehead, *Process and Reality*, 162.

FIFTEEN

A Process-Akashic Religious Naturalism

Leslie A. Muray

A LONG-STANDING CONCERN of Frederick Ferré was how to situate humans in the nonhuman natural world while simultaneously safeguarding the distinctiveness of human beings. He often articulated this tension as between "organicism" and its emphasis on wholes, often in an impersonal way, and "personalism" and its emphasis on individuals, with humans standing above the nonhuman world. One question on which I will focus is the related question of how persons emerge from a supposedly impersonal nonhuman nature? I shall turn to Whitehead's understanding of "person," which he extends beyond humans.

Ferré, of course, used Whitehead's philosophy to resolve these issues. He espouses a panexperientialist position in which actual occasions are primary. According to this outlook, personal capacities have their analogs and continuities in the nonhuman natural world. Here, he uses the Whiteheadian notions of mentality, "soul," and freedom from the simplest forms of life to the most complex—if we are to maintain that the complex forms of life emerged from the simple. Ferré points out that we need not attribute a full degree of self-consciousness to acknowledge that it is experience. In typically Whiteheadian fashion, he maintains that even in our own lives as human beings we find varying degrees of self-consciousness; that most of psychic life even in human beings is at the subconscious level. If this is so, is it not arbitrary to deny the presence of mentality in nonhuman animals?

Ferré's Personalistic Organicism

Ferré maintains that "we take full personal existence, at the height of its expression in mature, healthy human beings, as characterized by six major capacities."[1] To him, "these are the powers of (1) enjoying consciously (including the ability to receive and appreciate experiences of senses or imagination); (2) thinking logically; (3) remembering; (4) planning; (5) preferring or judging; and (6) acting with moral responsibility."[2] He asserts that "these powers constitute the best and the worst—for the heights of aesthetic achievement and religious ecstasy, the depths of philosophic reflection and scientific penetration, the tenderness of regret, the eagerness of hope, the seriousness of choice, and the nobility (or baseness) of responsibility."[3] He states that "these capacities have been refined in human civilization over the millennia, while beauty has been created and profaned, opportunities grasped and missed, good achieved and destroyed."[4] He concludes poetically that "they constitute the humanist's pride and (all too frequently) the environmentalist's despair."[5]

Ferré, however, is quick to point out that personal capacities have their analogs and continuities in the nonhuman natural world.[6] He asserts that it is the Cartesian, mechanistic worldview that erected a barrier of bias against the possibility of an inner life for nonhuman animals.[7] He claims that it would be more empirical and more adequate to acknowledge through inductive generalization from the evidence of our own subjective interiority, at some level, to that of all actualities. Subjective experiencing is also present in all actualities, not only as valuing, but also as mentality, i.e., logic (thought as methodical discipline), in however rudimentary a form. To illustrate this form of logic, or capacity for thought in the nonhuman world, Ferré uses the example of the cat crouching before the mouse and anticipating the mouse's every move. Ferré also shows that memory and anticipation are present at some level in all actualities. In this regard, all actualities exhibit the capacity for valuing, for expressing preference.[8]

Ferré maintains that "my argument against the extremes of personalism, then is that if human persons rightly can claim intrinsic value by manifesting subjective interiority, logical thought, memory, anticipation, and judgment, then humans should not fail to honor the same capacities when found elsewhere in the organic world."⁹ However, he does think there may be an appropriateness to drawing a greater disjunction between the personal and the nonhuman as far as ethics is concerned.¹⁰ Nevertheless, even here there is continuity between the human and the nonhuman, the difference being one of degree and not of kind.¹¹

It is in the context of his affirmation of the *intrinsic* value of all actualities, human and nonhuman, that Ferré makes what I consider his most important move. He describes it in the following manner:

> Still, it is reconciling the organic and the personal, both domains of intrinsic value, that principally concerns us here. We have seen how key traits that personalists admire can be recognized in nonhuman organisms; is there a reciprocal move from what organicists see as the 'wisdom of healthy life' to the personal? I believe so. All healthy organic life shares three great characteristics, worthy of admiration in their interactive tension: creativity, homeostasis, and holism.¹²

The meaning of these words may be found in the following: (1) *creativity* as the growth, innovation, spread, devouring, evolution of healthy life; (2) *homeostasis* as the self-defense of healthy life from both overgrowth and collapse at both the individual and popular levels; and (3) *holism* as what in healthy life makes both creativity and homeostasis possible through networks of information in which diverse elements are linked in a manner pertinent to the benefit of the whole system.¹³

Whitehead's Understanding of the Person

Although we have already alluded to Whitehead's understanding of the person by way of Ferré's appropriation of that notion, in this section, I will discuss the Whiteheadian concept of personhood at greater length.

First, for Whitehead, a "person" is a personally ordered society of momentary experience.¹⁴ This personal order is a serial sequence of actual occasions, each inheriting a common character from its predecessor. In this understanding, human beings as well as atoms and molecules fit the description of "person."¹⁵

John Cobb maintains that up to this point, Whitehead saw personal order as a form of social order which in turn he saw as the common element of form inherited from previous occasions.¹⁶ It is with the introduction of hybrid prehensions, the combination of physical and conceptual feelings, that we have the possibility of a different kind of society, one that is both alive and capable of seeking novelty.[17] Thus, there are societies that Whitehead describes in terms of personhood that repeat the past, while others, differing in degrees of complexity of organization, are capable of greater novelty and have the capacity for greater richness of experience.

Whitehead equates societies with a dominant or regnant center of experience with a "living person."[18] For him, this entails both a summing up and inclusion of the past, providing continuity, while at the same time seeking novelty.[19] "Living person" is also what Whitehead identifies as the soul. For our purposes, these are the two key features to personhood, namely, (1) the inheritance element of form inherited from the past, providing for continuity as well as (2) the capacity to respond to the organism's environment with increasing sensitivity and responsiveness, especially with greater degrees of complexity of organization.

Thus, animals with central nervous systems, a dominant society of occasions, are "living persons," with a soul.[20] Cobb alludes to discussions among Whiteheadians as to whether or not creatures without central nervous systems can be considered to be "living persons"—to have a soul. He states that process thinkers will be guided on this question by the evidence, and the evidence suggests unicellular organisms are such "living persons."[21]

This provides an opening for my larger argument. Whitehead provides an ecological metaphysics in his philosophy of organism. In other words, he delineates a worldview that is intelligible, coherent, and adequate to the facts of experience. This means, at least in part, that what is said needs to apply consistently at all levels of experience. It would imply mentality and freedom are qualities not only of humans or "higher" animals but also present, at least at a rudimentary level, in the tiniest energy events. It also means that all actual occasions, all momentary experiences, are of intrinsic value (although not necessarily of equal value).

It means, as we have already seen in Ferré's appropriation of Whitehead's understanding of person, that personhood is decidedly not restricted to humans and animals, but is present in rudimentary, incipient form in all experiences. This I maintain is a consequence of Whitehead's "panexperientialism" (which, unlike some Whiteheadians, I would not hesitate to call "panpsychism").

Perhaps the following will help. One tendency among evolutionary biologists is to stress human uniqueness. This is often accompanied by a mechanistic view of nonhuman nature. Even when not mechanistic, humans are seen as separate and superior to nonhumans and are unique in being the only creatures who think, use language, have culture. Humans are the only ones with personhood.

If human beings emerge from nonhumans, if the complex forms of life emerge from the simple, how can humans whose *defining characteristics* have nothing in common with nonhumans emerge from those species? Is this the scientific origin of a "deus ex machina?"

Instead of human uniqueness, I prefer to use "human distinctiveness," which preserves the specialness of humans, alongside the specialness of all species. Humans are distinctive—but so are all other species. It avoids anthropocentrism. Of course, it is not sufficient to assert such claims; we need to follow empirical evidence that provides backing for claims of continuity between humans and nonhumans, that the difference between humans and nonhumans is one of degree and not of kind. The works of such scientists as Jane Goodall, Franz de Waal, Marc Beckoff, and Nancy R. Howell are especially helpful in this regard.[22]

In contrast to advocates of human uniqueness, Goodall, de Waal, Beckoff, Howell, and others try to show that the gap between humans and nonhumans is narrow. For instance, chimpanzees not only have over 99% of the genetic make-up of humans, they can learn sophisticated sign language with which to communicate. They, as well as other species, do have culture. Examples are chimps that use sophisticated tools to crack nuts and for other uses. If they do not use them correctly, they might hurt themselves.[23] Other examples are the death rituals of elephants and other species. When an elephant dies, the others gather around it in a circle, cover it with branches, brush, and plants, and start wailing in a sad tone, all in a ritualistic fashion.

While animal culture can be observed among wild animals, so can distinctive personalities.[24] I certainly invite my readers to reflect on their experiences with their companion animals as I indulge in some personal anecdotes.

I have an 18-year-old three-legged cat that I have had since she was three weeks old. She is very loud in her meowing, almost bellowing. That is just one of her ways of communicating. Although she runs well, she limps and can no longer jump. When she wants attention, she will start bellowing in the middle of the living room. That is her signal (she has me trained) for me to go to my rocking chair. Within seconds of sitting down, she is by the side of the chair meowing, requesting that I pick her up. She then sometimes sits on my lap. More often than not, she will sit next to me brushing against my hip, sitting in a position reflecting equality.

In the course of the last few years, I have had some health problems that required frequent hospitalizations. Upon my return home, I usually sleep the first couple of nights on the living room couch rather than my bed. My cat—Sasha—seems to know that something is wrong. Instead of bellowing or asking to be put on my side or my lap, she lies at the foot of the bed, quietly, as though she were guarding me.

I am certain all of us who have companion animals could tell similar stories. Some scientists would maintain that such descriptions of animal behavior are anthropomorphic, making nonhuman animals humanlike. In other words, we see what we want to see. I would maintain that we describe and interpret what we see. It is common sense. Instead of seeing this kind of interpretation as anthropomorphic, it can be considered a form of animism, seeing all living things as having a soul (to some degree). A process panexperientialism is precisely the kind of animism we need to lure us toward an ecological civilization.

A Caring Universe

Let's consider the concept of "care," especially "being cared for." To have a sense that we are cared about to the point where our lives make a difference to the lives of others, to be loved, is life giving, life nurturing, empowering, liberating. Studies have shown that when infants and even older children do not receive such loving care, they live emotionally stunted lives, get ill, and may even die. We need a sense of our lives mattering not just to us but to others who stand with us through life's ebb and flow, its joys and sorrows. Nonhuman animals care for their young and each other. They protect each other, teach the young. They have distinct personalities. Having a sense of being cared for carries intimations of a divine caring, a cosmic dimension to being cared about. This sense of being cared for is vital to the development, long and short term, of the sensitivity and receptivity that is involved in personhood.

To develop the cosmic dimension of being cared about let's bring in the recent work of Ervin László and others concerning the Akashic Field. For László, influenced by a synthesis of process thought and systems theory, the Akashic Field is an indispensable element in his version of "a theory of everything." Taking the word *Akasha* from the Sanskrit language and Indian culture, he defines Akasha as the "all-encompassing medium that *underlies* all things and *becomes* all things."[25] It cannot be perceived through sense experience but can be reached through such spiritual practices as yoga.[26]

László maintains that "in-formation" is present throughout the universe and is best thought of as a field. Like other fields, such as the gravitational, electromagnetic, and Higgs, the-in-formation field is not available to sense experience. Nevertheless, the in-formation field, like all fields, has effects that can be perceived. It conserves and conveys in-formation.[27]

László claims that it is appropriate to identify the in-formation field with the Akashic Field. He states that "the Akashic vision of a cyclic universe—of a Metaverse that creates universe after universe—is essentially the vision we now get from cosmology."[28] He writes:

> It is the original field out of which emerged particles and atoms, stars and planets, human and animal bodies, and all the things that can be and touched. It is a dynamic, energy-filled medium in ceaseless fluctuation.[29]

Moreover, he asserts that in this original field there is a cosmic consciousness in which everything is preserved.

> consciousness does vanish when the functions of the brain and body cease. It persists, can be recalled, and, for a time at least, can also be communicated with. . . . It's capable of receiving inputs from the manifest world and responding to them. In this interpretation, the perennial intuition of an immortal soul is no longer inconsistent with what we are now beginning to comprehend though science about the true nature of reality.[30]

László's eloquent words provide an excellent summary of his understanding of the Akashic Field:

> The universe is a memory filled world of constant and enduring interconnection, a world where everything in-forms—acts on and interacts with—everything else. We should apprehend this remarkable world with our heart as well as with our intellect.

> [This chapter] recalls the ancient intuition of an information-filled cosmos where everything is conserved and affects everything else. It offers... a poetic vision of a cosmos where nothing disappears without a trace, and where all things that exist are, and remain, intrinsically and intimately interconnected.[31]

László makes his argument, profoundly influenced by process thought and systems theory, using evidence from quantum physics, non-sensory perception, near-death experiences, out of body experiences, altered states of consciousness, and parapsychology.[32] His understanding of the Cosmic Consciousness, that is, the Akashic Field, is his version of Whitehead's consequent nature of God, in which God experiences all experiences, human and nonhuman, and preserves them everlastingly.

I have to confess that my previous exploration of the theme of "being cared about" owes much to the work of Schubert M. Ogden, who maintains that if we truly care about and love someone, then that person makes a difference to us; a difference to our very self-constitution. And if God is a God of love, then we make a difference to God and affect the very inner being of God, God's inner self-constitution. Ogden argues that for life to be meaningful, we need a sense of contributing beyond ourselves. Contributing to family, the lives of friends, community, history, etc. are insufficient since they, like us, are subject to "perpetual perishing." Thus, we need a sense of contributing that gives an ultimate significance to our lives beyond the ravages of time. Ogden writes:

> If the only contribution our lives could make were the contribution they make to other creaturely lives as limited as our own, they would make no abiding difference and, in that sense, would be meaningless. Death and transience—the perpetual perishing of all things in the ever-rolling stream of time—would be the last word about each of us, and about all of us together.[33]

He continues:

> But if the difference we make is not only such difference as we can make to our fellow creatures but also, and definitively, the difference we each make to God, the one to whom *all* things make a difference and to whose life each thing can contribute *all* that it is, then our lives and all lives are redeemed from meaninglessness by being given an imperishable meaning in the everlasting of God.[34]

The eloquent words of John Cobb provide an excellent summary of Ogden's position: "What happens really matters only if it matters ultimately, and it matters ultimately only if it matters everlastingly. What happens can matter everlastingly only if it matters to him who is everlasting."[35]

I need to point out that, for Hartshorne and Ogden, being preserved in the divine memory everlastingly does not imply subjective immortality, continuing subjective experiencing after death. In fact, for Ogden, worrying about one's subjective immortality provides an ultimacy to our most intense self-preoccupation.[36] Being preserved in the divine memory, objective immortality, is sufficient to ground our confidence in the meaning of life, in the sense that life is worth living. It endows all creatures with an ultimate sense of their dignity.

At this point, I want to make a quick comment about the significance of each actual occasion regardless of its contribution beyond itself. I want to emphasize emphatically the value of a momentary experience in and for itself, quite apart from what it may contribute beyond itself. In process thought, every moment seeks the experience of beauty, its own completion, "satisfaction." In a manner similar to Buddhism, impermanence, "the perpetual perishing" of actual occasions characterizes the passage of time. Each moment is its own birth and its death. All we have is the experience of the moment—to be embraced for its own sake as the gift that it is. In a fashion typical of the "both/and" orientation of process thinkers, there is no reason why we cannot emphasize the present moment of experience for its own sake and enjoyment as well as a sense of contributing beyond ourselves.

The point of this discussion is that there is a cosmic dimension to our sense of being cared for, whether it be in the form of Ervin László's adaptation of the Akashic Field or Schubert Ogden's adaptation of Whitehead's concept of the consequent nature of God. In my own recent work, I have attempted to develop an understanding of God that is in between an orthodox Whiteheadian view of God and religious naturalism. Influenced by Ferré, Loomer, László, Donald A. Crosby, and Jerome Stone, I have come to identify God with the *drive* toward creativity, novelty, beauty, and complexity, as well as *sensitivity* and *responsiveness* (again, this bears a striking resemblance to Whitehead's idea of the primordial and consequent natures of God). It is this *creativity, sensitivity, and responsiveness* that elicits and lures the development of persons, human and nonhuman.

Lest this sound pollyannaish, as though I am ignoring the cruel, indifferent, and ugly dimension of nature, I would argue that our lives matter to the universe in spite of and within its ambiguity or, perhaps better put, within its particular ambiguities. When we die, we literally go back to the universe. In a real sense, we get "recycled." And the universe "remembers" us—not necessarily in a self-conscious way (except to the degree there is some degree of consciousness in all actualities) or one that provides for subjective immortality, or preserves the details of our experiences. Nevertheless, just as the Big Bang lives on in us, so do we become part of the universe forever.

Knowing that our lives matter, that we are cared about, whether by a cat, fellow humans, or the universe is life giving. The sensitivity and responsiveness of the universe in its life-givingness is the Holy Spirit, "the lord and giver of life." I believe Fredrick Ferré is correct: "the reality of caring is woven into the texture of the Universe."[37]

Endnotes

Editors' Note: Les Muray passed away before his could see this chapter in print. The editors remember Les fondly and affirmingly quote Jay McDaniel's tribute:

> Les Muray passed away, or shall [we] say moved forward, on July 21, 2019. He was a powerful and influential partner in the process circle, and an exemplar of the process way at its best. He did not promote himself, he was not feverish for 'recognition.' He was a humble, open, compassionate man who loved cats, the Boston Red Sox, his mother and father, the Boston Celtics, his friends, Hungary, the eucharist (he was an Episcopal priest), democracy, Buddhism, classic rock, process philosophy and theology, humor, Paul Tillich, the mountains of New Mexico, and Nicholas Berdyaev. When kindred process thinkers turned to him for guidance, they often sought his views on politics and political philosophy. He was quick to be an advocate of biocracy: that is, a society that listens to the voices of all, not human beings alone. But he also had a mystical side, a quiet side, a side that knew aloneness and sometimes loneliness. He was a complete human being, ahead of his time even as having passed away. We do well to follow his example. We remember him and anticipate becoming more like him. Thank you, Les. We miss you."

See J. McDaniel, "Remember Les Muray: 1948–2019," available at https://www.openhorizons.org/remembering-les-muray.html.

1. F. Ferré, "Personalistic Organicism: Paradox or Paradigm?," in R. Attfield and A. Belsey, *Philosophy and the Natural Environment* (New York: Cambridge University Press, 1994), 65.

2. Ferré, "Personalistic Organicism, 65.

3. Ferré, "Personalistic Organicism, 65.

4. Ferré, "Personalistic Organicism, 65.

5. Ferré, "Personalistic Organicism, 65.

6. Ferré, "Personalistic Organicism, 65.

7. Ferré, "Personalistic Organicism, 65.

8. Ferré, "Personalistic Organicism, 65.

9. Ferré, "Personalistic Organicism, 65.

10. One of my few disagreements with Ferré here and in other places is that he tries to accentuate the distinctiveness of human beings more than I would accent the differences between the human and the nonhuman. Our positions, nevertheless, remain very close. See my "The Transformation of Ethics: A Response to Frederick Ferré," *American Journal of Theology and Philosophy* 23.1 (January 2002): 3–12.

11. There are differences of opinion among Whiteheadian process thinkers on this matter, some claiming that differences of degree amount to differences of kind. Ferré and I agree that these differences are of degree and not of kind.

12. Ferré, "Personalistic Organicism," 69.

13. Ferré, "Personalistic Organicism, 69–70.

14. A. N. Whitehead, *Process and Reality*, Corrected Edition, ed. D. R. Griffin and D. W. Sherburne (New York: The Free Press, 1978), 34–35.

15. Whitehead, *Process and Reality*, 34–35.

16. Whitehead, *Process and Reality*, 34–35.

17. Whitehead, *Process and Reality*, 34–35.

18. Whitehead, *Process and Reality*, 34–35.

19. Whitehead, *Process and Reality*, 45.

20. Whitehead, *Process and Reality*, 44.

21. See J. B. Cobb Jr., "The Resurrection of the Soul," *Harvard Theological Review* 80/2 (1987): 213–27.
22. In particular, see J. Goodall, *My Life with Chimpanzees*, Revised Edition (New York: Byron Preiss Visual Publications, 2002); and F. De Waal, *The Ape and the Sushi Master: Cultural Reflections of a Primatologist* (New York: Basic Books, 2001).
23. De Waal, *The Ape and the Sushi Master*, 239–72.
24. Refer to Goodall, *My Life with Chimpanzees*.
25. Ervin László, *Science and the Akashic Field: An Integral Theory of Everything*, 2nd Edition (Rochester, VT: Inner Traditions. 2007), 76.
26. László, *Science and the Akashic Field*, 76.
27. László, *Science and the Akashic Field*, 73.
28. László, *Science and the Akashic Field*, 77.
29. László, *Science and the Akashic Field*, 77.
30. László, *Science and the Akashic Field*, 138.
31. László, *Science and the Akashic Field*, 129.
32. László, *Science and the Akashic Field*, 129–69
33. Schubert Ogden, *Faith and Freedom: Toward a Theology of Liberation* (Nashville, TN: Abingdon Press, 1989), 70.
34. Ogden, *Faith and Freedom*, 70.
35. J. B. Cobb Jr., *God and the World* (Philadelphia: Westminster Press, 1969), 84.
36. This was relayed in an audiotape lecture in the late 1970s. Original source unknown.
37. F. Ferré, *Living and Value: Toward a Constructive Postmodern Ethics* (Albany, NY: State University of New York Press, 2001), 330.

Contributors

John Pickering received a first degree in psychology from Edinburgh and a doctorate in experimental psychology from Sussex. He worked in the US at Rochester and Stanford, then returned to the UK to lecture at Warwick, where he still teaches. His interests are centered on consciousness in general and on human experience in particular. Pickering is a founding member of the Consciousness & Experiential Psychology section of the British Psychological Society. His investigations into consciousness led him to study Eastern traditions of thought in Sri Lanka, China, Korea, India, and Thailand. Pickering takes process thought, especially that of A. N. Whitehead and C. S. Peirce to be the natural basis for bringing his interests in consciousness together with contemporary developments in science and with environmental geopolitics. Pickering hopes his work will help promote more sustainable ways of life.

Luca Vanzago is a full professor of theoretical philosophy at Pavia University in Italy, where he works mainly on the phenomenological traditions and on the various trends in process thought. Vanzago has widely published in Italy and abroad. Among his publications are eight books and more than sixty articles. He is member of the European Society for Process Thought, the Merleau-Ponty Circle, and the Italian Society for the study of Merleau-Ponty's philosophy. Vanzago is also director of the Theoretical series for Mimesis publisher and a member of several international philosophical journals.

Jason Brown is a neurologist and writer of works in neuropsychology and philosophy of mind. He is emeritus Clinical Professor of Neurology at New York University Medical Center and a fellow of the Royal Society of Medicine. He has been a reviewer and recipient of grants and fellowships from the National Institutes of Health and the Alexander von Humboldt Foundation. He has served on the editorial boards of leading journals in his field, written 15 books, edited 4 others, and contributed over 200 articles. His many books include *The Self-Embodied Mind* (2001), *Process and the Authentic Life: Toward a Psychology of Value* (2005), and *Mental States and Conceptual Worlds* (2019). Follow his work at https://www.drjbrown.org/.

Herman F. Greene is executive director of the Center for Ecozoic Societies in Chapel Hill, North Carolina. He was the founding executive director of the International Process Network and presently serves on its board of governors. Greene is on the board of advisors for the Center for Process Studies and the Institute for the Postmodern Development of China, both now in Salem, Oregon. He also maintains a part-time practice as a corporate, tax, and securities lawyer through Greene Law, PLLC. Greene received his JD degree from the University of North Carolina at Chapel Hill, a DMin from United Theological Seminary, a MTh and MDiv from the University of Chicago, and an MA in political science from Stanford University. His dissertation was titled "Creation Season in the Life of the Church." Greene has lectured widely and published numerous articles on ecology and culture and the meaning, mission, and future of process thought.

John B. Cobb, Jr. taught at the Claremont School of Theology from 1957 to 1990. He is the co-founder, with David Griffin, of the Center for Process Studies, which has especially promoted the thought of Alfred North Whitehead as an alternative perspective to that of modernity. Cobb helped to organize the Institute for Postmodern Development of China, which has focused on the creation of an ecological civilization. He was lead organizer of the 2015 conference, Seizing an Alternative, Toward an Ecological Civilization, out of which Pando Populus and the Institute for Ecological Civilization emerged. His current projects are organized through the Cobb Institute of Claremont, CA.

Maria-Teresa Teixeira holds a PhD in contemporary philosophy from Faculdade de Letras da Universidade de Lisboa. She is a researcher at Universidade de Coimbra. Teixeira is the author of two books on Whitehead: *Ser, Devir e Perecer A criatividade na filosofia de Whitehead* (*Being, Becoming and Perishing Creativity in Whitehead's Philosophy*) and *Consciência e Acção Bergson e as neurociências* (*Consciousness and Action Bergson and Neroscience*). She has translated *Process and Reality,* by A. N. Whitehead, into Portuguese and has published many papers in international journals. Teixeira serves as the International Process Network director-elect, and was the organizer of the 2017 International Whitehead Conference.

Moirika Reker holds a Master of Fine Arts from Columbia University, New York (2001). She studied Free Media at Gerrit Rietveld Academie in Amsterdam and completed the Advanced Course in Visual Arts in AR.CO, Lisbon. Reker is currently a PhD candidate in philosophy at the School of Arts and Humanities, University of Lisbon, with a thesis on the philosophy of the garden based on the Italian philosopher Rosario Assunto. She is a student member of the Centre of Philosophy of the University of Lisbon. Her main research interests include the philosophy of the garden, philosophy of landscape, ethics, and aesthetics of the public space.

Mark Dibben is a retired academic known for his work in applied process thought, the thorough-going, serious-minded, common-sense application of process metaphysics to topics in the sciences and social sciences. A Distinguished Fellow of the Schumacher Institute, Dibben is a former Head of School and Deputy Chair of Academic Senate at the University of Tasmania. He argues that only a process-relational worldview, one that regards all individuals within all species as having inherent value and subjective experience, can overcome the challenges we face at the ending of the modern age. This requires localism and person-centered economy and communities to arrive at sustainable systems that are inherently resilient, resourceful, and recoverably regenerative.

Arran Gare is Associate Professor in Philosophy and Cultural Inquiry and founder of the Joseph Needham Centre for Complex Processes Research, Swinburne University, Melbourne, Australia. After graduating from the

University of Western Australia and Murdoch University and completing a Fulbright Post-Doctoral Fellowship at the Center for Philosophy and History of Science at Boston University, Gare lectured at Murdoch University, Curtin University, and the University of Western Australia before taking up his present position at Swinburne University. The focus of his research is on transforming culture to create an ecological civilization. He has published widely on the philosophy of nature, process metaphysics, the metaphysical foundations of the sciences, the philosophy of mathematics, complexity theory, human ecology, the emergent theory of mind, social and cultural theory, the history of European and Chinese cultures, and social and political philosophy. Gare is also the founding editor of the online journal *Cosmos and History: The Journal of Natural and Social Philosophy*.

Charles Walter is a philosopher, mathematician, and theoretical biologist known for his work on science, jurisprudence, and the applied arts in his nonprofit institute supported by his patent law practice in Houston, Texas. His friendship and collaboration with Ilya Prigogine in Austin at the University of Texas integrated physics and biology into fundamental processes in nature, such as homeostasis and the "disystem." Walter designed clinical trials and modeled cellular differentiation while on the biomathematics and biochemistry staffs at MD Anderson Hospital; and engineered the technical requirements for a carbon-free, hydrogen-based US economy while professor of chemical engineering at the University of Houston. After completing law school, Walter taught computing power, legal reasoning, legal language, and jurisprudence. He organized international conferences on legal informatics and integral jurisprudence while directing the first Law & Technology program in the U.S. at the UH Law School. His interest in Whitehead's metaphysical cosmology derives from Whitehead's collaboration with the American pioneer of sociobiology and preeminent myrmecologist, William Morton Wheeler, eighteen years after Professor Wheeler brought the concept of homeostasis explicitly into sociobiology. This late contact between Whitehead and Wheeler at Harvard is well-known to biologists but not so much to philosophers.

Andrew M. Davis is program director for the Center for Process Studies at Claremont School of Theology at Willamette University in Salem, Oregon. He holds a B.A. in Philosophy and Theology, an M.A. in Inter-religious Studies, and a Ph.D. in Religion and Process Philosophy from Claremont School of Theology. Davis is author or editor of five books, including *How I Found God in Everyone and Everywhere: An Anthology of Spiritual Memoirs* (2018), with Philip Clayton; *Propositions in the Making: Experiments in a Whiteheadian Laboratory* (2019, with Roland Faber and Michael Halewood; *Depths as Yet Unspoken: Whiteheadian Excursions in Mysticism, Multiplicity, and Divinity* (2020), with Roland Faber; *Mind, Value, and Cosmos: On the Relational Nature of Ultimacy* (2020); and *Process Cosmology: New Integrations in Science and Philosophy* (forthcoming), with Maria-Teresa Teixeira and Wm. Andrew Schwartz. Follow his work at andrewmdavis.info.

Robert Gnuse (Vanderbilt, Ph.D., 1980) is the James C. Carter, S.J., Chase Bank Distinguished Professor of the Humanities and Full Professor of Hebrew Bible at Loyola University in New Orleans, LA. Gnuse is also chair of the Department of Religious Studies (2003–09, 2019–). He is the author of eighteen books and numerous articles and an ordained Lutheran minister. Gnuse is married (Beth) with three adult children (Becky, Jake, and Adam).

Farhan Shah is a Muslim philosopher who is influenced by the philosophy of Muhammad Iqbal. Shah is currently working on his doctoral dissertation, at the University of Oslo, Norway, which revolves around the philosophy of Iqbal, with a special focus on Iqbal's process-driven concept of God, the human self and cosmology. Another important dimension of his thesis is the prospects for a shared Christian-Muslim ecological attitude, an ethics for freedom, responsibility, and care for nature and the nonhuman communities of life.

Wm. Andrew Schwartz is executive director of the Center for Process Studies (CPS) and assistant professor of Process Studies & Comparative Theology at Claremont School of Theology, as well as co-founder and executive vice president of the Institute for Ecological Civilization (ecociv.org). Schwartz earned his Ph.D. in Philosophy of Religion and Theology at Claremont Graduate University. His academic interests include comparative religious philosophies, process thought, ecology, and education. His recent work has been focused on high-impact philosophy and the role of big ideas in the transition toward ecological civilization. As executive director, Andrew has overall strategic and operational responsibility for CPS, including development and implementation of the CPS mission, programs, and strategic vision.

Leslie A. Muray was professor of Philosophy and Religious Studies at Curry College (MA) and coordinator of the Philosophy and Religious Studies program. He is author of *An Introduction to the Process Understanding of Science, Society and the Self* and *Liberal Protestantism and Science*, and eighty articles in five languages. Les was an incorrigible fan of cats, especially his three-legged 17-year-old Sasha, rock 'n' roll, the blues, the Boston Red Sox, the Boston Celtics, and the New England Patriots.

www.ingramcontent.com/pod-product-compliance
Lightning Source LLC
Chambersburg PA
CBHW071957110526
44592CB00012B/1124